Multi Unit Leadership

The 7 Stages of
Building High-Performing
Partnerships and Teams

by Jim Sullivan

To Cita, Richie & the Bean

Copyright 2007 **Sullivision.com**

Published by Indian Creek Press
A Division of **Sullivision.com**
PO Box 7042
Appleton WI 54912

Printed in the United States of America

Library of Congress Cataloging-in-Publication data is available.

ISBN: 978-0-9715849-1-4

> ***Multi Unit Leadership* is the gift that can be opened again and again.** This book makes a great gift for your leadership team at every level. Visit our website at **www.sullivision.com** for information on volume discounts.

Keep my words positive:
Words become my behaviors.
Keep my behaviors positive:
Behaviors become my habits.
Keep my habits positive:
Habits become my values.
Keep my values positive:
Values become my destiny.

M.K. Gandhi

INTRODUCTION
The Invisible Warrior

Cautionary Tale

"I was recruited to be an area director at a manager meeting. The VP of Operations asked for a show of hands if anyone was interested. Me and another person raised ours. After I was hired—over the phone by the way— the VP mailed me a copy of a really bad time management book and wished me luck in writing on the front page. He told me nothing, showed me nothing and every time he came in he wanted to change something about my stores. That, in a nutshell, is how I was 'developed' as a multi unit manager."

The 7 Stages of Building High-Performing Partnerships and Teams

Preface

Let's be honest. The "Preface" in most business books is little more than glorified thank you card that reveals less than an Amish swimsuit.

While I will offer some well-deserved thank-you's, I first promise not to waste your time; the content herein is designed to be all killer, no filler.

The dozens of research projects, hundreds of consulting opportunities and the thousands of seminars our company has done over the last 10 years has given us unique insight into the roles of multi unit managers and leadership in both the foodservice and retail arenas. We've had the opportunity to both teach and learn from the best and the brightest. So *Multi Unit Leadership: The 7 Stages of Building High-Performing Partnerships and Teams* is a joint effort between **Sullivision.com** and all the creative and talented people we get to work with everyday, and to whom we are deeply grateful.

Not to thank those whose insight and expertise made this book possible would fail to reflect the collaborative project that it is. So we begin by tipping our hat to the hundreds of multi unit managers and CEOs across North America who shared their time and talent with us during our research for this book. I would also like to extend a sincere merci beaucoup and hearty howdy-howdy to Dick Gaven for patiently and fastidiously helping edit the text. Finally, I'd like to thank the colleagues, clients, and friends listed below for their collective mentoring, inspiration and support:

Alan Gould	Jim Collins	Ted Fowler	Chris Muller	Creed Ford
Norman Abdallah	Bill Walsh	Tony Hughes	Alice Elliot	Gretel Weiss
Lewis Hollweg	Joni Doolin	Doug Brooks	Annette Boulay	Joleen Flory Lundgren
Frank Steed	Toni Quist	Sam Rothschild	Hans Lindh	Harvey Brownlee
Howard Schultz	Chris Lowe	Rodney Morris	Jon Luther	Paul Rich

The 7 Stages of Building High-Performing Partnerships and Teams

A quick note about names and nomenclature in this book: we define a multi unit manager as any supervisor who is directly responsible for the performance of two or more foodservice operations, whether they are company-owned or franchised. For instance, if you're an independent owner or franchisee and you've opened a second restaurant, you are now a MUM (multi unit manager). If you're a franchise business consultant helping franchisees develop and grow a chain brand on behalf of a franchisor, you are also a MUM.

While all multi unit managers have both a challenging role and a common goal, their business cards reflect a variety of different titles, usually determined by the size of their company. A ten-unit chain might have two multi unit managers, each overseeing five stores, reporting to the owner. They might each have the title of Director of Operations. A chain of six hundred units could have as many as one hundred multi unit managers that they might call Area Directors, reporting to Regional Managers, who report to VPs of Operations. The bigger the company, the greater the need for additional management layers between the unit and the executive offices. Industry-wide the multi unit manager job titles include, but are not limited to:

- Area Director
- Area Manager
- District Manager
- Area Supervisor
- Franchise Business Consultant
- Regional Manager
- Director of Operations
- Territory Manager
- Area Coach
- Division Manager

Business guru Peter Drucker probably defined the role best when he called them "the Manager of Managers." Since foodservice companies

The 7 Stages of Building High-Performing Partnerships and Teams

use so many different titles to define essentially the same position, we have chosen to use the term *multi unit manager*, or **MUM**, to describe this important leadership role. Whatever they're called, the roles and responsibilities are essentially the same: to develop, coach and grow people, performance, and profits throughout their territory through indirect influence and leadership.

Our company (**Sullivision.com**) designs service, sales, marketing, training and leadership programs which have been used by *American Express, Walt Disney Company, Coca-Cola, McDonald's, Applebee's, Target Stores, KFC, Marriott, Starbucks, Panera Bread, Home Depot, TGI Friday's, Pizza Hut, Perkins, 7-11 Stores, Sam's Club, Famous Dave's, Denny's, Texas Roadhouse, Holiday Inns, Nordstrom, Ritz-Carlton, Burger King, Outback Steakhouses, Johnny Carino's, Mitchells and Butlers, Chili's,* and hundreds of other successful companies. You can visit our website at ***Sullivision.com*** to see our client list, product catalog, consulting services and access tons of additional free MUM learning resources.

Finally, I'd just like to say that if you have half as much fun reading this book as I had writing it, then I had twice as much fun as you. Thanks so much for your continued support and for being part of the greatest industry in the world.

Jim Sullivan

The 7 Stages of Building High-Performing Partnerships and Teams

Introduction **The Invisible Warrior**

They are hidden to the customer, unknown to stockholders, and invisible to most of the hourly staff. Yet without them, foodservice executives or owners would most likely struggle, and most certainly fail. CEOs would be helpless, VPs aimless, and boards of directors pointless. Chain restaurants or stores would surely stagger and fall without their guidance and leadership. Their influence keenly shapes and orchestrates the success—or failure—of the very people they report to and those who report to them. But ironically, shareholders overlook them and many owners or CEOs rarely or barely know them by name. The key leadership level they represent—steering growth and administering scalability between the unit level and the home office (from street to suite)—is critical to operational success but astoundingly overlooked when it comes to recognition, training, development and reward commensurate to their effort. Why have we overlooked the selection, development and performance processes of multi unit managers for so long?*

Like Batman, MUMs seem to dwell and execute from the shadows, hidden from customer and crew, always alert, armed with instinct, conviction, and a variety of leadership weapons in their "utility belt." They are ready to spring into action day or night to assemble teams, right wrongs, and collectively build a bigger bottom line.

Each day multi unit managers walk a leadership tightrope stretched taut between shifting priorities from above and producing results below. Pressure? They do their job diligently on a sea of distraction in a highly competitive business that is equal parts high-performance and high-anxiety. Being a multi unit manager is not for crybabies, because our industry is tough. How tough? *You don't quit it, it quits you.*

---

* The multi unit manager is virtually invisible not only to customers and crew, but apparently to our industry as well. Trade magazine editors and conference planners: where are the Multi Unit Manager panels, recognition and awards?

The 7 Stages of Building High-Performing Partnerships and Teams

Let us now pause and praise the multi unit Manager. I say: *All Hail the Invisible Warrior.*

Perhaps because they toil so far from the limelight, or because of their relatively small numbers, or since they are seen as "middle managers" by unenlightened investors, multi unit managers have routinely and unfairly been under-served, over-told and under-taught. There has been way too much learning-by-doing and precious little development-by-design; too much "execute the plan" and too little "what do you need?" They're expected to grow their stores and people from point A to point B through pluck, luck and nerve, but often without enough resources, training and clear direction from the executive team. And if they are given succinct plans, Headquarters will frequently change directions more often than a politician during re-election. (One MUM described his guidance thusly: "full speed ahead in all directions!") We need a better way.

If you talk to a lot of Multi Unit Managers (MUMs) a distinct persona emerges. First, the multi unit manager position is unique in that it's a thinking—not a "doing"—job. Second, most MUMs work crazy hours, juggle insane schedules, rack up more miles than a traveling circus, fuel growth, raise families, and have fun, all while supervising a multi-million dollar business from a combination automobile dashboard, corner booth and home office. They are fast-thinking, numbers-crunching, paper-pushing, service-driven mobile leaders with a brain and a Blackberry as weapons of choice. Third, they are effectively "regional/area CEOs" of eight-figure-multi-million dollar businesses. They collectively influence and shape the experience and success of thousands of managers, hundreds of thousands of hourly crew members and millions of customers. And they do it by indirect

The 7 Stages of Building High-Performing Partnerships and Teams

influence, not hands-on control, a fantastical skill oft admired and rarely mastered. They embrace technology, energize the system, keep operations safe, put a premium on "soft" skills, generate revenue, operate through the customer's lens, and mentor the future leaders of Generation Next. And that's just on Tuesdays.

Multi Unit Managers are the face and the steward of the Brand in the most important marketplace: in the store, where the company meets the customer. MUMs are true brand architects, today's change agents and tomorrow's CEOs. Most learn their job the hard way—trial by fire—because their companies have neither the patience nor the resources to develop them slowly, prudently, and with guided practice. Instead, most MUMs are "promoted on the battlefield," and left to the Darwinian development process of sink-or-swim. Most are survivors, not born teachers, because their companies left them to figure it out pretty much on their own. Most companies invest more time and money training their hourly associates and store managers than they do their multi unit managers.

If the MUMs job was an automobile, it would most likely feature a giant gas pedal, a tiny, barely workable brake, and no rear-view mirror.

It's time to better understand the challenges and opportunities we have to improve how we select, develop and nurture the performance of multi unit managers in the 21st Century. Who on your team—if not MUMs—are more deserving of leadership skill enhancement? What better level of supervision to invest in, get better at, and build bunkers of leadership in? Which level of leadership delivers the greatest return-on-investment? MUM's the word.

The 7 Stages of Building High-Performing Partnerships and Teams

Where's the road map?

While meeting, coaching, and working with MUMs around the globe over the last decade, I routinely heard the same request: *"When are you going to write a book about multi unit leadership? There's nothing out there for us."* I thought they surely were mistaken. There *had* to be a wealth of resources available through their companies or in book stores to help them hone their skills, right? After all, multi unit managers may be outnumbered by unit managers, but they are still the critical leadership link in any organization. Was it possible that Operators and Owners had overlooked creating effective training materials and daily development tools for their multi unit managers? Sadly, it seems they have and unfortunately they still do. Looking for MUM training tools is like passing through a small town in the sticks...there ain't much to look at. As we sought out and researched available and MUM-specific resources we were very surprised. The MUMs we met through our consulting and seminars, as it turned out, were absolutely right: the cumulative *effective* MUM material out there was smaller than the period that ends this sentence.

Every company and franchisor we studied invests sizable resources to create scalable training for their hourly crew and managers across multiple learning platforms including manuals, DVDs, flash cards, live trainers, role-playing, pre-shift meetings and most recently, e-learning.

Not so, MUMs. Many, if not most, of the MUM training resources we saw at the corporate level describe a role of "Inspector Compliance" versus Head Coach. They tell the new MUM how to checklist, but not how to coach. Their training materials suggest that MUMs should be visiting "stores", not people, when in fact, just the opposite is true.

The 7 Stages of Building High-Performing Partnerships and Teams

The live seminar programs we've witnessed address "leadership-in-general" but not much "MUM-in-specific", rendering a good bit of the content ethereal, if not plain meaningless. MUMs have a lot of data spewed at them daily, but little relevant education: *they are drowning in information, but starving for knowledge.*

Stranger still, our research shows that rarely, if ever, are multi unit managers' best practices routinely solicited, shared, and documented *within* companies and franchise groups. It's depressing to think how much hard-won corporate memory has been and *is being* routinely lost. There are almost no MUM-specific inter-company conferences that provide a forum where they can commiserate with colleagues over common challenges, seek collaborative solutions, and learn new skills to help them grow. Of the 21 companies we surveyed (see below), we found only one wise enough to invest in sabbaticals or annual leadership retreats for their MUMs to help them rejuvenate, re-focus and "refill the well."

The 7 Stages of Building High-Performing Partnerships and Teams

Research yields keen insight

As an initial step to building a *Leadership Ladder* to a better way, our company began an in-depth survey and investigation of the multi unit manager role. We focused on identifying the core competencies, best practices and behaviors of high-performing MUMs, how they grew into their roles from the junior level, and the kind of training and development resources they need to evolve from "managers" to leaders.

We executed our 13 month-long MUM research project across hospitality and retail industry segments ranging from casual-theme to QSR, family-dining to fast-casual, from fine-dining to hotel and nightclub-bar, and both big-box retailers and category-killers. Not surprisingly, our clients and customers were both intrigued by and eager to participate in the MUM research. There is a collective thirst from chain operators and their franchisees for relevant insight into how to advance and transform the multi unit manager position for the unique challenges in the 21st Century workplace. Those challenges include inspiring a multi-generational workforce, out-thinking a competitive marketplace and embracing new technology that changes more often than Elton John at a Las Vegas Liberace tribute.

Our methodology was straight-forward, our insight revealing. First, we collected samples of all the MUM-specific training materials we could find. Then, we partnered with a well-known university research team to help us design a statistically valid research tool and comprehensive questionnaire for MUMs across industry segments and experience levels. We combined online, in-person (and often on-camera) interviews with hundreds of multi unit managers who shared specific best practices, real-world expertise, insights, advice, and truth from the trenches.

The 7 Stages of Building High-Performing Partnerships and Teams

We were given access to and interviewed 282 high-performing multi unit managers from 21 different companies. We addressed, assessed and detailed their experience, skillsets, competencies, fears, frustrations, hopes, challenges, and best practices. We learned and documented what the best ones did and what the worst ones fail to do. At the same time, we also interviewed 102 award-winning General Managers (GMs) from those same companies, assessing their unique skillsets and competencies. The goal was to determine what GMs expect leadership-wise from their multi unit supervisors, and also which characteristics of high-performing GMs may indicate or predict future success (or failure) as a MUM. A key learning: just because you're a successful GM is no guarantee you will make a successful transition to the multi unit manager role without the right blend of innate skills, guided practice and a willingness to *unlearn* what made you successful as a GM to begin with. More on this later.

> **"Average" means that you are either best of the worst or worst of the best.**

The competencies and practices detailed and the voices shared in *Multi Unit Leadership: The 7 Stages of Building High-Performing Partnerships and Teams* are powerful because they are authentic. The ideas rock because they're based on real-world application. The *Leadership Ladder* is effective because it's built on documented expertise from the field, not consultant's guesswork.

Some of the questions that framed our research include:

- What are the best practices of high-performing multi unit managers?
- What behaviors do high-performing and low-performing MUMs have in common?
- Are we focused on solving the right, or the wrong, problems?

The 7 Stages of Building High-Performing Partnerships and Teams

- What traits should we be looking for (or not looking for) in our GMs to indicate future success as MUMs?
- What are the characteristics of purposeful store visits that get measurable and profitable results?
- What are the characteristics of store visits that are a waste of time?
- Why are most MUMs fixing the same performance problems over and over in their units?
- If the same problems tend to re-occur after MUM store visits, is the process broken? What does a "better way" look like?
- How can companies better collect, share and archive the best practices of their multi unit managers?
- Are MUMs being taught and developed on a model developed in the mid-1990's that is now out-of-date and out-of-touch with today's 21st Century workforce and marketplace realities?
- Are we asking our MUMs to focus on the right things and teaching them how to do the right things right?
- How does the leadership role of a multi unit manager differ when he or she oversees a franchisee versus a company store run by an employee-manager?
- What are the 5 most important and least important things a multi unit manager should be doing every day?
- How many stores are ideal (and how many are *too many*) for effective multi unit leadership?
- What are the best practices relative to time management, calendar development and schedule-making for MUMs?

The research and feedback has yielded a treasure-trove of best-practices and competency data related to the two most critical levels of foodservice supervision: unit leadership and multi unit leadership. From

The 7 Stages of Building High-Performing Partnerships and Teams

this wealth of data, this book, and companion DVDs, audios, seminars, research report, and e-learning courses were born. We will repeat this research annually in order to create an effective benchmarking survey to help us better understand and serve the needs of MUMs as our industry changes and the multi unit manager role evolves.

Summary of Research Results

Here's a top-line summary of what we learned from our MUM research across industry segments:

- While it's challenging to determine an exact number, there are approximately 90,000 foodservice multi unit managers working in North America's 700,000-plus units/stores in the foodservice industry. This includes both company-owned and franchisor/ franchisee operations.
- Average industry tenure for a typical multi unit manager is 5.9 years. Some of the MUMs we interviewed were in their jobs less than one year, others had 20+ years experience.
- Average number of units that foodservice MUMs oversee is 8. (We met one multi unit manager in Canada who is responsible for 26 units. Pray for her.)
- Foodservice MUMs are overwhelmingly male (68%) and Caucasian (64%). Women make up just 32% of the MUM workforce in North America. There are obvious diversity opportunities within this leadership level.
- The key challenges our 282 MUMs research subjects cited (in order of most frequent mention) are:

1. Geography: too many stores across too wide a market.
2. Focus: shifting priorities from above, paperwork and data overload.
3. Disorganization: time management, new technology.

The 7 Stages of Building High-Performing Partnerships and Teams

4. Ability to execute effective store visits.
5. Learning how to better coach and train their associates.
6. Staffing/ bench strength/ turnover.
7. Marketing proliferation (Limited Time Offers, etcetera).
8. Energy.
9. Work-Life-Family balance.
10. Personal development, training, "re-charging".

- The MUMs role is more tactical and directive (do this) than strategic (why and what) today than it was ten years ago. Most MUMs think it should be the opposite.

- Most chain operators have no effective training program that shows MUMs how to progressively improve performance and results over time.

- Paperwork is over-shadowing people-work.

- MUMs we researched visit their stores an average of once every 2.5 weeks. The MUMs with the most profitable stores visited an average of once a week.

- Many MUMs are unable to identify the specific behaviors before, during, and after store visits that will most effectively improve store performance.

- Franchisor multi unit managers (sometimes called Franchise Business Consultants or FBCs) who oversee franchisee-run operations whose operators are not "employees" have a significantly different set of leadership challenges than company multi unit managers who oversee company-owned stores whose managers are employees and can be fired for non-performance or non-compliance. FBCs have a critical role, not just as brand stewards, but also as advisors, psychologists, negotiators and innovation-spotters.

- Most MUMs surveyed (89%) felt their company's tools and training resources for their position are "below average" or "inadequate".

The 7 Stages of Building High-Performing Partnerships and Teams

- Tools and resources to help *veteran* MUMs re-energize, re-focus, and re-invigorate after two, four, six, or ten years on the job are practically nonexistent. Few companies have developed resources for enhancing the unique challenges, needs, skills and competencies of MUMs who have been on the job more than 5 years.

- Since MUMs effectively help operate stores that can generate anywhere from $20 million to $40 million in gross sales annually (or even hundreds of millions when you consider Area Directors for companies like Wal-Mart), they are stewards of operations that dwarf most small businesses or the much-heralded entrepreneur. So why are their training resources so meager?

- Most companies spend more time and resources detailing *career path opportunities and development plans* for their hourly crew and unit managers than they do for their MUMs. When you consider other positions, MUM-specific training time and resources pales in comparison:

   1. QSR hourly associates receive an average of 6 days of job-related training.

   2. Full-service restaurant servers receive an average of 7.5 days of job-related training.

   3. Unit managers receive an average of 28.5 days of job-related training.

   4. Multi Unit Managers receive an average of 4.5 days of job-related training.

- Custom-written training materials for new MUM orientation range from minimal to non-existent.

- Most MUMs learn as they go. Rarely did we find detailed stages of orientation and development plans or formally assigned mentors on both "vertical" (supervisor) and "horizontal" (colleague) scales.

- MUM's stores are usually spread across a wide territory (anywhere from 200 to 500 miles apart in some cases) and they

> **If we don't change the direction we are going, we're likely to end up where we are headed.**
>
> –Chinese proverb

The 7 Stages of Building High-Performing Partnerships and Teams

travel great distances to visit their operations. Their ability to manage their calendars, schedule and strategically plan ahead to make the most of their time on the road and at their stores is a critical skill. Most new MUMs are not coached enough in this discipline and art.

- The art of meaningful store visits—arguably the most important part of a MUMs job—is a widely misunderstood and under-executed skill.

- MUMs are often assigned too many stores to realistically and effectively supervise, coach and guide.*

- A top-line review of our General Manager research shows there are over 565,000 foodservice General Managers in North America.

- Most GMs report that they receive "better than average" training (68%).

- The majority of General Managers surveyed (71%) hoped to become MUMs someday.

- Most GMs (63%) said they'd supervise their GMs much differently if they became MUMs.

- The top 4 complaints GMs had about their MUMs:

  1. Not enough face time.

  2. Store visits where MUMs worked positions rather than offering relevant direction, coaching and feedback.

  3. Pre-occupation and distraction on the MUM's part during store visits via constant cellphone and e-mail interruptions.

  4. Too much "direction" not enough "development."

- Just because a general manager is really good at running one restaurant doesn't mean they will be similarly effective at supervising multiple locations. The leap from "telling what to do" to "telling how to do" is a unique and learned skill that takes patient coaching, guided practice and innate skill.

- The comprehensive and current full MUM survey and report can be reviewed in more detail at *Sullivision.com*.

> **The Multi Unit Manager is both a high-performance and high-anxiety role.**

---

*What is the ideal number of restaurants to realistically supervise? Consider that there are only seven days in a week. If you take one day off, that leaves MUMs six days in which to effectively coach and lead their team. Let's presume that MUMs should affix a 1:1 ratio for coaching; spending one day per working week focused on one of his or her stores. If that logic is realistic, an effective MUM should have no more than six units to oversee.

The 7 Stages of Building High-Performing Partnerships and Teams

Conclusions

Too much of what passes for MUM direction and development today was developed in the 1990s when the industry, the customer, the crew and the marketplace were radically different. What tools are needed for today's realities and tomorrow's likelihoods? Customers change, markets change, learning styles change, and competition changes, so the way we select, develop and coach our multi unit managers has to change as well. We need to "skate to where the puck is going, not to where it is now." This book will not only detail solutions but we'll also identify creative ways to groom the multi unit leader for the likely challenges of tomorrow.

The Role MUMs Play in the Leadership Hierarchy

If you operate a single restaurant, there's only one degree of separation between administration and operations. In a one-unit company, the owner will either hire the GM, or *be* the GM. Either way, the span of control is minimal; one building, one market, one team, one concept, one kitchen, one menu, one set of books. But open a second location, and things suddenly get more complicated very quickly. The skills you acquired growing one unit successfully can actually be detrimental if uniformly applied to operating the second and third or thirtieth one. Evolving your leadership styles from hands-on to indirect-influence is a skill that sadly eludes—and sometimes destroys—many first-time multi unit managers and franchisees.

If success grows your concept further–from two units to four, forty, four hundred or four thousand–the span of control between owner and operations increases not incrementally, but exponentially. Things quickly become more complex and complicated. As sales, size, and geography

The 7 Stages of Building High-Performing Partnerships and Teams

expand, communication and organization grow more complex, calling for increased administration, accountability, scalability, and effective sub-levels of leadership. MUMs are expected to responsibly govern the span of control and scalability of systems between the store and the home office. They implement, supervise and execute the people, performance, and systems which drive growth and revenue.

Before we rock, let's examine the role

Multi unit management, at least in theory, can be as down to earth as Home Plate: fundamentals in place, basics being executed, period goals being achieved, marketing plans in effect, managers leading, team focused, nobody hurt, money in the tills, everything running sharply, and every customer leaves happy. Those are the good days.

On other days, multi unit management can resemble an octopus on rollerskates; there's a lot of activity but you can't tell if it's going to be up, down, forward, backwards, sideways, or out of control. It's a role characterized by determined-and-creative personalities who are comfortable leading indirectly through potential chaos, uncertainty, multiple objectives and multi-directional demands. (Says one MUM we interviewed: "Why do I bang my head against the wall? Because it feels so good when I stop!") Remember that MUMs are in fact "Area CEOs" who run multi-million dollar companies that generate more revenue than 95% of small businesses in North America.

The Game Plan

As mentioned earlier, the goal of this book is direct and relatively simple. We want to share both classic and creative ways to help you

The 7 Stages of Building High-Performing Partnerships and Teams

re-think, re-shape and respect the critical role that multi unit managers play in our industry. It is organized around the seven core competencies and stages of high-performing multi unit managers we've identified through our research. These 7 stages make up the **Leadership Ladder**: *Brand Ambassador, Talent Scout, Servant Leader, Head Coach, Marketing Guru, Synergist and Goal-Getter.*

At the beginning of each chapter we will share a verbatim cautionary tale of bad MUM development, and then share substance, relevance and detail about each competency stage. Expert practitioners on MUM development and leadership will contribute perspective throughout each chapter. Periodically throughout the book we'll also refer to a short video to watch or podcast to listen to on our website at **www.sullivision.com** that will illuminate each stage of leadership development even further. At the end of each chapter you'll find a brief Workshop exercise that will allow you to assess and gauge your own personal strengths and challenges relative to that particular competency.

Read this book with a pen or highlighter in hand to get the most out of it. Circle what you want to remember, underline it, yellow it in, mark it up, and then—and this is most important—teach it to someone else. Use it to change the way you think about the multi unit manager position and how you can adapt, innovate, improve and *change* your behavior to lead rather than merely manage your team. The more time you invest into applying and integrating the ideas, the greater likelihood that you'll use these ideas to transform yourself, your company, your career. *Information is good, but transformation is better*. The world does not pay for what a person knows, but it pays for what a person does with what they know.

The 7 Stages of Building High-Performing Partnerships and Teams

This book is intended to be a useful resource for everyone in a leadership role in the industry, not just MUMs. CEOs, General Managers, kitchen managers, and even hourly shift leaders can benefit from it. If you're already the world's best MUM, consider that one doesn't have to be sick to get better. What you know now has been built on what you were once ignorant of. The book is the cumulative result of research, resources, and years of trial-by-error. It is a compilation of hard-gained knowledge from expert practitioners in the art of multi unit leadership. The content is a collective expression of the hearts, minds, and experience of hundreds of real multi unit managers. Listen and learn from their voices.

Shoshin The Power of the empty mind

The best multi unit managers approach new ideas like beginners, not experts, as they grow and evolve into their role. They know that if you don't learn something new everyday in this business, you're just not paying attention. MUMs are curious, interested, patient, and willing to admit they don't know everything, no matter how long they've been managing managers. They know that to keep leading is to keep learning and school is never out for the pro.

"Knowing it all" can be a dangerous place from which to lead when it comes to improving an organization. In fact, the best MUMs have learned that constantly identifying both personal and company-wide knowledge gaps are the building blocks of daily growth. While identifying what you "don't know" is an important first step, the best multi unit managers go a level deeper. As one MUM we interviewed explained: "He doesn't even know what he doesn't even know".

The 7 Stages of Building High-Performing Partnerships and Teams

The Japanese have a great word called *shoshin* which means "beginner's mind." Author Shunryu Suzuki explains it thusly: "this does not mean a closed mind, but actually an empty mind and a ready mind. If your mind is empty when it comes to learning, it is always ready for anything. It is open to everything. In the beginner's mind there are many possibilities; in the expert's mind there are few."

So whether you've been a MUM for ten years or ten minutes, please read this book through your shoshin lens. Clear the clutter. Suspend what you know and empty–don't just "open"–your mind in order to better access new ideas, concepts and behaviors. Think about how you and your company can collectively improve the process of MUM selection, MUM coaching, MUM development and MUM performance. (Maybe a good place to start is by asking the question: what's the opposite of "what we always do"?) Twice a year, every year, companies should *shoshin* their multi unit manager role. Every six months ask your MUMs what's working, what's not working, and which tools and resources they need today, tomorrow and the day after that to get better in the hyper-competitive world we do business in. What you know matters less than how often you share it. "Knowledge" is not power. Shared knowledge is power. After all, when we teach, we learn twice.

> Freedom is actually a bigger game than power. Power is about what you can control. Freedom is about what you can unleash.
>
> – Harriet Rubin

The Leadership Ladder of High-Performing MUMs ™

Interview hundreds of them, assess the cumulative research, and you will learn one thing for certain: no two MUMs are alike. But there are specific patterns of behavior that characterize and differentiate high-performing multi unit managers from low-performing ones. The detailed research, realities and best-practices we've conducted and collected confirm it.

The 7 Stages of Building High-Performing Partnerships and Teams

We did our best to identify these best practices (and how they translate into action-able behavior) in a way everyone reading this book can benefit from. We identified and separated *need-to-know* from *nice-to-know* content relative to MUM competencies, performance, and development stages. We surveyed the mountain of data our research revealed and soon distinct patterns and behavior groupings began to emerge. We grouped them into seven stages, and then contacted 34 of our original MUM survey subjects and asked them to review each stage (and their sub-competencies) to assess their validity based on their experience. These seven stages that form the rungs of the Leadership Ladder were not arbitrarily assigned by our research team but confirmed by the expertise of the MUMs we originally interviewed. Stringing these 7 growth stages together produces a progressive stepladder of leadership.

Brand Ambassador ™
Talent Scout ™
Servant Leader
Head Coach ™
Marketing Guru ™
Synergist ™
Goal-Getter ™

Let's now turn the page and collectively re-discover — with shoshin-fresh eyes —the 21st Century roles and responsibilities of *Multi Unit Leadership.*

STAGE ONE
Brand Ambassador™

Cautionary Tale

"My development—if you could call it that—as an area manager consisted of the VP leaving me voice mails three times a week alternately accusing me of trying to do too much and then not doing enough. Every thing our company said it stood for in its training materials, he was the opposite of. The only training I ever got from him was what not to do if I ever became an area manager. And that's what I eventually learned from him: first make a list of all the things a supervisor did to you that you hated. Now don't do those things to anyone else, ever. Next, make a list of everything a supervisor did for you that you loved. Do <u>those</u> things for your team always."

"Does the right things and the right things right."

The key competencies of a "Brand Ambassador" include:

- Culture Keeper: standard bearer who models the way
- Authentic and disciplined
- Aligned with company goals
- Runs it like they own it
- Habitual Consistency
- Brings Energy (doesn't take it away)
- Embraces technology
- Clear grasp of the non-negotiables
- Meets financial goals

"If someone were to ask me 'what kind of company are you?' I like to think I can point to any one of my area managers and say 'See her—or him? That's who we are and what we're all about'." That quote, from a regional VP at a multi-national quick-service foodservice chain says it best and says it all. The best multi unit managers are standard bearers, "ambassadors of the brand," who know the way, show the way, and go the way.

A *Brand Ambassador* is someone who buys wholeheartedly into the philosophy and culture of the company he or she works for and the brand they represent. They both model the way and preach what they practice. They know that the "Shadow of the Leader" determines the behavior of the team. If you're not a role model, in sync and aligned with the company's culture, the other 6 stages are useless and you're most assuredly in the wrong job.

The 7 Stages of Building High-Performing Partnerships and Teams

You are who you hire

Brand Ambassador MUMs do not act like clones of one another. Nor should they. Different style and character among multi unit managers brings a company greater dividends than an org-chart full of corporate clones. Every MUM is unique and his or her leadership style reflects who they are. They should act and even think differently. As one military leader once famously said: "If we're all thinking alike, then someone isn't thinking." The personality, people and performance of a MUM's stores directly reflect who they are and how they lead. People like to associate with and work for people who like them and are like them. Show me a disciplined, authentic and passionate MUM and I'll show you a profitable set of operations built on fundamentals, focus, and fun. Show me an unfocused, detail-blind, and dispassionate MUM and I'll show you high turnover, sloppy GMs and underperforming units.

There should be no inconsistency between your company's values and the multi unit manager's behavior. If I read your company's mission statement I should recognize your MUMs. The MUMs who get the best performance and profits from their people are habitually consistent in their actions, words and demeanor. They are fair, honest, moral, committed, and disciplined.

Characteristics of Brand Ambassadors

Our research and resources have uncovered the following traits as being the most consistently valued by both MUMs ("this is what we should be") and General Managers ("this is what I want from a leader").

Authenticity. The "real deal" MUM is credible, competent and committed. "Authenticity" means being aligned with corporate goals, policies, procedures and expectations. It extends to being moral and accountable for

"Does the right things and the right things right."

one's actions and words. It means telling the truth. (By the way, authenticity is granted by the people the MUM supervises, not by the MUM proclaiming how "genuine" they are.) If a MUM's words and deeds around their internal customers (employees) is inconsistent with the brand promise your company makes to your external customers (guests), the credibility and integrity of the MUM will always be suspect. And lack of credibility is a shaky lake to sail from.

Integrity. If you have integrity, nothing else matters. If you don't have integrity, nothing else matters.

Knows the difference between principles and rules. *Brand Ambassadors* recognize the difference between rules and principles. Rules tell you what you can do, principles tell you what you can't do. Who we are *not*, also defines who we are. Your words, deeds and actions must always support and reflect—never contradict—brand values, policies, and procedures. Do the right things and do the right things right.

Energetic. Leaders are never "energy-neutral." You are either giving people energy or draining it from them. When visiting your stores or meeting with managers you should always bring energy, don't take it away.

> One job of a leader is to help people identify what habits and assumptions must be changed for the company to prosper—and to ask, "Which values and operations are so central to our core that if we lose them, we lose ourselves?

Flexible and fair. Authentic MUMs can both cruise in the calm and perform in the storm. They're adaptable to challenge, change, and shifting priorities. Being cool, calm and collected under duress is highly valued by a MUM's direct reports. The ability to evaluate performance fairly and reasonably (looking at the Big Picture and having a balanced perspective) are traits GMs value highly in their supervisors. Never evaluate mistakes when you are angry.

The 7 Stages of Building High-Performing Partnerships and Teams

Self-esteem. Who believes in leaders who don't believe in themselves?

Disciplined. High-performers are tough on standards, but easy on people. They have a clear grasp of the *non-negotiables* and never confuse being disciplined with being a "jerk." They know that what they (and their managers) permit, they promote. They keep rules to a minimum, and enforce the ones they have. They do not avoid conflict, they move swiftly to resolve it; they never leave a nail sticking up where they see it. By acting as a living embodiment of the brand, they demonstrate that actions speak louder than rules. The best companies we've studied are characterized by a *strong culture and thin rulebook.*

Problem-solvers. Every store manager likes a supervisor who can help solve new challenges by helping fix the problem without assigning blame, or berating them for asking for help. When a problem arises in a store, a new MUMs natural reaction is to "fix-it-and-fly," but that urge must be resisted if you're to realistically expand your people's capacity to grow. You've probably heard the classic Irish folk saying: "give a man a fish and he'll be full for a day, teach him how to fish and he'll never be hungry again." Leadership is like that. There's a big difference between helping someone solve a problem and doing it for them. A parent can teach a child to fish but cannot catch the fish for them. A football coach can show the team how to run, block, kick, punt and pass, but cannot go on the field to make the play. When a store manager is faced with an operations or performance problem, they should brainstorm ways they can fix the challenge they're struggling with. If time or circumstances don't allow for counseling and thinking it through together, then fix it yourself if you can, but *don't forget to show them how you did it.* Smart MUMs have learned that transferred knowledge (show-how) trumps innate knowledge (know-how) every time. We'll re-visit this idea again in the *Head Coach* chapter.

"Does the right things and the right things right."

Problem-givers. The best MUMs are also problem-givers in the sense that they set s-t-r-e-t-c-h goals for their direct reports; not too hard, not too easy. They understand the importance of being *thoughtfully unreasonable* from time to time, assigning challenges the manager may think to be unattainable until they actually try it, usually succeeding, thereby enhancing both performance and self-esteem. This builds confidence as well as *capacity* for problem-solving; the more we solve complex problems that initially challenge us, the further we enhance our capacity to solve even more complex problems. Just like exercising muscles.

> **You cannot live a perfect day without doing something for someone who will never be able to repay you.**
>
> —John Wooden

Sweat the small stuff in operations. Etch this in stone for you and your managers: NEVER GET BORED WITH THE BASICS. Make certain your managers know what the fundamentals are and how to execute those fundamentals every shift. The devil is truly in the details. A *Brand Ambassador* never underestimates the importance of their managers executing the "little" things daily, shift in and shift out. They know if they and their managers sweat the small stuff, their customers won't have to. Most of what customers define as good service is made up of dozens of little details the customer doesn't even notice...*until you don't do them*. The most profitable stores are the ones whose managers and team are brilliant at the basics.

Run it like you own it. *Brand Ambassador* MUMs will manage their territory, stores, equipment, customers, team and budgets with as much care and consideration as they do with their own money. They approach all decision-making as an owner (whose home is the on the bank loan guarantee) would, thoughtfully, thoroughly and with resolve. They learn to model the way and teach the "owner-mindset" to their store managers so that the managers will teach it to the hourly associates as well.

The 7 Stages of Building High-Performing Partnerships and Teams

Be an innovator. The *Brand Ambassador* knows that "good enough never is." A strong management role model is always looking for a new way, a better way, a smarter way. They challenge the process daily at their own operations, they watch what other companies do, and "steal" good ideas to adapt, innovate and improve upon in their own restaurants. They keep a keen eye on their own stores or franchisees to spot innovative ideas that could be shared system-wide.

Celebrate diversity. What do we have in common? We're all different. What defines our collective strength? Our differences.

Embrace technology. In today's competitive world, we compete not just in products and quality but also in operational processes and informational systems. Master the intricacies—not just the "basics"—of Excel, Outlook, Word and Power Point. Be curious about and research new and developing technologies that can enable better productivity, especially in the areas of hiring, training, scheduling, inventory, financials, throughput, service and sales. P.S.: A word of caution here: personal productivity tools like "Crackberries" and smartphones are critical resources for the modern MUM, but knowing how and when to use them is just as important. There's always the danger of becoming "Inspector Gadget" and investing too much time serving technology instead of your people. Find the balance and resist the temptation to be constantly checking or replying to your e-mail when you're in your stores or in meetings with your managers.

Market your brand to the primary audience first. A *Brand Ambassador* markets and sells his or her product, promise and purpose to the "home team" first and foremost. Fail at internal branding and you may waste a lot of money on advertising campaigns that make promises your employees can't—or won't—keep. "It is not good enough for your brand

"Does the right things and the right things right."

to have quality and value for your external customers," says Josh Davies, Director of Training and Development for Denver, CO-based Sage Hospitality. "Your internal brand must provide quality and value for your internal customers, too." Seems simple until you consider that you can't define what quality and value are, only your customers can. So find out what your internal customers value most about your company's culture, and give them more of it.

Our two objectives this year are to improve service and cut costs.

–actual annual goal of a restaurant chain who shall remain anonymous

Natural Historian. A core competency of Brand Ambassadors is their interest in preserving corporate memory as a tool to improve their team, territory, and company. They recognize the importance of retaining, recording, preserving, and sharing key learnings and best practices of their team on a weekly basis. It helps them to grow incrementally better every day. Preserve not just what you and your team learn on a daily basis, but also the physical memorabilia of your operations, including menus and photos. If key supervisors leave voluntarily or retire be certain to capture their recollections of your company's early days or solicit perspective and advice on which mistakes not to repeat. More on this topic later in the *Head Coach* chapter.

Sensibility of shared fate. Recognizing that we're all in this together helps effective *Brand Ambassadors* make decisions that align with both today's priorities and tomorrow's goals. If you ever want to demonstrate the importance of solidarity to your team or franchisees, here's a strong visual metaphor you can use. Buy a box of pencils. Take out one pencil from the box and show the audience how easy it is to snap it in half. Now take out the rest of the pencils in a bundle. Try to snap the bundle. You can't do it. The moral is direct: individually we can make decisions or do things which alone can challenge us or break us. But collectively, sticking together, we cannot be broken.

The 7 Stages of Building High-Performing Partnerships and Teams

"Don't fight in front of the kids." This classic advice applies not only to parents but also to supervisors. Visible discord among MUMs and their managers affects morale and team performance. Praise publicly, critique privately.

Understand how small changes affect the global template. Effective *Brand Ambassadors* know the importance of challenging the process, of making small adjustments and daily improvements. They learn to first gauge how the small change might affect the global brand template, to look before they leap. Sometimes small changes (the right kind) can positively transform an entire business. Likewise small changes (the wrong kind) can just as easily ruin one. For instance, managers or franchisees should never change, modify or refuse a spec, standard, or policy because they "don't like it" or they believe that they can get it cheaper elsewhere. Know why it was chosen in the first place and how changing it might change the customer's experience with your company or brand. Making even small changes to spec food, beverage and brand standards for the sake of price may be "penny-wise but it's pound-foolish."

> The manager who makes a mistake and then blames circumstances or others has now made two mistakes.

What you reinforce is what you get. What's the first thing you focus on when you open your manager meetings or visit one of your restaurants? Numbers? Labor? While financials are certainly important, know too there's a dark side to the "numbers, numbers, numbers" mantra. If you believe training and service are important but "numbers!" are the first thing out of your mouth in all conversations, don't be surprised when the main thing your managers work on is cutting labor, even at the expense of training and service. The more you focus solely on labor and numbers, the greater the likelihood Store Managers may decide to work an hourly position themselves to save the labor dollar and attempt to hit their bonus. Of course that means zero training, zero

"Does the right things and the right things right."

coaching, and zero customer service focus during the shift because the manager is working as an hourly associate not as a coach. Keep an eye on the numbers and manage to the financial goals certainly, but also encourage your managers to keep an eye on the Big Picture. Great companies don't build "business," they build people. *People* build business.

Keep regulators on your side. Having to deal with any government agency, especially over things that could have been avoided and done right in the first place, is a depressing, time-killing and resource-draining affair. Sloppy oversight on compliance issues which causes local, state or federal government officials to get involved in your operations results from lack of discipline; a serious and rookie mistake. Operational oversights or straying from standards that attract regulatory agencies to your business will bring you (and your manager's) world to a screeching halt. Be sure you and your teams fastidiously audit all compliance issues daily so that the government spends its time with competitors instead of you.

Clearly define the non-negotiables. What are the non-negotiable standards in your company? Do your store managers and hourly crew clearly know what they are? A short list might include (but not be limited to):

- Quality, Service, Cleanliness.
- Safety, security.
- Customer-Centric focus.
- Commitment to diversity.

- Contributing to community.
- Daily training and coaching of each associate.
- Always telling the truth.

Be honest, be discreet. Know when to share information and who to share it with. Be ethical. Tell the truth and research facts before sharing opinions. One lie does not cost one truth, one lie costs *the* truth.

The 7 Stages of Building High-Performing Partnerships and Teams

Don't bad mouth the executive team (or the competition). Multi Unit Managers who speak derisively about executives or executive decisions to managers or fellow MUMs don't endear themselves to those people, it just makes your character suspect and those people uncomfortable. Have you ever heard the phrase "if he gossips to you, he will gossip about you?" Constantly denigrating the competition as inferior also affects your integrity.

Habitual Consistency. It's one thing to "know" the behaviors of high-performing *Brand Ambassadors*, it is another thing entirely to *do them* on a daily basis. Habitual consistency is all about being brilliant at the basics and establishing a results-driven daily success routine. After all, a successful restaurant or store is the result of the endless repetition of perfect and near-perfect shifts, day-in and day-out.

Makes the company money. Building the bottom line is the bottom line for measuring and evaluating high-performance. Healthy ROI is the reward and result of doing everything else right. No *Brand Ambassador* ignores the importance of contributing to and being part of a profitable organization. An organization that routinely meets or exceeds its financial goals is an organization that best serves its customers, crew and managers. Profitability is both a means *and* an end; the means to grow further and the end result of executing the basics of being a *Brand Ambassador.*

Summary

Brand Ambassador is the critical first stage rung on the Leadership Ladder of high-performing MUMs for a very simple reason: *your team may not always listen to what you say, but they never fail to imitate what you do.* Actions speak louder than words. Every unit manager and frontline team member should clearly understand what the company is dedicated to and those characteristics should be embodied in the words, deeds and behavior of their multi unit leader.

"Does the right things and the right things right."

Self-assessment: **Brand Ambassador™**

"Does the right things and the right things right." Review the list of defining Brand Ambassador competencies below. Assess your personal strengths and challenges relative to each competency in one of the boxes to the right. Review the boxes again in six months. Any progress?

Competency	Good At	Average	Needs Work
Am I a standard bearer that models the way?			
Am I authentic and disciplined ?			
Do I bring energy (not take it away)?			
Am I habitually consistent?			
Do I embrace technology?			
Do I have a clear grasp of the non-negotiables?			
Are my actions and words aligned with company goals?			
Do I run it like I own it?			
Do I routinely meet or exceed my financial goals?			

Actions Speak Louder Than Rules

Put 5 monkeys in a cage. Inside that cage, hang 1 banana on a string and place a ladder under it. Soon one of the monkeys will spot the banana and start to climb the ladder. As soon as he does, spray all of the other monkeys with cold water. Now, replace the banana. After a while another one of the monkeys will probably go for the banana. Again, spray all of the other monkeys with cold water.

The 7 Stages of Building High-Performing Partnerships and Teams

Monkeys are fairly smart, so pretty soon whenever one of the monkeys tries to climb the ladder all the other monkeys will try and prevent him from doing it. When this happens, put away the cold water. Remove one monkey from the cage and replace it with a new one. Then put another banana at the top of the ladder.

The new monkey will spot the banana and make for the ladder. To his surprise all of the other monkeys will attack him. After a couple more tries result in further beatings, the new monkey will not make any attempt to go for the banana.

Remove another of the original monkeys and replace it with yet another new one. Then replace the banana. Again, the new monkey will make a grab for it. Like his predecessor he will be amazed to find that all the other monkeys attack him. The previous newcomer will take part in his replacement's punishment with some enthusiasm.

One at a time, gradually replace all of the original monkeys with new ones. Each of the newcomers will go for the banana. Each one will be attacked by the other four. Most of the new monkeys have absolutely no idea why they were not allowed to climb the ladder, or why they are participating in the assault on the newest monkey. When all of the original monkeys have been replaced, none of the remaining monkeys have ever been sprayed with cold water. Nevertheless, no monkey ever approaches the ladder. Why not? Because as far as they are concerned that's the way it has always been done around here. And that is how a company policy begins.

Moral: Challenge the process daily. Why do we do it that way? What if we didn't? What was the origin of the policy? Does it still make sense for us? For our customers? Does the process or policy make it is easy for customers to do business with us? If not, why? Change it. Does it make it easier for us to do business with us? If not, why? Change it.

"Does the right things and the right things right."

Expert Opinion: Chris Muller

Chris Muller is Professor and Director, Center for Multi Unit Restaurant Management, Rosen College of Hospitality Management at the University of Central Florida in Orlando. He has been studying multi unit foodservice managers globally for over a decade and is recognized world-wide as an expert on the topic.

Q: You've done a significant amount of research over the years on the competencies of multi unit managers. Can you describe the stages of developing high-performers in this critical role?

Over the past fifty years, there is general agreement on the use of a lifecycle approach to understanding change created by either experience or maturity. In our research we have applied this idea to the development of the multi unit manager as well. Since almost all restaurant multi unit managers have mastered the skills of a single unit manager, their perspective is based on this experience. Great general managers acquire the competencies of a general manager, which they bring with them to their new position. What they need, though, are the skills of a "manager of managers."

The first stage of multi unit manager development then, is the transition from being a great GM to being a MUM. This critical development stage is often the hardest to make because the skills they bring with them seem to be easily applied to the new job. Unfortunately, many people get stuck at this stage, because they quickly evolve into a "super operator" and not a true multi unit manager. This stage relies on a keen understanding of unit operations, from food and labor cost control to staff scheduling, from driving customer counts to passing mystery shop inspections. A first stage MUM will often work two, three, or four times harder than they did as a single unit GM, primarily because they are still doing the same job, but now they have four units to manage instead of one.

The 7 Stages of Building High-Performing Partnerships and Teams

They are still thinking tactically, with a short-term horizon, and only using the skills they already possessed when they were promoted.

If they survive this stage, (and many do not), they will transition to the next level only after they let the "super operator" fade away and the "manager of managers" to emerge. This second stage liberates them from focusing completely on the daily operations of their units, and they soon come to realize that their new job requires an integration of each individual restaurant into a cohesive network, area or district. The primary requirement for this transition is understanding that integration requires a mastery of complex financial skills. These skills reveal the relationships among the three key accounting reports—the Income Statement (or P & L), the Balance Sheet, and the Cash Flow Statement. Where a GM spends time looking at unit level operating income (primarily because bonuses are based on this line item), the MUM has to see how an investment in one specific unit this quarter will have a positive economic impact in three months, or six months, or longer. The MUM comes to see that financial management is not just about managing "the numbers" but is about the allocation of scarce resources. Profits are not just generated from unit operations, but also come from wise investment in plant, people and promotions. It has been said that "any dummy can cut costs by 10%, but it takes a genius to spend money wisely." This second stage of MUM development is about seeing the "whole" and not just the "parts" and grasping how cash flows from the restaurants into the corporation.

After they begin to recognize this complex network of relationships, high performance multi unit managers may transition to the next stage of personal development. At this point the financial investment in the area will have become stabilized, and a new perspective will begin to come into focus. This is when the MUM turns their attention to the customer, not the units.

"Does the right things and the right things right."

The competency required at this level is an understanding that the position calls for the maximization of brand value through marketing and customer retention. The MUM must now understand the linkages among operations, financial results and guest satisfaction. The goal, of course, is to increase district revenues through building frequency and loyalty, the two key factors in successful restaurant management. Marketing, in all of its components, reaches out to customers where they live, creates in them a desire to become trial users. The execution of great operations then creates in them a reason to return. Regular, loyal customers reward the company with their patronage, which then creates sound and profitable financial results.

The final stage of high performance multi unit management transition is made when the MUM focuses on achieving results through the development of people. Truly successful "managers of managers" are those individuals who see the creation of talented teams, deep and diverse bench strength, and high retention rates (not low turnover rates) of all district employees. At this point in a career, which in the best of multi unit managers should take no longer than 24 months of personal development, almost all of the work of the MUM is spent investing in the people who truly create customer value—their staff across all levels. Basically, great operations lead to great financial results because great marketing has built strong brand identity which attracts great people who develop to their full potential and help to create great operations. The high performance "manager of managers" has now become an enlightened multi unit manager.

Q: What are 3 most common things that companies overlook when hiring or developing new Multi Unit Managers?

As described above, the skills that made a unit manager successful are not necessarily the same as the ones that will make someone a successful "manager of managers." So what attributes should be sought out when looking for the person ready to make the leap to the next level?

1. An ability to understand the difference between being motivated by outside forces (extrinsic factors) and being motivated by inside forces (intrinsic factors). Specifically, the kind of procrastination which is overcome by the intensity and formal structure of unit level operations will suddenly becoming paralyzing to a new MUM who must face the highly unstructured and self-scheduled role of an area manager. People who thrive in the routine and regular daily cycles of a restaurant will find it difficult to figure out what to do when they start their day as a district manager. Unit managers are surrounded by people seeking their advice, MUMs work alone and set their own pace. Companies need to find out if this trait is present in the MUM candidate before a promotion is offered.

2. An ability to "let go" of tasks, responsibility, and authority. Unit managers might delegate the small stuff, but they thrive in the role of "boss" making dozens of decisions, large and small, every day. multi unit managers make suggestions, and succeed by being persuasive, not giving commands. In order to be successful the "manager of managers" needs to truly be able to delegate, hold people responsible for their decisions, and to give away the necessary authority so this can happen. Identifying this attribute in an individual will go a long way to accelerating their moving from the first stage "super operator" to the next three stages.

3. The final attribute to surface in new multi unit managers is an attitude of "servant leadership." Where a top general manager might be focused on the staff, they are also driven to succeed on a personal basis. Most are highly

"Does the right things and the right things right."

competitive, with themselves, other GMs in the system, and other competitors in their market. Top multi unit managers need to be "other directed" and cognizant that their success now depends entirely on the success of the people who they manage. They will exhibit a desire for organizational success not their own individual achievement. Finding people who exhibit this trait is often not a priority when looking for the advancing GM, but should be for advancing companies.

Q: *How will the role of multi unit foodservice manager most likely change in the next 5 years? What should we be looking for in GMs?*

How often have we all heard that nothing is certain except for change? Now that restaurant meals have become a crucial part of the American lifestyle, the changes that effect society in general will have significant impact on the multi unit environment. One such change is the increasing "pluralism of consumer demand," meaning that customers continually want more choices of better and more differentiated product offerings. With this has also come a "pluralism of the supply of talent." This means that the labor force becomes less and less homogeneous in education and shared cultural knowledge or experience, more diverse, and more demanding each day.

So, what will be the key success factors for future general managers looking to be promoted to the next level? First, they will have to become true "generalists" with a strong mastery of organizational complexity and managing in a less structured and more insecure market. Generalists will need to be able to move rapidly from downloading on-line computer reports to meeting with community activists, from conversing in at least two languages to creating in-store merchandising campaigns, all the while dealing with a more mobile work force who see their jobs as little more than a temporary stop on the way to somewhere else.

The 7 Stages of Building High-Performing Partnerships and Teams

A big part of this complexity will come with the need to understand the principles of customer relationship management. This means, for example, having the ability to create, manage, and track local store email campaigns which are integrated into a total neighborhood marketing program. Promotional activities, public relations, sales blitzes, and the integration of the community into the daily routines of the restaurant will become a major component of every general manager's job description. They will become the de facto Sales and Marketing Manager for their restaurant unit.

As I mentioned earlier, GMs will be required to manage their business units by understanding not only a simplified P & L statement, but how the total Income Statement drives positive Cash Flows, which in turn create increasing value on the Balance Sheet. Where this level of financial sophistication used to be reserved for senior executives, competencies in all aspects of the business will soon be expected of general managers in most corporate units. The GM will also wear the hat of the Chief Financial Officer for their restaurant unit.

Finally, as in so many areas of modern society, restaurant managers will need to master layer upon layer of newly emerging technologies. From a simple labor cost to capital improvements looking to replace labor, and from just-in-time purchasing software to cook-chill systems, technology will drive the skills of the restaurant manager.

For example, within a very short time, a significant portion of the cost structure for restaurants will revolve around energy management. Restaurants will need to monitor all manner of energy, waste, and other environmental factors, either because of changing laws and government regulation or pressure from the investment community for cost reductions. Miniaturization of kitchen equipment through advance computing will soon

"Does the right things and the right things right."

arrive. Where a simple understanding of refrigeration technology used to be a plus for GMs, now they will be required to understand the workings of remote digital wireless sensors, heat pumps, co-generation equipment, and blast chillers.

Computers will no longer simply be collectors of information from the POS system, they will be used to monitor every activity in the restaurant from time cards to use-by dates for dairy products. And, while technology will be changing the hardware, demand will rapidly expand the software side of the restaurant business. Local product procurement, organic food sourcing, nutritional composition of all menu items, and basic food science will all become part and parcel of the GM's daily workload. To be promoted to a multi unit level, all of these skills, and many others, will need to be mastered. The GM will become the Chief Technology Officer for their restaurant units.

Basically, there will be more technological change during the next decade than there has been since Escoffier designed the hierarchical kitchen brigade system at the end of the 19th Century. Companies, and managers themselves, will need to find the means to gain the education necessary to master all of these factors. Change will indeed require new skills, and the role of the GM will change too. Needless to say, the "manager of managers" will have to have mastered these skills, and be able to explain them all, before they will be eligible for promotion.

STAGE TWO
Talent Scout™

Cautionary Tale

"My first day on the job as an Area Manager, my Regional Director of Operations took me on a whirlwind tour to the 8 restaurants I would be overseeing. I swear we did it in less than 90 minutes and then he had me take him to the airport. As I was dropping him off he told me I needed to hire 2 new managers in the next 7 days, and that he'd be back in three weeks. The next day he called and told me that he'd just hired the managers for me from a competitor and that they would start on Friday. That was how I learned the importance of selecting, not hiring, the right person for the job. He wasn't a bad person, but he was a really bad recruiter."

"Stop 'managing' people. Get better people."

The key traits of a "Talent Scout" include:

- Establishes a talent strategy
- Strengthens the Bench
- Prunes the Deadwood
- Hires s-l-o-w, fires *fast*
- Builds their own replacement
- Identifies tier talent daily
- Recruits to cultural fit, talent gaps and knowledge gaps
- Knows the value of inside-out and outside-in expertise
- Hires noticeably better people ("A" Players only)
- Meets financial goals

Goal-Getter™
Synergist™
Marketing Guru™
Head Coach™
Servant Leader
Talent Scout™
Brand Ambassador™

A leader's lasting value to any organization is measured by succession. And the strength of your team is directly proportional to the quality of people you select, develop and groom daily. Finding, developing and retaining talented people speaks volumes about your competence as a multi unit leader. That's why *Talent Scout* is the second stage on our Leadership Ladder.

Without having aces in their places you're in dire straits as a leader. Great MUMs know that being a *Brand Ambassador* (Stage 1) is the connective tissue of attaining and retaining talented high-performers; who you are is who you attract. It is not exaggerating to say that your long-term personal and company growth is determined by how well you and your managers

The 7 Stages of Building High-Performing Partnerships and Teams

develop "A-Teams" in your stores. The depth of your bench strength and talent pool is the foundation of any sound strategic plan. MUMs with Talent Scout awareness quickly recognize that job #1 is finding, developing, and retaining high performers. Job #2 is to fill the pipeline with more high performers. Job #3, ironically, is building your own replacement.

One of the greatest compliments any organization can earn is this: "look at the awesome people who come out of there.

In today's competitive marketplace, every restaurant says its food and beverage is the best, they all claim "quality". And so what happens? As far as the customer is concerned, when everyone claims quality, no one "owns" it anymore. Quality becomes the "greens fees" of doing business with you; it's an expected, a given. And the reality is that when quality is perceived as a commodity, the battleground shifts to your **people**. Where are you and your company relative to filling up and grooming your talent pool?

Talent Scouting is not easy. Multi Unit Managers can—and must—build teams from a veritable Freudian smorgasbord of personalities and range of abilities, often with too few resources and always with not enough time. Building bench strength and coaching better performances from their team daily is a necessity, not an option, because the reality is that MUMs are hired by the people they report to but fired by the people who report to them. The best multi unit managers work wonders, bringing consistency to chaos, building bottom lines, wringing good things from bad locations, and strengthening the span of control between owner and operations. The worst can just as easily bring the company down through inattention, inexperience, and ineptitude, forgetting that all operation problems boil down to people problems. What's the difference between the best MUMs and the worst ones? *It's the people, stupid.*

"Stop 'managing' people. Get better people."

Recruiting is a philosophy, not a department

Until you prioritize the skill of Talent Scouting for the *right* people, you'll be forever "managing things" instead of leading teams. Nothing is more time-consuming and energy-draining than having to constantly recruit, re-train, and replace bad hires. Every other leadership competency we'll cover in this book is meaningless if you don't first put a premium on having enough talent (of the right kind) and then learn to *groom* the right people and broom the wrong ones.

The best MUMs are pro-active talent scouts 24/7/365, seeking both internal (inside-out) and external (outside-in) expertise. And the smartest MUMs have learned that the key to more time and greater productivity is to stop "managing" people and start *hiring better people.*

Talent Scouts hire to make a difference not merely to "fill a slot." Look around your restaurants and stores at the managers and crew who make up your talent pool. What do you see...potential or uncertainty? A little of each? Or are you unsure? The best MUMs know exactly where their knowledge and talent gaps exist and coach or recruit to improve them. Here are a few questions to consider and answer as you evaluate your territory or company's *Talent Scout* prowess:

- As our company grows, do we have the internal capacity to provide enough leaders for that growth?
- Where are we currently strong and weak in management?
- What is the current MUM selection process in our company?
- Do we have room for improvement?
- Are we promoting people from within and also enriching the mix with outside talent?

The 7 Stages of Building High-Performing Partnerships and Teams

- Do we have the talent to meet our 5 year strategic goals? Will we have it?
- How successful are we at recruiting, internally and externally?
- Do we have a great program in place to train/develop MUMs?
- If so, how will we improve it in the next 12 months?
- If not, what are we going to do differently starting today?
- Do we have a system in place for MUMs to share and collect best practices so that we continuously improve?
- Are we recognizing and rewarding behavior we want to see more of?
- Do we or should we have a third party company assist us in the selection process? If so, how do we get started?

Building the Dream Team: a Blueprint

There are two kinds of new MUMs: 1) high-potential (hi-po) GMs who already work for you and are being promoted, and 2) MUMs who have worked as multi unit managers for another company and have been recruited and hired by your organization. Each person has a different set of challenges as he or she assimilates to the position, so let's briefly look at some different scenarios and suggested strategies.

"Stores" can't change, people can. The veteran MUM hired from *outside* your company will normally be strong on experience but potentially weak on your systems and company culture. Outside MUM hires usually bring fresh perspective, additional expertise and ingrained good and bad habits. From a supervisory perspective, the veteran new MUM will need high support and low direction. On the other hand, the *internal* hire (a newly promoted GM-MUM) brings enthusiasm and excitement, but little experience as a multi unit manager. They will initially

"Stop 'managing' people. Get better people."

need high direction and high support. Later in this chapter we will detail the best ways to orient new MUMs into their roles by re-examining the orientation process from a leadership, not a "management," perspective.

While each of these MUM-types have different nurturing and development needs, there are some critical competencies you should be looking for in any new MUM candidate, whether the talent is home-grown or brought in from the outside. Here are some best practices of *Talent Scouts* to consider as you're drafting your dream team, building your bench and putting your aces in their places.

Start with this question. "Who on my management team would I most like to clone? Why?" List their attributes and behaviors in detail. Know what your *heroes* look and act like. Now you've got a reasonable screening tool of characteristics to seek out in your next management hire, interview or search. Know what your *zeroes* look and act like. What are the attributes and characteristics of the worst hires you (and your managers) ever made? Keep these competencies top of mind. If you interview someone for an opening who exhibits those desirable positive or undesirable negative traits, trust your instincts and hire on or move on.

> The amount that can be consumed and executed by a team is controlled by the weakest person on it. While others can give him physical help, he has to do his own thinking.
>
> – Vince Lombardi

Build your Dream Team on paper first. What kind of talent do you need for your personal "Dream Team" or "A-Team" in your restaurant? What would they know, how would they act, what would they teach each other, why would they make your job easier, how would they treat customers and how would they make more money for your company? What and where are the talent and knowledge gaps on your current team? Once this list is detailed

The 7 Stages of Building High-Performing Partnerships and Teams

in writing, you know what to look for in terms of hiring and what to do in terms of coaching. You're looking not just for different skills, but better skills. Different is not always better, but better is always different.

Select for Corporate or Company Fit. Hiring someone for a manager or crew position who doesn't fit your company's culture and then trying to train them to "adapt" to it is like teaching a pig to sing; it's complicated, time-intensive, and ends up just really annoying the pig. Look instead for people who already live and breathe your standards, have the requisite leadership skills that the team needs, and exhibit the behaviors of a *Brand Ambassador*. Once you spot these qualities, whether they're from the outside or inside, hire them. Experience is important, but cultural fit is critical. Training can always be used to enhance expertise, but training cannot be used to "teach values" if they haven't already taken root in a person.

Know why your stars stay. Talk to the people who have already "bought" your product (your current team members). Find out why your managers like working for your company; is it the culture, growth, people, pay? Make a list of those positive attributes and next time you have an opening, look for candidates who have similar affinities. And by the way, if your current team values those elements enough to mention them as reasons why they stay, be sure that you're reinforcing and enhancing those things every day, week, and period with your team.

Work your social networks to build talent pools. When's the best time to plant a tree if you want shade? Five years ago. When's the best time to plant a tree if you want shade five years from now? *Today.* Smart operators know that the best possible future talent for their organization is currently working somewhere else. So they constantly build, maintain, and expand relationships among and between their social and business

"Stop 'managing' people. Get better people."

networks. They instinctively scour and search for talent among friends, family, churches, synagogues, schools, customers, vendors, local businesses, retail stores, current team members, and chambers of commerce. They invest time weekly expanding and maintaining their social network in and among competing restaurants. If high-performers working elsewhere are currently happy with their jobs, smart MUMs know someday they may not be, and let it be known that they're always in the market for talented people. The truth is, you're never really fully staffed if there's great talent available. They also ask distributors and vendors to keep their ears and eyes open for leadership talent at other operations who may have become dissatisfied with their current jobs and are looking for greener pastures. Developing a strong social network is important not just for finding talent but also for marketing and growing your business. A social network is not limited or finite like a pie. It grows—it doesn't diminish—the more you use it. Your social network is like a muscle; the more you work on it, the bigger and stronger it will become. ***Hot tip:*** drop in on local job fairs that the Chamber of Commerce, or local colleges, or retailers like Home Depot may be staging. Note what's working to attract fresh talent to these companies. Read periodicals like *Inc.* and *Forbes* and *Fast Company* and *Wired*. Steal their best ideas related to recruiting and retention. Share the insight with your managers and make recruiting a line item discussion topic at every manager meeting.

Be patient. Hire s-l-o-w, fire *fast*. If you hurry-hire the wrong person because of impatience on the front end you'll end up doubling or tripling your time investment on the back end trying to correct all the problems generated by the bad hire, not to mention the time you'll spend having to find yet another replacement. Patience is a virtue. This mindset of patient hiring is one you must not only personally master but also teach to your

The 7 Stages of Building High-Performing Partnerships and Teams

GMs because it applies to selecting and developing *all* team members. Commit to hiring noticeably better people each time you fill a position.

Be disciplined: seek top tier talent only. Whether you have a position open for $7 an hour or $70,000 a year, there are 4 types of candidates who will apply for jobs with you: A, B, C, or D players. A's are the high performers, D's the low performers. The challenge is that 90% of job applicants (whether they're applying for hourly positions or managerial positions) are C and D players. Less than 10% of applicants are A's and B's, so be patient and disciplined in seeking and selecting these high-performers.

Q: Why are some employees so difficult to work with?
A: Because they're allowed to be.

(Another good reason to only hire A and B players: C managers don't hire C hourlies; they hire D hourlies.) Where MUMs make their biggest mistake is when they hire C or D players rationalizing that "training will fix them." Training will not "fix" D players, only smart hiring—or strategic firing—will. Again, your objective is simple: stop "managing" people...hire *better* people. *Don't spend all your valuable time trying to make below average people average people.* Average means you're either the worst of the best, or best of the worst.

Teach managers and hourly crew to actively seek and recruit talent. To fill the talent pipeline with more A players at every level requires an enlightened staff talent-scouting for you every day in every tier. Which of your high-performers have the biggest social networks? Engage them to help the talent search; high-performers always know other high-performers. Successful companies make it a priority to teach all managers and hourly team members how to recognize and attract more talent to the team. Recruit everyone on your team to be a Talent Scout. ***Note:*** remember that other Talent Scouts will likely be coveting *your* top talent too, so be certain to recognize your high-performers on a regular

"Stop 'managing' people. Get better people."

basis, keep them engaged, excited and feeling appreciated.

How well do I want this job done? If you can't measure it, you can't manage it. First assess your current high-performers and your low performers. What did they have in common? Was there one quality lacking (or in abundance) that made a difference? "Managers often miss out on the right people because they fail to set standards of performance," says writer Dorothy Leeds. "Interviewers typically ask themselves 'What job do I have open?' A smarter question—*the question that would get the best person is—'How well do I want this job done?'* Most of us have only a vague notion of the performance level we require in a job." Raise your sights. Every time you interview your goal is to hire noticeably better people.

> **Once you hire the wrong person there is no right way to develop them.**

Use 3rd Party expertise to hire right. There are a wealth of effective third-party search firms and companies offering effective electronic screening and hiring tools that can save you considerable time and expense by helping you find, screen, and select candidates for your management and hourly positions. Visit our website at **www.Sullivision.com** for a list of companies that do a great job finding and screening high-performers.

Hire people bigger than you. Some MUMs (and GMs too) will actually pass over exceptional manager candidates because they feel threatened by their resume, expertise or capabilities. Consistently seek out and hire people better and bigger than your current team and you will become a company of giants.

Get your aces in their places. Contrary to what you might have heard, "people" are not your most important asset; the *right people* are. We should always hire to make a difference, not merely to "fill a slot."

The 7 Stages of Building High-Performing Partnerships and Teams

Who you are is who you attract. We touched on it in the previous chapter, but it's wise to remember that people like to work with people who like them and are like them. Your managers and stores ultimately reflect the values, commitment, resolve and personality of the MUM supervising them. So the question is: are you hiring the kind of people that you—and more importantly your *customers*—would like to hang out with?

> Strengths are enhanced by our experiences, our skills, and our knowledge. But the most important underlying component is talent. Without the right talents, all the experience, training, and knowledge will never turn us into world-class performers. We cannot understand or develop our real strengths until we understand our underlying talents.
>
> –Benson Smith, author

Hire and retain people who have a natural affinity for hospitality. Why? Because training people to be "nice" is a major pain in the ass.

Prune your deadwood. Why do we retain managers in our company who are not good at team-building and people development? *Would we tolerate an accountant that wasn't good with numbers?* One really good manager is equal to three or four mediocre ones, but the problem is that the three to four mediocre ones usually think they are top performers. The smart MUM knows the difference. They rate and assess their management teams quarterly to determine who is in the top 30%, the middle 60% and bottom 10% of performers. They first recognize and sustain the performance of the Top 30%, attempt to move the middle 60% upwards, and then try to improve the performance of the bottom 10% through coaching, resources and direction. If the performance of the manager is still unsatisfactory after coaching and direction, then you must humanely and steadfastly prune your deadwood. MUMs learn quickly that high-performing managers and team members like to work with other high-performers and that *high performers hate to work with low performers.* Low performers drive away customers, sales,

"Stop 'managing' people. Get better people."

and your high-performers. They cause all kinds of problems that everyone else—especially high-performers—have to fix. Most importantly, if you don't terminate people who are not working out, you increase the possibility of having to let go of the people who are.

Maybe you think your low performers are "not-so-bad." In which case I'd suggest you remember the words of author Marcus Buckingham who says: "the opposite of bad is not 'good', the opposite of bad is 'not bad'." Managers and MUMs spend way too much time dealing with difficult employees. Make the tough choice and let go of the people who bring your company, customers and crew down. Don't avoid confrontation by deciding to push the low performer onto another MUM or manager; *do not rotate bald tires.* After all, it's not the people you fire who will make your life miserable; it's the people you *don't* fire. Don't linger long with a bad hiring decision that will negatively affect your team's progress and internal DNA. How do you and your managers identify the deadwood in your operations? See the next point.

The Life Raft Exercise. This clever mental game can help you identify your high performers, average performers and your deadwood. Here's how it works: in your mind, fire everyone who works for you; your best, brightest, and least productive. Imagine they have all been thrown into the "sea of unemployment." Picture them literally bobbing around in those troubled black waters, uncertain of what has happened. Now imagine you suddenly appear, paddling along in a giant life raft, scudding across that dark water. As

There are four main sources of employee pride, all of which reflect facets of a single attribute—excellence:

1. Excellence in the organization's financial performance
2. Excellence in the efficiency in which the organization's work gets done
3. Excellence in the organization's products…and quality
4. Excellence in the organization's moral character

The first two of these factors relate to doing well and the latter two relate to doing good.

– David Sirota, *The Enthusiastic Employee*

The 7 Stages of Building High-Performing Partnerships and Teams

you look over the team members bobbing about, who would you *first* search out to pull into the life raft with you? Who is the second person you'd look for? Now prioritize who you'd pull in, chronologically. Who's third? Fourth? Tenth? Seventeenth? Twentieth? Now this is the most important part of the exercise...who would you clearly *leave bobbing out there*??? There's your deadwood. If you wouldn't pull them in your life raft, why do you let them continue to affect your lifeblood of customers and crew?

Don't confuse correlation with causation. Resist impulse hiring based solely on resumes alone. The truth is that a managerial candidate may have worked for a successful company without actually contributing a thing to its success. Research and analyze resume claims, performance results, and actual achievements by thoroughly checking references. Whenever you don't get a top-notch reference in reply to a request, consider it a negative one.

Seek fresh talent from all directions. Developing and promoting talent from within your company is crucial. It demonstrates a commitment to growth, recognition, and reward for service and performance. It reinforces the career-path promise (you *do* map out and reinforce the growth opportunities in your company with your managers and hourly team members every day, right?) Knowing, however, when to look *outside* your company for the right talent is just as important as grooming internal talent, too. Hiring managers from other companies (outside-in expertise) can contribute fresh approaches and add new layers of perspective, insight and problem-solving to your team that your home-grown talent may not currently have. Finding the right balance of outside-in and inside-out expertise is what builds a great company. Beware of "vertical tunnel-vision," warns author Scott Eblin, "the tendency to only pay attention to what those above you and below you are doing. Look left and right as you lead to see a wider talent pool."

"Stop 'managing' people. Get better people."

Sullivan's Twin Laws of Team Selection and Performance. 1) When hiring key employees, there are only two qualities to look for; judgment and honesty. Almost everything else can be bought by the yard. 2) There are two kinds of people who never succeed: one cannot do what they are told; the other cannot do anything unless they are told.

Actively seek and identify tier talent. Which server, cashier or cook do the other servers, cashiers or cooks turn to when they have a question or a problem? Which employees are held in high esteem because of consistent caring behavior toward the guest or fellow employees? Why? Which employees have the greatest success selling appetizers, desserts, beverages? Why? How did they learn to do it? What behavior of theirs can be taught or repeated? Always formally recognize your informal leaders, and of course, encourage your unit managers to do the same. Recognize performers as well as the performance. Identify your future leaders among the hourly crew at every manager meeting.

> There's something rarer than ability — it's the ability to recognize ability.
>
> – Tom Rector

Commit to developing your talent early and often. "Most people are enthusiastic when they're hired; ready to work and eager to contribute," says author David Sirota. "What happens to dampen their enthusiasm? Management, that's what. Employee enthusiasm is not just a feeling or an attitude. It is a motivated state, impelling people to action. Companies with an enthusiastic workforce are more successful simply because it is so much less costly to manage them." Don't wait until "official" orientation to mentor, coach and encourage your new hires. Make the hiring ritual itself a motivational event. Make them feel chosen, not "hired." And keep the praise and encouragement flowing. Talented people seek feedback and affirmation on a regular basis. By acting quickly

The 7 Stages of Building High-Performing Partnerships and Teams

to help coach or develop them you not only enhance their enthusiasm, but early interaction can also help determine if you've hired a potential mismatch, an error you want to discover as quickly as possible.

Excel at retention, not just recruiting. Most MUMs have a hiring strategy. The best have a *retention* strategy too. Finding and recruiting talented people is important, but the care and nurturing of talented people you already employ is just as critical. Why spend all that time and effort selecting the right person and then lose them due to supervisory oversight or neglect? Do you fight to retain talented team members? *If you don't recognize your performers, somebody else will.* Great MUMs know that brains, like hearts, go where they are appreciated, so they put a premium on "re-recruiting" their own high-performers everyday. Do you know who it is on your team that you want to retain? Do you know what you need to do to retain them? Have you asked them? Are you actively pursuing their retention through competitive pay, training, and coaching? Your "ROR" (return-on-retention) is as important as your ROI (return on investment).

Don't forget to teach the coach. Our research shows that MUMs who are offered additional outside training courses annually perform better, produce more and stay with their companies longer.

Managing Transition Stages for New MUMs

What kind of GM makes the best MUM?

As mentioned earlier, there are two kinds of MUM candidates: 1) veteran multi unit managers from outside the company and 2) new multi unit managers recently promoted from GM ranks within the company. We've discussed the many characteristics to look for in a high-performing MUM, but how

"Stop 'managing' people. Get better people."

can we best decide who's the best GM candidate for internal promotion to a multi unit manager? The easy answer is "the one who will do the best job."

Unfortunately however, no one can predict the future (which is why you never see a newspaper headline that says *"Psychic Wins Lotto"*). But you can reasonably predict the new MUMs future performance based on past GM performance. Our research with hundreds of high-performers at both the MUM and GM levels confirms certain behaviors of store leadership that are indicative of future success (or failure) as a Multi Unit Leader. These competencies and behaviors are both myriad and complex. One of our MUM research subjects put it this way: "A great GM who will successfully transition to multi unit management is consistent, fair, understanding, passionate, mentally stable, self responsible, tells the truth, wants the truth, respectful, great communicator, willing to adapt, a risk taker, as good at the end of a task as they are at the beginning, gets results through positive reinforcement, and detail oriented." That's certainly quite a list of competencies to consider, but it's still incomplete. Here's what our research reveals as to whether high-performing GMs will excel at Multi Unit Leadership too.

> Not facing your hiring mistakes or your inherited problems is your responsibility. Face it, or someone will conclude that you're not an 'A' player.
>
> – Brad Smart

- **Seek out the automatic operations.** Look for the GMs whose unit runs perfectly even when they're not there. Or, in fact, they may operate even better when they're not there, because the assistant managers and hourly team will work even harder in the GMs absence to prove they're both proud and able. This is a sign of great GMs. They know how to get the best out of their crew because they recognize that all work is teamwork. On their days off, they're off, not calling in or dropping by their stores.

The 7 Stages of Building High-Performing Partnerships and Teams

- **Look for vocal advocates.** General Managers destined to move up the ranks are often the ones who speak up in meetings, advocate and apply the company's best practices in all areas of their operation. They teach themselves to master other disciplines of restaurant operations, such as accounting and marketing, and may even volunteer to cover shifts for other general managers on leave or vacation. If you notice certain GMs exhibiting keen interest in further leadership responsibility, develop some typical MUM-decision matrices and put them forward to the GM, asking "What would you do in this situation?" You can learn a lot about their analytical and strategic thinking mindsets.

- **Compare and contrast.** Consider the 7 stages of outstanding MUMs *(Brand Ambassador, Talent Scout, Servant Leader, Head Coach, Marketing Guru, Synergist, and Goal Getter)* and apply them to your current high-potential GMs. How many of these MUM competencies do your GMs already exhibit? Fast-track the GMs whose behavior reflects all or most of the Leadership Ladder stages.

A good way to further identify potentially effective MUM candidates from your current talent pool is to compare and contrast the behaviors of both above-average and below-average GMs. Begin by knowing what your high-performing and low-performing GMs have in common. Based on our research, here is a comparison table that allows you to compare and contrast hi-po (high-potential) GMs from lo-po (low-potential) GMs relative to the multi unit manager role in your company:

"Stop 'managing' people. Get better people."

Top Performing GMs	Bottom Performing GMs
Quality Food and Beverage	Poor QSC, complaints, low health dept. scores
Tons of fans	Tons of excuses
Feel the energy when you walk in	No energy in customer interaction or staff
Team smiling and appearance sharp	Dirty uniforms, frowns
See vendors as partners	Sees vendors as adversaries
Tough on standards, easy on people	Variable standards and treatment depending on who's managing that shift
Runs it like they own it	Runs it like it's a Monday, or Thursday o
Habitual Consistency	Hot or cold or average mood depending on
Trains team daily	Trains during orientation
Staffing and Scheduling is optimal	High turnover, Low morale, Lack of direction
Managers see what the customer sees	Manager has blinders on
Brilliant at the Basics	Sloppy, inconsistent fundamentals
Shift leaders with Passion	Shift pullers/no passion
Tenure	Turnover
Hires to make a difference	Hires to fill a slot
Accountable, disciplined	"Not my fault"
Mistakes made but learning occurs	Blames the system, the people, the boss. Is surprised by unpredictability of the business

The 7 Stages of Building High-Performing Partnerships and Teams

Top Performing GMs	Bottom Performing GMs
Owns the Community	"Marketing is someone else's job"
Focus, Goal-setting, Execution	Whatever. "I can't believe you guys today"
Invests in relationships: Crew/Customers/Community	Invests in getting through the shift
Communicates well up & down, inside and outside the organization	Fails to work on public speaking skills to get better at reaching the community and crew
Conflict resolver	Conflict maker; hasty, indecisive, avoider
Not surprised by trouble or troubled by surprise	Sports a pit-bull-on-crack expression when stressed
Evaluates first and then acts	Full speed ahead in all directions
Every shift, they talk each team member into position, through the position, and out of the position	Lets the shift "happen" with little or no pre-prep, thought, or planning. Lets crew define the shift by the moods they bring to work that day
Crew is loyal, committed	Crew's home page is Monster.com
Teaches everyone something new each shift	Makes them watch a video when it's time to "train"
Turned on, tuned in	Has "quit" the job but still picks up a paycheck
Pre-Shift meetings are mandatory	Pre-shift? (What that?) Didn't have time
Net result: Profit and Growth	**Net result: Problems and Turnover**

"Stop 'managing' people. Get better people."

Bottom line, if you had only one restaurant to supervise instead of six, seven or eight, *is this person the GM you'd want running it?* If not, what changes need to be made?

The art of upward leadership: orienting GMs to the MUM Role

Our company has helped dozens of foodservice and retail companies improve their multi unit manager selection and development process over the last ten years. We incorporate detailed needs assessments with electronic pre-screening, pre-testing, case studies, problem-solving, life coaching, guided practice and job simulation scenarios. We have also developed effective self-assessment tools to help the wannabe MUM to identify which skills they may presently lack and how to gain proficiency in those skills within a graduated timetable and with a prescribed development curriculum that features guided practice. Visit our website to take a free online assessment to gauge your skill levels. Nurturing the aspirational GM who may not quite yet be ready for the MUM role is a critical process for every company with ambitious growth plans. Don't just say "no", show them how to grow. You have to keep the pipeline full not only with talent but also with skill. Build your bench and "farm team" of future MUMs by careful pre-selection, nourishment and growth. Let's closely examine a four-phase graduated development process that will help new MUMs (and veteran MUMs too) successfully adapt to each growth level of the position.

The 4 Transition Phases of GM to Multi Unit Manager

The transition from GM to MUM happens in a blur to most of the newly-promoted. You're scrambling to finish up the details of your GM job while simultaneously stepping in to learn and get a handle on the new one. Companies need to be aware of this stressful period and provide the right resources, support, and a patient and progressive development plan for their

The 7 Stages of Building High-Performing Partnerships and Teams

new MUMs at this critical juncture. There are four phases that new hi-po (high-potential) GMs move through on the road to becoming successful multi unit managers: 1) Pre-Selection, 2) Orientation, 3) Taking Charge, 4) Growth and Re-Orientation. Let's look at each phase in detail and discuss the right and wrong ways to successfully shepherd each person through the transition.

| 1. Pre-Selection | 2. Orientation | 3. Taking Charge | 4. Growth & Re-Orientation |

Phase 1 **Pre-selection.**

There are few things sadder to see—and needless to happen—than when a company promotes a high-performing GM into the MUM role with "high hopes" only to watch that once-promising talent suddenly fail in the new position. *(Note to readers: "hope" is not a strategy.)* The scenario is sad because you've effectively crushed their ego and spirit and also probably forced them from the company; how many freshly-failed MUMs will choose to return to the GM role in their company under these circumstances? The scenario is needless because it was preventable. The company is to blame for two reasons: 1) they failed to properly screen the candidate and then compare the GMs abilities, skills, competencies and expectations against the MUMs competencies, skills and deliverables, or 2) the new MUM was given only encouraging words and token training (what we call "sink-or-swim support"). The thinking goes that if they were really good with one unit, they'll be awesome with six more. This is patently absurd rationale but it happens all the time. There <u>is</u> a better way and it involves patience, persistence and graduated assimilation into the role. Transitioning high-

"Stop 'managing' people. Get better people."

performing GMs into the MUM position must never be rushed. But all too often it is. Why do we show more patience developing our new store managers and hourly crew than we do our new multi unit managers?

Our research reveals that some companies transition their GMs to MUMs in as little as a day. Enlightened organizations take a thoughtful, patient and long-term approach to new MUM development. Some invest as much as two years to the development process. They know that if you don't have a detailed screening and development program in place for new MUMs that creates a high-quality internal pipeline of talent, you'll always be searching outside the company for these leaders. Invest time upfront patiently screening the potential MUM candidate from among your store managers, and know that not every great GM makes a successful MUM.

Once you identify high potential GMs in your company slowly and methodically begin teaching them the relevant skillsets and roles and responsibilities of the MUM position. Develop and share typical MUM scenarios or challenges with them every month and see if they have an affinity and aptitude for leadership via indirect influence versus hands-on. Those who respond well should be assigned to a more formal second stage MUM development program. Those who don't should be given a specific development plan that outlines the skills or competencies which they may currently lack and need to keep working on. Give them the roadmap.

This patient, holistic, and "slow-drip-learning" approach to MUM development pays big dividends. Most of the industry, however, still sadly transitions their new MUMs much too hastily, forcing them to learn on the job and worse, *practice on their store managers.* "Sink or swim" development is for chumps not champs.

The 7 Stages of Building High-Performing Partnerships and Teams

Don't develop the wrong person

Remember the key is selecting the right person to begin with so you're not spending time and money developing the wrong one.

Finally, before choosing or assigning a new MUM to a territory, the company must always consider the different *replacement scenarios* the new MUM will be walking into. The territory supervisors must carefully assess the situation, evaluating the strengths, weaknesses, attitudes and needs of the people the MUM will be leading. Each store and team will have different leadership and development challenges based on the market, location, unit, age and especially what the previous supervisor did or didn't do. Don't forget to consider the circumstances under which the previous MUM left the company. Will the new MUM be replacing...

...A strong leader who was promoted?

...A strong leader who left the company for a competitor?

...A weak leader who was transferred or re-assigned because of performance?

...A failed MUM who was fired?

...Or is this a new territory with no previous MUM leadership track record?

Each replacement transition scenario must be considered thoroughly and managed properly. Each scenario requires different guidance, orientation, mentoring, and preparation.

"Stop 'managing' people. Get better people."

Phase 2 **Orientation.**

The two most common mistakes companies make are choosing the wrong internal MUM candidate, and failing to design and execute a *graduated* orientation curriculum for the transition between general manager and multi unit manager. The transformation from high potential GM to new MUM is not a neat and clean "one-size-fits-all" linear learning process. Each growth stage on the 7 rung Leadership Ladder we prescribe in this book requires unique conditioning and assimilation, with peaks and troughs of needs, coaching and absorption. Some master one stage quickly but struggle in the next. Always build in time for reflection, trial-and-error, "perfect" practice, custom coaching, and self-assessment.

Transitioning from 1) applying for the MUM position to 2) being considered for it to 3) being selected to 4) taking charge to 5) growing in the role the first year and then 6) evolving into a veteran MUM through the next many years requires unique infusions of guided practice, adapted learning and patient coaching from MUM supervisors at each of these distinct stages. Every new multi unit manager will have different mental, learning and assimilation challenges at each stage.

New MUM orientation "officially" begins with being formally offered and accepting the MUM job and it formally ends only when you stop being a multi unit manager.* Too many organizations characterize "orientation" as a one day drive-by-and-visit of the stores the new MUM will be overseeing, plopping a hefty three-ring binder in their lap along with a set of keys and an org-chart, followed by a brief chat ("Any questions?"). That's chaos, not coaching.

---

*Orientation never truly ends for enlightened companies that are intent on going from good to great. After 3 years, 5 years, 10 years, even 20 years, multi unit managers should be re-oriented to the unique demands of a maturing role. This stage of MUM transition is perhaps the most critical, and ironically, this phase is where our research shows most companies fall way short.

The 7 Stages of Building High-Performing Partnerships and Teams

The company should first carefully assess the knowledge base and knowledge gaps of each candidate relative to multi unit leadership. Role plays, case studies, interviews and questionnaires (especially via an e-learning platform*) can be used to effectively help the candidate self-assess and confirm that they have the realistic expertise and intestinal fortitude necessary to proceed.

Next, the executive team should share long-term company growth strategies and objectives with their top-tier candidates. Give them the same strategic information your current MUMs have. This way they have insight into what their future responsibilities will entail and can realistically assess their own physical, mental and emotional abilities to perform up to those objectives.

Mentoring the new MUM is a process, not a project. The Orientation phase should begin with a thoughtful and detailed learning syllabus that combines both blended learning built on expertise and heavy doses of realistic guided practice. A variety of subject matter experts in your company—ranging from the CEO or franchise owner to the training department and regional VP—should be effectively trained (not merely told) to orient and coach every new MUM. Anyone involved in formally coaching the new MUM must be trained on the principles of Adult Learning 101 and be known for their coaching prowess. Define and assign both vertical (boss) and horizontal (colleague) mentors from which and with whom the new MUM can learn, neither of whom should be their immediate supervisor. The multi unit manager coach or mentor must take his or her role seriously; we suggest that part of their bonus be tied to how well they coach the newbie MUM. Remember, when you teach, you learn twice, and never practice on a new MUM!

---

*We have found that E-learning is a very effective platform for developing both your new and veteran MUMs to another level. E-learning affords them realistic simulation, self-assessment, and the opportunity to both practice and fail at new concepts when the stakes and risks are small. Plus e-learning assures that the whole learning process and progress can be tracked and self-paced. See a sample at Sullivision.com.

"Stop 'managing' people. Get better people."

If your company or franchise group is currently in the sink-or-swim mindset relative to new MUM development, how can you change direction or obtain the necessary buy-in for a more realistic and effective new development program for your MUMs? Robert Tomlinson, Senior Vice President of Operations for ACG Texas, an IHOP franchisee, faced a similar challenge. Here's how he went about the change:

> "We began with a remedial program. We interviewed each multi unit manager and assessed their strengths and weaknesses and also surveyed their needs in order to find the right tools to help them. Next, we scheduled the new Area Directors to spend time in each department in the company: teams, operations, leadership, marketing and HR Management to help them understand each department's core values and key issues. These would be critical in helping them determine what the common mistakes were and how not to repeat them."

We then worked in reverse to figure out how we could avoid those problems from re-occurring. There are too many times, for example, that multi unit managers assume they know how to properly handle a human resources issue, but may not. By sending our multi unit managers to visit with the heads of the different departments and having them go over every possible challenging scenario, area supervisors were able to self-assess how they measured up to common challenges and key issues.

We then put a five-week training program together. The first seven days is nothing but bonding time with the heads of the organization: one day with HR, one day with IT, one day with the director of operations, one day with the administrative director. That is where the area supervisor really starts to build their knowledge base. They spend that time in the office with each department head, but they also go to stores. After the first seven days, they get matched with an area director; in our company that's the level

The 7 Stages of Building High-Performing Partnerships and Teams

You can teach without being natural at it. It may not be your highlight. You may have to have some reinforcement. But you must remember: Good people come to companies and stay because they believe they have a chance to expand their capabilities and fulfill their destiny. You have an obligation to help them. So don't keep a person in a job too long just because he or she is excellent at it; give her another assignment so she can expand herself. Ultimately, you generate your own management future by virtue of working as hard as you can to fulfill these people's expectations. Expand people's capability through coaching.

–Larry Bossidy

between the SVP of Operations and the area supervisor. Each area supervisor now spends four weeks with the area director, talking to people, doing walk-throughs, line checks and system checks that allow the individual to see operational readiness in action. The four weeks they spend in the field are invaluable. At the end of the four weeks, we do an evaluation to see where they are in various areas compared to where they think they are. We ask, "Is the training over?" If not, we help them to work on their weaknesses. Since we instituted this new multi unit manager orientation program, we've reduced management turnover by over 60 percent which saved us nearly $150,000 each year. Comprehensive multi unit manager development not only makes you more money, but it saves you money too."

Here's some suggestions on who to integrate into the new MUMs orientation. Make the most out of your internal human capital resources, here are some suggestions on who the new MUM should meet with and what they should cover together.

With the CEO or Owner

- The new MUM should be officially welcomed and briefed in person by the chief executive of the company. A "30,000 foot" perspective of strategic goals should be discussed.
- A welcome gift or basket and packet of benefits coupled with written gratitude for joining the team from the CEO should be sent to the new MUMs home and family.

"Stop 'managing' people. Get better people."

With the Training Department

The training team should build a bedrock foundation of trust, expertise and executional know-how in the new MUM. Here are some of the skills they should transfer:

- How to use—and *master*—the laptop, cellphone or Blackberry and the software on it.

- How to design and organize an effective home office and filing system.

- Detail and discuss the common challenges (and solutions) they'll likely face relative to issues surrounding HR, Operations, R&M, Marketing, Compliance, Reporting and Scheduling in their stores. The training department should find out what these challenges are by polling each department head and asking them to list their Top 10 issues.

- How to use the most effective and productivity-enabling features of Microsoft Office (if that's what your company uses); especially Outlook, Excel, Word, and Power Point. A lot of potential productivity and time is wasted when MUMs and unit managers only know the basics of these programs.

- Accounting and financials 101; don't presume they know or understand multi unit financial management just because they successfully managed the P&L for a single store.

- Explain how to assess, prioritize and budget funds for repair and maintenance issues across multi units.

- Discuss and role-play the art of conflict and dispute resolution and the art of conflict and dispute *prevention*.

- Learn the fundamentals of effectively managing multiple priorities.

- All relevant HR information including payroll, benefits, worker's comp, operations support, etcetera.

The 7 Stages of Building High-Performing Partnerships and Teams

With the MUMs Supervisor (i.e. RVP or RM)

- New MUMs should spend several days with their new boss visiting stores and clarifying job responsibilities, expectations, priorities, communication preferences, appropriate business expenses, time management, common reports, diversity goals, code of conduct, leadership development stages, quality assurance, KRAs (Key Result Areas you'll be measured on) and hierarchy.

- The new MUM and RVP should review and discuss both good and bad quarterly business plans (QBPs). The new MUM should clearly know the difference between the two. (QBPs are detailed in Chapter 6.)

- Review the process of designing time-effective and cost-effective schedules and calendars. Examine right and wrong samples.

- New MUMs should know how much time they are expected to spend in their stores and what should be targeted and accomplished during visits.

- The RVP should conduct sample store visits with the new MUM, clearly outlining and teaching the stages (Pre-Visit, During the Visit, Post Visit Manager One-on-One, Post-Visit Assessment) and the relevant paperwork. Time should be spent together de-constructing and de-briefing each store visit afterwards. Chapter 6 will also detail the art of purposeful store visits.

- Together they should review the parameters of effective one-to-one manager coaching sessions either after store visits or during period financial reviews.

- The RVP and the new MUM should conduct a S.W.O.T. (strengths, weaknesses, opportunities, threats) analysis of each restaurant.

- They should discuss the peculiarities of each location and the surrounding market area, including a store history, recent store visit reports, and any works-in-progress (people-wise or project-wise) at each location.

"Stop 'managing' people. Get better people."

- Discuss the art of time versus activity management (coming up in the *Head Coach* chapter) and how to make the most of your day.

One-on-one collaborative time during the orientation phase between the Supervisor and MUM is critical time well spent. Listen to his or her needs and understand the nuances between the person and the performance in the early months of the new job.

There are key questions that every new MUM—whether a veteran multi unit manager from the outside or a newly-promoted GM—should ask their supervisor during the Pre-Selection phase. The questions below are paraphrased from Michael Watkins excellent book *The First 90 Days* (HBS Press, 2003):

- What are the biggest challenges our company is likely to face in the near future?
- Why are we facing (or going to face) these challenges?
- What are our best unexploited opportunities for growth?
- What would need to happen for our company to exploit the potential of these opportunities?
- If you were me, what would you focus attention on?
- If you were me, what would you not focus as much attention on?

Your goal in seeking these answers is to share the same reality as your team and supervisors do. To attempt leadership without understanding your team's expectations and perspective is folly. By the way, these questions will benefit the new CEO as well as the new MUM.

The 7 Stages of Building High-Performing Partnerships and Teams

With the outgoing MUM

- Presuming the territory's former MUM is leaving in good stead, the new MUM should spend a few days with them in the stores they're taking over.

- Together they should clarify job responsibilities, expectations, priorities, communication preferences, appropriate business expenses, time management, common reports, code of conduct, leadership development stages, and hierarchy. *This reality-check discussion should be in exact sync with what the RVP said.*

- Discuss the peculiarities of each location and the surrounding market area, including a store history, review of last 13 period results, recent store visits, and any works-in-progress at each location.

- Together they should conduct an informal S.W.O.T. analysis of each manager and each restaurant.

With a veteran MUM who is also a trainer

The new MUM should spend at least a week working with an experienced current MUM who is also nuanced in the art of adult learning. (This person may or may not be the former territory MUM). Here's a short list of what they should be covering with their new MUM trainer:

- The vet should show them how to plan and prioritize their schedule/calendar and share insight on the kind of things that can cause that plan to change.

- How to effectively use a home and mobile office. List all the tools (from PDAs to paper clips) they should keep with them in the car, in their briefcase, in their shirt pocket, purse or trunk when they're traveling between restaurants or stores.

- How to help set effective performance goals with their GMs.

"Stop 'managing' people. Get better people."

- How to conduct effective and productive GM meetings.
- How to effectively juggle administrative paperwork and people work.
- How to effectively assess, prioritize and apportion funds for repair and maintenance or remodels.
- How to efficiently use indirect influence versus "Super-GM-ing" to get the best results.
- Tips, tricks and techniques of effective time and activity management.
- How to balance succession planning with staffing, labor, diversity, turnover and tenure goals.

The MUM trainer, like the RVP before them, should conduct sample store visits with the new MUM, clearly outlining and teaching them the stages (Pre-Visit, During the Visit, Post Visit Manager One-on-One, Post-Visit Assessment) and the relevant paperwork. Time should be spent together de-constructing and de-briefing each store visit afterwards with the GM or MOD (manager on duty). The Vet MUM trainer, former area MUM and the RVPs messages and expectations should all be synchronous and not contradict one another.

With your unit managers

- A new MUM should set aside time during the Orientation phase to spend time meeting with each GM and associate manager at every store or restaurant.
- Learn their goals, earn their trust, show them you know how to listen. Get a sense of their focus, abilities, career hopes, and interests, both at work and outside of work. Ask them what they see as the strengths and challenges of their restaurant and team. Ask them what they'd like to know about you or your goals.
- As the new MUM takes on the new role and gets their message out, remember that your new manager direct reports are focused on other

The 7 Stages of Building High-Performing Partnerships and Teams

issues, both past, present, and future. They're sizing up your every move, word, actions and intent. They are asking themselves things like: *"Will this new person be good or bad for me?" "How will this new person affect my store and my work routine?", "How will this person affect how I use and spend my time?", "Are you worthy of my respect and trust?"* Some new MUMs compile a FAQ (frequently asked questions) sheet for their use only that considers the questions that your team are probably asking themselves (or questions that you would be asking if you were in their shoes).

- Always ask "Active Listening" questions during orientation. If you're a new MUM, a veteran MUM about to begin a new job, or a CEO about the take the reins of a new company, there are five questions you should ask both your GMs and senior managers, according to authors James Citrin and Thomas Neff in their book *You're in Charge—Now What?* (Crown Business Press 2005):

  1. What are the most important things (top 5) about the company that we should be sure to preserve and why?
  2. What are the top 3 things we need to change and why?
  3. What do you most hope I do?
  4. What are most concerned that I might do?
  5. What advice do you have for me?"
  6. Take careful notes and synthesize your learning.

Also meet with these people:

- Key company vendors and consultants.
- The HR, Marketing, R&D, Training, Operations and IT departments for your region or company.
- Key hourly employees, alumni and customers (regulars) too.

"Stop 'managing' people. Get better people."

As you can see, this comprehensive and holistic approach to orientation will make the transition smoother and the productivity swifter for any new MUM. Graduated and customized coaching will maximize successful transitions during each stage of orientation and growth based on the MUMs progress, personality and performance. This "shadow of the leader" learning process is most effective when it is carefully planned, executed with detail and alternates between classroom learning and real-life examples in the "field." The coaching must be framed in the context of guided practice (training interspersed with real-world immersion) and not just "classroom" learning. You cannot create a better MUM merely by assigning them to "take some training courses." This is like teaching a person how to swim with a textbook and never letting them near the water.

The end goal of effective MUM orientation is that expectations are clear, all parties are singing from the same page, and the new MUM clearly understands what is necessary to be successful or what will potentially lead to failure. And perhaps it goes without saying, but during orientation new MUMs should always listen more than they talk; key and critical information being shared at this leadership stage can make or break a career.

Now write a "100 Day Plan" personal road map

When new U.S. presidents are elected they are measured by their progress in the first 100 days in office. This time-frame assessment is relevant for MUMs too. After 100 days on the job you'll know if you have the right person in place. But why wait and see? Be pro-active and engage the MUM candidate in picturing his or her success. Ask new MUM candidates to compile a personal written "100 Day Plan" that outlines their leadership and business objectives for the next three periods. The document should reflect all they've learned through their orientation with the different executives and trainers. It should detail both the strengths they have and the knowledge gaps they'd like to spend the first 100 days filling. It could note the specific challenges in

The 7 Stages of Building High-Performing Partnerships and Teams

the territory as they perceive them and how they'll address them. This document will provide insight into how well they research, assimilate and align long-term strategy and goals to short-term planning, and also gives the company insight into how well the candidate thinks, plans and communicates.

Hot Tip: If you're trying to choose between several GM candidates for one MUM opening, our research and experience has shown that the best written "100 Day Plan" usually indicates the best potential candidate.

Phase 3 **Taking Charge.**

This phase is characterized by moving from orientation to assimilation. It's framed on one end by the first day on the job and ends approximately 6 to 12 months later depending on the person and progress (some new MUMs successfully take charge in as little as 90 days). Our research shows that this is the make-it-or-break-it stage for most new Multi Unit Managers.

The first three months of Stage 3 are critical. Begin by reviewing and approving the "*100 Day Plan*" together and use it as the Road Map. Now assign formal vertical and horizontal mentors to whom the new MUM can turn with questions or unexpected challenges. Next, executives or trainers should get your current team of MUMs together and ask them what *they wished they knew or had* resource-wise during their first 90-180 days on the job. Create a comprehensive development plan for new MUM assimilation based on their input. The seeds of confidence and determination that you plant at this development stage will reap a huge harvest of productivity down the road. Here are a few ideas to help new MUMs get smarter faster.

"Stop 'managing' people. Get better people."

Get set to learn. A successful GM has probably not conscientiously committed to learn specific new skills in a long time, so the MUM transition can come as a shock to the dormant mind. The *shoshin* mindset is key at this stage because you not only have to approach new concepts with an open mind, but you also have to abandon some facets of leadership that made you successful as a GM but can be detrimental to being an effective MUM (i.e. hands-on versus indirect influence leadership). Know what you have to learn and also what you have to un-learn. Keeping a detailed journal can help the new MUM sift through the learning and gauge their understanding and assimilation. Most of the successful MUMs we interviewed keep meticulous journals that capture their learning progress.

Prepare yourself emotionally. Authors Thomas Neff and James Citrin cite the following actions as the most important for getting new leaders—whether MUMs or CEOs—off to the right start.

- Absorb information.
- Define the company's challenges.
- Establish credibility and win employee's trust.
- Assess the senior management team.
- Prepare yourself emotionally.

They warn that the last action is the one most frequently neglected, so help your new MUMs anticipate, address, and focus on this issue early and often.

Ask lots of dumb questions. Each new MUM has to adjust and adapt to a different culture, management style, market, and personalities. One of the first things a new MUM should do is ask a lot of questions. In fact, it's probably your one and only time to feel comfortable asking lots of dumb questions.

The 7 Stages of Building High-Performing Partnerships and Teams

Implement change early. Being a change agent is a common competency of high-performing MUMs. There are two schools of thought here: 1) don't make changes early on because you may not understand the "big picture" or 2) make changes early because it's expected. We prescribe the latter choice if you're thoroughly oriented and trained. Implementing change during the "taking charge" stage of MUM development is important for a key reason: the people you'll be supervising *expect* you bring about changes as you begin your new role. Take advantage of this unique opportunity. In the first three months, most of your decisions are less likely to be challenged because your team will naturally presume you'll be doing things differently. But make sure you make the right changes; ones that are both needed and logical. Don't make change just for the sake of making change alone. Be thoughtful. Be wise. And always explain the change in the context of how it benefits the customer.

Know the Break Even Point. Within the first three months of taking charge, a new MUM is in what behavioral psychologists call a "temporary state of incompetence." They don't have all the answers and can't expect to, so guided practice and collaborative coaching from above is critical. There is a point in every new MUM's "Taking Charge" stage where all the development and training time investment during the orientation phase suddenly transforms into performance and ROI. Author Michael Watkins refers to it as the *Break Even Point* and defines it thusly: "the point at which new leaders contribute as much value to your organization as they consumed from it. They are net consumers of value early on as they learn. As they begin to take actions they create value." Regional Managers and RVPs (supervisors of new MUMs) must learn how to recognize this evolution point, because it means that their coaching style

"Stop 'managing' people. Get better people."

and content must now evolve to a different level; transforming from high direction/high support to low direction/high support. Also, if after 12 months you haven't seen a break-even point occurring, you've possibly hired the wrong person…or failed to provide adequate coaching.

Phase 3 (Taking Charge) continued:

The Fatal Flaws of Newly-Promoted MUMs

While there are different kinds of challenges in each phase, at this phase <u>not</u> succeeding is far more potentially damaging to both a company and a career. Therefore MUM supervisors, coaches, and mentors (as well as new MUMs) should keep the following performance traps in mind as they observe new MUM development or grow into the role. These "fatal flaws" have de-railed many a promising multi unit manager.

- **Acting like "Super GMs."** This is the number one mistake new MUMs make. Trying to micro-manage each store's operations instead of exerting indirect influence via coaching, feedback and goal-setting is deadly. This awareness is challenging for any former superstar GM. Not all will succeed. How often in professional sports does the star quarterback or pitcher make the successful transition to coach?

- **Running every store like they did their own restaurant.** Like a person, every restaurant is different in character, needs and nuance, and so is their management team. If you have kids, you know each one is motivated by different things, and the same is true for your team. Our earlier suggestion of conducting a S.W.O.T. (strengths, weaknesses, opportunities, threats) analysis for every restaurant and the GM of each restaurant in your area will give you keen insight into what the store's unique needs are.

The 7 Stages of Building High-Performing Partnerships and Teams

- **Won't ask for help or guidance.** Most new MUMs are overwhelmed by the responsibilities of their new role, and most new MUMs are too proud or fearful to ask for help. This common pitfall can be avoided two ways: 1) create comprehensive checklists for new MUMs that detail the activities and responsibilities in each period of the first three months, and 2) assign official mentors the task of answering the questions that the new MUM may be reluctant to ask.

- **Fail to connect with the community.** Every restaurant has a small community within the four walls and is part of a larger community outside the four walls. Effective MUMs must show their managers how to understand and connect with both the internal and external social networks that make up and surround each of their stores. Building social capital with the internal and external communities of each restaurant is the key to connectivity and success.

- **Fail to mentally accept the new role.** If you get promoted from GM to MUM in the same company, you'll be leaving some manager colleagues behind. To some, you're now going from "us," to "them." New MUMs must feel certain and secure that the perceived losses are worth the gains, because you can't move forward—or be happy where you are—until you face these emotional issues. As the philosopher says: "You'll never get what you want until you're willing to let go of what you have."

- **Not managing time.** Good GMs are masterful at time management—they have to be—but going from one restaurant to six or more means multi unit managers are in a whole new realm of time and activity demands which require a whole new level of thinking, prioritizing, and planning.

"Stop 'managing' people. Get better people."

- **Trying to be liked rather than respected.** New MUMs should avoid accepting favors from the people they manage. It's OK to do special favors for your performers to recognize contributions, but not merely in an effort to be liked. Don't try for popular decisions when tough decisions need to be made. Don't be soft on discipline. Don't party hearty with subordinates. And don't forget your sense of humor. You'll need it.

- **Fail to keep criticism constructive.** When something goes wrong, do you tend to assume who's at fault? Do you control your temper? Do you praise—and pause—before you criticize? Get all the facts first. Listen to the other side of the story. Suggest specific steps to prevent recurrence of the mistake. And don't make binding decisions while you're upset. Forgive, forget, move on. Always allow a person to retain his or her dignity. We're all in this together.

- **Fail to show appreciation.** Show people you appreciate them by making a weekly commitment to send one manager, employee, colleague, or customer a handwritten note offering positive feedback, sharing an idea, or expressing thanks. A couple of lines on a card or Post-it will be enough to make people feel good about themselves...and you. Use e-mail or voice mail if you are time-crunched. Engage in random acts of kindness to help create a culture of caring in your operations. It's sure to rub off on your customers too.

- **Fail to delegate.** Good GMs succeed because they're the best at getting the job done. A successful MUM is good because they get others to be the best at getting their jobs done. Delegate or fail.

The 7 Stages of Building High-Performing Partnerships and Teams

- **Fail to prioritize and file communications.** MUMs are bombarded with paper, reports, instant messages, e-mail, voice mail, memos, and one-way and two-way communication daily. Learn quickly the best way to review, prioritize and respond to this communication, and when not to. Learn how to communicate and store information succinctly so that you're not wasting time having to repeat what you need to say.

- **Not being patient.** multi unit managers tend to not give their GM's enough time to solve their problems. We take over, they don't learn, they fail, we follow. Give them more patience than you allow for yourself. Coach more. Direct less.

- **Management by intimidation.** This style reflects insecurity more than leadership. And your team knows it too.

- **Management by too much direction.** Let your team clearly know what's expected, help them determine reasonable options for what they need to do (resist the temptation to simply tell them what to do) and then get the heck out of their way. Everyone knows a Dad or Mom who did it all themselves when intending to show a child what to do. They fixed it or built it but the child never learned how to. Remember this: "Give a man a fish and he'll be full for a day, teach him to fish and he'll never be hungry again."

- **Baby-ing (or bullying) their home unit.** If you've become a MUM in a territory that includes your original store, you will naturally face a multitude of challenges from your former colleagues. Don't encourage skeptical thought by granting repeated favors or extended visitation rights to your home unit. Conversely, don't be overbearing on your home unit just to prove how "fair" you are.

"Stop 'managing' people. Get better people."

- **Loneliness.** Going from "Star of the Store" to The Invisible Man/Woman can be challenging emotionally for some new MUMs. Going from the thick of things (GM) to observing from the outskirts (MUM) takes some getting used to. This transition is especially tough on new multi unit managers who are stimulation junkies.

- **Failing to budget enough time to conduct Meaningful Store Visits.** No job is more important to do right and no job is more often done wrong in our industry. We will discuss this critical skill in detail later in chapter 6.

- **Paralysis by analysis.** You will drive your store managers and supervisors crazy by over-analyzing, fretting and failing to make a move. Not to decide is to decide...to be indecisive. Choose a path and then move down it. Better to make the wrong decision and correct it than to make no decision at all and let the problem fester and grow.

- **Focus only on the small picture.** Effective MUMs stay current with both local and national business trends, and local and Federal laws. If you work for a company that operates multiple branded concepts, know the key operating processes and best practices of your sister brands as as your own.

- **Letting problems grow.** Many new MUMs doom their leadership role by avoiding or delaying conflict-and-dispute resolution. We're in a people business; resolving peer-to-peer, manager-to-crew, or customer-to-company conflicts should always be a priority. A MUM should never leave a nail sticking up where they find it.

The 7 Stages of Building High-Performing Partnerships and Teams

1.
Pre-Selection

2.
Orientation

3.
Taking Charge

4.
Growth &
Re-Orientation

Phase 4 **Growth and Re-Orientation.**

After a year or two on the job and positive annual performance evaluations, most companies are content to let their MUMs learn, grow, and get better on their own. It's called "maturing on the job". This may have made sense 20 years ago but if you're standing still you're walking backwards in today's marketplace. Failure to re-invest and routinely upgrade your MUMs knowledge capital will surely put your company behind in this *faster-smarter-harder-more!* world we work in. Most companies are content to assume that hitting their numbers is the end-all measure of high-performing veteran MUMs. But would the numbers and the team's progress have been even better if they'd had additional learning opportunities? Even—and especially—-veteran MUMs need training, recognition and ongoing development. At every level of employment: no train, no gain. Our research shows that companies which reward veteran MUM's performance with additional pay or bonuses *along with training* achieve better retention and higher sales than companies who recognize veteran MUMs with pay/bonuses alone. As one MUM told us, "A raise may be nice, but it won't make me better at what I do."

"Good is the enemy of great." I'm certain your veteran MUMs are good. But feeling good about our collective talents can sometimes be a liability, keeping a company motionless, holding us back from being better, perhaps even greater. Gather your MUMs *at least* once a year (we recommend twice) to engage solely in a best-practices-sharing forum and ideation sessions. The focus of the meeting should be "What do we need to *know next* and *do next* to make us better and more competitive?"

"Stop 'managing' people. Get better people."

A core component of a company's value is the sum total of its MUMs smarts, and the deeper the smarts, the greater its value to customers, owners or shareholders. Invest in outside vendors to design training programs that will enhance your veteran MUM's leadership skills and help them grow to the next level quicker than your competitors. Don't presume that a MUM who's been in the same role for ten years or more won't benefit from additional coaching, input and growth skills. At the very least they should share the same industry briefings the executive team gets relative to segment growth, industry trends, mergers and acquisitions, and marketing, demographic and product trends.

Re-engage your veteran MUMs. The veteran MUMs we interviewed all wished their companies provided ideas, resources, insight, and training commensurate with their experience, and nearly all of them said they had to seek it on their own. Most companies have no formal development plan or curriculum for MUMs with multi-year tenure. Toni Quist is the Senior Director of Training & Development for Perkins & Marie Callender's restaurants, supporting over 650 teams. She is well-versed in the skills and development necessary to build high-performing multi unit leaders. I asked her what companies can do to re-invigorate MUMs who have been with you for 10 years or more. Here's her reply.

"The first thing to keep in mind is that these tenured players deserve the same attention and energy as newly hired MUMs. That being said, here are a few suggestions:

- Continue to support their individual strengths and goals. Appreciate their contribution and respect their unique style and abilities. Keep the focus on what is right with them.

- Encourage and develop peer-to-peer networking and learning with their fellow MUMs.

The 7 Stages of Building High-Performing Partnerships and Teams

- Challenge them to be students of the industry and expand their understanding of businesses and companies outside of the organization.

- Reconnect them, on a regular basis, to the core attributes and principles of your brand. It's most likely why they joined you in the first place.

- Make them better trainers. Seek opportunities to help them refresh by seeing the organization through the newest member's eyes. Teach them ways to conduct action orientation for new managers and assign them mentorship roles, have them participate as training leader for new store openings. The fresh perspective and new hire excitement is contagious!"

Each one teach one. Your veteran MUMs are treasure troves of insight and advice for new MUMs, but often overlooked when the training department begins researching the role. In our research project, the last question we asked every veteran MUM we interviewed was: *"What do you know now that you wished you knew your first year as a new multi unit manager?"* Here are some of the insightful replies they shared (see more at Sullivison.com):

Give a lot, expect a lot, and if you don't get it, prune.

- Ask for help. It's okay to say "I don't know."
- Results take time.
- The big picture is bigger than I thought.
- It's OK to let them do it different than you.
- You are always on stage, be careful what you say.
- Your people make you what you are going to be.
- Clear communication—make sure your message is heard and understood.
- Build relationships inside and out.
- Listen better. Do less. Delegate more.
- Don't be afraid to be great.
- Moving forward can start today.

"Stop 'managing' people. Get better people."

- When you have a day off, take the day off.
- Know why you're visiting a store before you visit.
- It is difficult to impose your work ethic onto others.
- Allow your people to make decisions and come up with solutions.
- Get better at Time Management.
- Accept criticism.
- Some turnover is good.
- Celebrate success.
- Be more patient.
- Know what both your top and bottom performing units have in common.
- Use support people better.
- When you offer incentives to managers for crew retention...be careful they don't keep bad hires just to win a prize.
- It's OK to make mistakes. But learn from them.

Summary

A MUM's ultimate goal is to assemble talented teams and then coach and direct those teams to accomplish a greater good together. Being a *Talent Scout* is the direct path and best way to effectively manage the present and set up a successful future. It amazes me to see the amount of time, focus, attention and care that a MUM (or unit manager) will give to managing, maintaining, repairing and improving the restaurant building itself. Yet give these same people the invaluable precious potential and appreciating asset of a human being to manage and they will not administer proportional time, care and improvement. Find the right people, groom 'em or broom 'em, then love 'em and lead 'em.

The 7 Stages of Building High-Performing Partnerships and Teams

Alice Elliot is the CEO, The Elliot Group (**www.theelliotgroup.com**), and Co-Founder and Chairman of The Elliot Leadership Institute. Alice has decades of experience sourcing, selecting and developing next generation leaders for our industry. I think it's appropriate to give her the final word on what a *Talent Scout* should look for in the multi unit manager role:

"Many companies, when recruiting high performers for the multi unit manager role, look strictly at technical and operational performance. They don't always put as much emphasis on an individual's ability to think strategically or assess their track record in areas like leadership and business expertise. While operational and financial results are extremely important, they aren't always indicative of one's ability to lead others and communicate a strategy and vision that a team will follow. We recognize that some of the best multi unit leaders are those who can inspire and motivate others. They have a unique ability to not only be empathetic, but they also hold others accountable for their actions and results. The most accomplished multi unit managers are natural 'coaches.' They are comfortable teaching others and are able to instill a shared 'mission' and sense of purpose to those around them. These Multi Unit Managers are also financially savvy and have an outlook that is typically proactive and inclusive. The more progressive companies realize that these individuals are best suited for continued advancement in their respective organizations. multi unit managers will also be called upon to be 'agents of change.' The next generation of leadership must be nimble, welcome new ideas and new opportunities for growth, be responsive to their superiors, peers, and direct reports. They will inspire and teach those around them both culturally and consistently."

"Stop 'managing' people. Get better people."

Self-assessment: Talent Scout™

"Does the right things and does the right things right." Review the list of core **Talent Scout** characteristics below. Assess your personal strengths and challenges relative to each in one of the boxes to the right. Review the boxes again in six months. Have you progressed? Where can you get help or guidance to get better?

Competency	Good At	Average	Needs Work
Do I have a strong bench of talent?			
Do I know my talent gaps and knowledge gaps?			
Do we prune our "deadwood"?			
Do we have a clear talent strategy for the year?			
Do we know what our "heroes" and "zeroes" act like?			
Are we hiring noticeably better people (A Players only)?			
Do we hire s-l-o-w, fire fast?			
Do we have programs to develop our veteran MUMs?			
Does the team meet its financial goals?			

The 7 Stages of Building High-Performing Partnerships and Teams

Expert Opinion: **Tony Hughes**

Tony Hughes is Managing Director, Restaurants, for Mitchells & Butlers, an organization headquartered in Birmingham, England, that operates 2,150 pubs and restaurants in the UK, and 50 Alex pubs in Germany. Mr. Hughes has held senior management positions with companies that include Whitbread, JA Devenish, B&Q and TGI Friday's.

Q: *When selecting multi unit managers what competencies do you look for?*

First, we need the person to 'walk the talk'. A multi unit manager must be a leader who sets the example for the staff and managers to follow. To do this the multi unit manager must have a deep understanding of the business and a track record of strong achievement as a unit manager. Our ideal candidate for a multi unit manager would be a single unit manager who:

- Consistently demonstrates flawless execution and results for his or her business.
- Develops their own people – with a depth of management team in the business that becomes a nurturing ground to create future unit managers.
- Has a passion for the business and its people—both team and customers.
- Has the respect of his/her peers, both for the operation of his/ her business but also the support and effort shown towards other businesses in the district.

Q: *When a multi unit manager visits an operation, what are the do's and don'ts of an effective store visit?*

First, a multi unit manager must arrive with a clear agenda of the issues to cover, and ensure these are followed through on the visit. They must set the example for the staff and managers to follow. Occasionally this includes the multi unit manager working the shift with the team, visibly demonstrating the highest standards of guest care and passion for quality. A store visit should leave a positive legacy. The entire front and back of house team (from the manager to the dish washer) should feel positively energized and 'touched' by the visit, and made to feel that their contribution is both valued and worthwhile.

A store visit is not just about platitudes but about addressing the core areas of business opportunity and improvement. He or she should never walk away from, or ignore, a wrong.

"Stop 'managing' people. Get better people."

Whether as part of a structured agenda, or simply observing practices for improvement, the multi unit manager should firmly identify and help correct improper business practices, yet always leave the team committed to higher future standards. Multi unit management involves 'tough love' and 'divine dissatisfaction'; meaning that 'good enough' never is. Overall a store visit should make a measurable difference. It is not about just "being seen". Whether it is the positive reinforcement of good practices, or the coaching of areas of improvement, the multi unit manager should leave a business visit confident that the visit has left a positive mark on the operation and the team.

Q: *How has the role of the multi unit management changed in the last 10 years?*
The role has evolved from one of audit and control, to one of business support and leadership. Historically much more emphasis would be placed on personally managing all the issues around control of cash and the cost centers across the P&L. With improvements in technology, we can now increasingly provide improved management information from the center that both sets and monitors effective cost control disciplines. This enables the multi unit manager to place greater emphasis on the more important issues of people and standards leadership. Consequently the role no longer fits into traditional '9-5' weekday office hours. The role now is about being visible and available when our guests are visiting.

Q: *What will be looking for in multi unit managers 10 years from today?*
The role will increasingly become one of business partnership, as we continue to develop, motivate and reward high caliber unit managers. Our guest's expectations will continue to rise. There is no excuse for a bad experience now, as our guests have an armory of choice for both in home and out-of-home quality meal occasions. As scale restaurant operators, the bar of required standards delivery is being increasingly heightened, and the multi unit manager is critical to delivering these raised expectations of standard and value. The market is also becoming more complex. Large scale brands will have to adapt to increasing market expectations for more local flavor, products and flexibility in their neighborhood restaurant. The multi unit manager will therefore have to develop greater skills as custodian and guardian of the overall brand standards, ensuring that any local flavor or product is not at the expense of either the expectations of standards or economics of the national brand.

STAGE THREE
Servant Leader

Cautionary Tale

"On the very first day I met him, the Regional VP took me to lunch at one of the restaurants I'd be supervising. He talked about the role of a multi unit manager for about 20 minutes, and then drove me past the 5 other stores I'd be responsible for. We never even went in to them. Then he took me to a strip club at 3 pm where he got hammered on tequila and told me all about how to be an area director and the importance of service. He borrowed $100 from me and threw up later in the parking lot of the restaurant we had lunch at when I took him back to his car. 'Oh, here,' he said as he was leaving. 'These are the restaurants keys you'll need and here's the folder with your paperwork and the benefits crap. My number's in there on my card. You'll figure it out. Let me know if you need anything'. I swear, that was my orientation from start to finish."

"My customer is anyone who isn't me."

The key traits of a "Servant Leader" include:

- Knows employees are the first market
- Collaborator (P2P sharing)
- Thermostat not Thermometer
- Expert Listener
- Knows that "Everything Speaks"
- Shares the same reality
- Excellence reflex
- Customer advocate/sees operations through the customer lens
- Meets financial goals

The 3rd competency on the leadership ladder of high-performing MUMs is ***Servant Leader***. It's based on a relatively simple premise: a multi unit manager accomplishes very little alone; their achievements are measured by how much or how little the *team* accomplishes. Leadership is a shared responsibility and framed around a simple notion: *my customer is anyone is who isn't me.*

Robert Greenleaf, the man who coined the phrase "servant-leadership" in 1970, described it this way:

> "The servant-leader... begins with the natural feeling that one wants to serve first. Then conscious choice brings one to aspire to lead. He or she is sharply different from the person who is leader first, perhaps because of

The 7 Stages of Building High-Performing Partnerships and Teams

the need to assuage an unusual power drive or to acquire material possessions. For such it will be a later choice to serve – after leadership is established. The leader-first and the servant-first are two extreme types. Between them there are shadings and blends that are part of the infinite variety of human nature.

The difference manifests itself in the care taken by the servant-first to make sure that other people's highest priority needs are being served. The best test, (and difficult to administer), is: do those served grow as persons; do they, while being served, become healthier, wiser, freer, more autonomous, more likely themselves to become servants? And, what is the effect on the least privileged in society; will they benefit, or, at least, will they not be further deprived?"

Autocratic or dictatorial leadership styles *("Why? Because I said so")* won't get you very far in the 21st Century workplace. A *Servant Leader* knows that the employee is the first market, and that the way we treat our team members determines the way they'll treat their team members and our customers. And if that's not reason enough to put service first, consider this: *you are hired by the people you report to but fired by the people who report to you.* In other words, if she works for you, you work for her.

Our research shows that *Servant Leader* MUMs are essentially *experience architects.* They help define and shape their team's (and their customer's) perception of, feelings for, interaction with, and emotional involvement in the brand, product and concept. After all, it may say "Joe's Restaurant" on the sign out front, but it's Mary, Doug, Rafael, Willie, Rosa, Lee, Ang and Sam—the hourly team interacting with the customer which has the biggest impact on whether or not the guest returns. A *Servant Leader* builds on the competencies of the *Brand Ambassador* and *Talent Scout*, practicing what

"My customer is anyone who isn't me."

they preach, and modeling the way for how their managers (and hourly team) should be treating our customers. The fact is that success in our business is not defined by how badly you beat your competitors, it's about how well you *serve your customers*. The **customer** is the competition.

Servant Leaders know the value of human capital and working as a unit. They never treat a customer better than they do an employee. Managers and crew like to report to MUMs who embody the characteristics and culture of the company *(Brand Ambassador)*, they appreciate the discipline and efforts of someone who surrounds them with like-minded high-performers *(Talent Scout)* and they like to work for someone who knows that *if you're not serving the customer directly you'd better be serving someone who is (Servant Leader)*. They recognize that our internal customers (employees) are just as important as our external customers (guests). Servant Leaders build a culture of caring from the top down, or is it *bottom up*? (See hierarchy pyramid, right.)

Customer
Hourly Crew
Unit Managers
Multi Unit Manager
Regionals · VPs · Executives

Based on our research, here are the key behavioral competencies of the Servant Leader growth stage in the multi unit manager role.

Be a Thermostat not a Thermometer. A thermostat <u>controls</u> the temperature; a thermometer <u>reflects</u> it: hot, cold, or somewhere in-between. Your team wants to work for someone with self-control and a steady hand on the tiller. This doesn't mean you're not passionate. It means you have patience, perspective, and grace under pressure. Grandpappy Sullivan always said that "you can judge the character of a person by the thing that makes them angry." Self-assessment question: when your team sees you coming do

The 7 Stages of Building High-Performing Partnerships and Teams

they think "Here comes help!" or Here comes trouble"? Our advice: be civil, not "Sybil.".* A good MUM is someone who, if things go wrong, doesn't go wrong with them.

Be nice. Above my desk for the last 10 years sits a sign that reminds me: "No greatness without goodness." A store manager's job is tough, so do everything you can to create and foster a Culture of Kindness in their workplace. Happy MUMs make happy managers. Happy managers make happy employees. Happy employees make happy customers. Happy customers keep coming back to buy more.

Catch 'em doing something right. What you reinforce is what you get, and outstanding performers love recognition, so remember that a pat on the back is just a few vertebrae up from a kick in the ass. Our industry's most under-utilized resource is recognition. High-performing MUMs know that brains, like hearts, will go where they're appreciated. When taken for granted, good managers will either decline in performance or leave, and if you don't recognize your people; be assured that someone else will. *Catch your people doing something right* (if you see it, say it). Traveling trophies for high-performance that unit managers compete for every quarter foster pride and friendly competition. A well-timed encouraging and gracious voice mail or e-mail at the end of a busy day can do the trick too.

> The first responsibility of a leader is to define reality. The last is to say thank you. In between, the leader is a servant.
>
> – Max De Pree

Make praise and recognition a part of every day's to-do list. Encourage your managers to recognize their hourly associates as well with small, unexpected rewards for jobs well done. A few suggestions for low-cost or no-cost hourly team member recognition ideas that unit managers could consider:

---

*We work in a crazy industry; it's been said that there are only two things to worry about our business: one, that things will never get back to "normal" and two, that they already have.

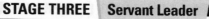

"My customer is anyone who isn't me."

- Verbal thank you
- Car wash gift card
- $5 international calling card
- Handwritten thank you
- Mass transit tokens
- iTunes gift card
- Candy bars that reflect the accomplishments that shift; i.e. LifeSavers, Extra gum, PayDay, 100 Grand, Zero bars, etcetera

Be a blowtorch, not a candle. "In the 21st Century workplace, energy, not time, is the fundamental currency of high performance," says author Jim Loehr. Bring energy to every store visit, *don't take it away.* Expand your capacity to energize and be energetic. The more energy you expend in your stores the more your team will energize the workplace.

Teach the team that everything is a useful gift. When challenges and problems occur, show your team the lesson and then discuss how to prevent the problem from occurring again. Problems are opportunities to learn from not get upset about. For instance, when a customer complains, consider it a gift. Research indicates that five other customers with similar complaints will just stop coming in and never tell you about it.

Know that "everything speaks." The cleanliness of your bathrooms, the friendliness on the phone, the brightness of a cashier or hostess's smile, the neatness of signage, the music levels, and the quality of food and beverage all add up to how a customer measures your restaurant's quality and worthiness for repeat business. It's not just one thing, it's all things that add up to a great customer experience, and the people closest to the customer have the greatest influence on their continuing patronage.

Focus on what's right instead of who's right. A *Servant Leader* is focused on accomplishing goals, not assigning blame. All policy changes should be filtered through and communicated relative to how it will positively affect the

The 7 Stages of Building High-Performing Partnerships and Teams

customer. The best MUMs learn, they don't blame, and when corrective action is necessary they always criticize the behavior not the person.

Lead from the middle. Be a strong leader, but also encourage collaborative growth. Embrace a "bubble up" rather than "top down" management style. The MUM who sits on top of a network is out of it.

Foster collaboration. A MUM's success depends on his or her ability to influence individuals and groups to achieve common goals by working together. It's critical for multi unit managers to create a coalition among their GMs and junior managers. Teamwork is essential for a productive company, and all work is team work. Stress cooperation over competition. Trying to do well and trying to beat others are two different things if not managed properly. *Servant Leader* MUMs have learned to keep their teams informed, involved, always sharing and always learning. Their manager meetings are dialogues, not monologues, and they always end with peer-to-peer (P2P) key learnings and sharing of weekly best practices.

Be a Connector. *Servant Leaders* are good at both know how and know who. They make a point of introducing their managers to other people who can broaden their professional or personal expertise. These people may be from the company or the community, but hooking them up with managers who will benefit from the relationship is a skill every MUM should master, and every manager will appreciate.

> **We make a living by what we get, we make a life by what we give.**
>
> –Winston Churchill

Invest in your public speaking skills. Fact: the better you are as a public speaker, the greater your leadership perception among your team. Fact: the better you are as a public speaker, the better you are in negotiations with vendors, and the better you are in coaching sessions with managers, the better you are in meetings

"My customer is anyone who isn't me."

with staff, and the better you are in articulating and presenting the case for change (whether it's in your stores or on your paycheck). There is **no downside** to investing in and improving your skills as a public speaker. So why aren't you doing it?

Judge people on their best days. Many managers do the opposite; they assess performance or pass out judgment based on a manager or employee's worst day. Be balanced, be fair, observe often, and consider all the grey areas before you make a decision in either black or white.

Search out and share best ideas. If I have a penny and you have a penny and we exchange pennies, now we *each* have a penny. But if you have an idea and I have an idea and we exchange ideas, now you have two ideas and so do I. Ask managers to bring best practices learned from the previous period or week to every meeting you hold with them. Discuss the ideas, write them down, archive them and distribute them. If you start this project next week, just think of the great ideas you'll have accumulated in just six months and a year from today! None of us is as smart as all of us. (Note: Never take credit for your manager's ideas or you'll never get another good idea from them.)

Possibility versus Probability thinker. Pessimists hear new ideas and think: "If I try that there's a 70% probability that I'm gonna fail." And they do nothing. Optimists think: "If I try that, there's a 70% probability I might fail, but a 100% *possibility* that I will succeed." Realistic Optimism is a key trait that Servant Leaders model and teach to their teams.

When I talk about servant-leadership, I usually pair it with these terms: being useful and being a resource. The Leader's responsibility is to insure that they need to do the work to accomplish the objectives, and the principal resource of the people is you, the leader. What does that mean? That means, in my view, to be the kind of leader who projects authenticity and vulnerability, is present, is accepting, and sees their role as being useful, as being the servant. I think what's key is that the leader makes every decision from a basis of values--what's the right thing to do, not what's the expedient thing to do--perhaps not even what's the most profitable thing to do, but what's the right thing to do.

– James Autry

The 7 Stages of Building High-Performing Partnerships and Teams

Losing good people costs more than you think. When good people leave, all the training everyone did goes with them too.

Excellence reflex. *Servant Leader* MUMs bring more value to their team by being uncompromising in brand standards and quality. Their mantra relative to food and beverage: "If it ain't a ten, make it again."

Meets financial goals. A great MUM knows that the best way to serve their managers and crew is by helping shape and define a great future for each and every team member. And the best way to accomplish that is by meeting or exceeding sales and profitability targets every shift, period, quarter and year.

Learn to listen to your managers. At every stage of growth a great leader makes the art of listening a priority. A recent article in *Fast Company* magazine said it best: "Great listening is fueled by curiosity. It's hard to be a great listener if you're not curious about other people. What's the enemy of curiosity? Grandiosity—the belief that you have all the answers." When you're visiting your stores or having a phone conversation or meeting with your managers do you listen to them? *Really* listen to them? (Letting your managers talk is not the same thing as listening to them). *Servant Leaders* work hard at the art of listening every single day, the same way they work at all the other skills that define a great leader. Here are some ideas to make you a better listener that we've adapted from Ragan Publications *Employee Recruitment & Retention* newsletter:

- **Put your work away.** As soon as a manager comes to you and wants to talk, put away whatever you're working on. Remove all temptation to do anything other than give your full attention to them.

"My customer is anyone who isn't me."

- **Bite your tongue.** One of the first signs that someone isn't listening is when he or she cuts off the talker in midsentence or midthought. Make sure your manager is finished before you begin speaking.

- **Smile and lean forward.** You'll be amazed at the effect a simple smile can have. By smiling and leaning forward, you send the message that you're fully engaged in what the person is saying.

- **Always ask questions, even if you don't have any.** Questions tell your manager or employee that you've been listening, and are truly committed to resolving whatever issue is being discussed.

- **Start your own comments by paraphrasing the employee.** Again, this shows the employee that you've been listening; it also helps you get the issues clear in your own head before you articulate your point-of-view.

Teach managers to see service through the customer's lens. The foundation of servant leadership is recognizing that service is our invisible product, and that we should serve the team as we would have them serve our customers. Good service is always evolving. When the customer changes, so does the meaning of customer service. We need to constantly adjust and adapt our service strategies to current workplace realities and utilize new training techniques appropriate to the next generation. Teach all managers how their teams can be customer advocates, not adversaries. Encourage them to lead each shift with an attitude of gratitude and manage to the 99% of our wonderful customers, not the 1% who may be a bit less appreciative of what we do for them.

> Teach anyone who moves a broom or operates a grinder everything the bank lender knows. That way they could really understand how every nickel saved could make a difference.
>
> –Jack Stack

The 7 Stages of Building High-Performing Partnerships and Teams

Fatal flaws of service-giving. When plotting customer service strategy and service delivery, many MUMs, managers and trainers focus on what they should "do" for their customers. I think it's just as instructive and illuminating to define first what not to do. Examine service from the customer's perspective, not the manager's or staff's. Look at the critical mistakes of service-giving as seen through the customer's lens. Eliminate those common service blunders, and you may no longer have the need to "teach" service at all. Why? *Because you will have eliminated the need for your customers to ask for anything.* And "not having to ask for anything" (i.e. the absence of complaints) is the ultimate definition of great service. Most customers don't actually "want service." Based on the thousands of customers we interview annually for the service projects we do for clients, what customers want first and foremost from businesses is to *eliminate dissatisfaction.* Yep, that's right. They don't want "excellence", to be "wowed", "delighted", "blown away," or whatever the service buzzword du jour is. Customers want consistent positive experiences characterized by the absence of complaints. So first focus your service efforts <u>lower</u> by answering and then resolving these two questions: 1) what are my customer's top ten complaints? And 2) what are my customer's top ten expectations? After you write down your answer, ask your managers and hourly associates the same two questions and compare all three responses. Your service challenges and opportunities will become crystal clear once you compare the synchronicity, overlap and/or disconnect among the different groups. Once you have eliminated dissatisfaction, now you can begin habitual satisfaction, then generate loyalty.

Further research reveals the following common complaints among foodservice patrons. Share this list with all your managers and customer-facing team members. You can find many more of these in our best-selling book *Fundamentals: How to Be Brilliant at the Basics.*

"My customer is anyone who isn't me."

1. **Cashier or Host absent or distracted when greeting or seating**. Most customer complaints can be traced back to disrespect or perceived disrespect. A distracted, visibly irritated or stressed greeter (or cashier) should not be the first thing a customer experiences when walking in the front door of a full-service restaurant. After all, they just drove past 10, 20, 30 or 40 other restaurants to come to yours. Hosts and greeters should be enthusiastic, focused, and pleasant, especially when they're busy. After all, the customer is not an interruption of their job. The customer is their job.

2. **Too slow when speed is expected.** Over 60% of Quick Service Restaurant (QSR) business in North American foodservice chains is now drive-through traffic, and **Go to serve not to shine.** studies show that shaving just 10 seconds off the drive-through wait time at peak periods increases throughput and annual sales by as much as $20,000 per unit. Show your managers and team how to be both accurate and swift during peak and slower drive-through meal periods. Make sure that you and your managers recognize the hourly associates when they improve accuracy and speed, and coach them how to get better when they don't. **Hot Tip:** always put a premium on accuracy over speed, "After all," says veteran foodservice executive Dave Schuh, "we're not in the business of serving the *wrong* food fast." Just try to woo back a customer who drives all the way home only to find a wrong or partial order.

3. **Too fast when ease and comfort is expected.** In tableside-service operations, assess first what time constraints—if any—your guests might be facing. Speed it up for guests in a hurry, but don't rush customers who want a leisurely experience. How do you know the difference? Train servers to first take the experience order. Greet each table in a friendly and calm manner; find out if they are in for a leisurely meal or have a tight time-frame. Now pace and layer your service accordingly. Customizing the service experience can't begin without first connecting to the guest and then assessing their expectations through questions and friendliness. Meeting expectations requires service. Exceeding expectations requires

The 7 Stages of Building High-Performing Partnerships and Teams

hospitality. What's the difference? Service fulfills a need; hospitality fulfills people. (Note: just because a guest tells you they're "not in a hurry" doesn't mean the server should then give priority to all their other tables. What the guest is really saying is "We're hungry but not in a hurry.")

4. **Server interrupting w/out permission.** Too many servers robotically hustle up to the "next" table and interrupt guest conversations with an abrupt "Ready to order?" backed with a forced smile. Teach servers to stand next to the table if guests are talking to each other until eye contact from the guest indicates they're ready.

5. **Manager interrupting with or without permission**. Managers are taught to do "100% table visits" but few have mastered the finesse of doing so. They too often interrupt guests in mid-bite with a brash "How is everything, folks?" Suggestion: wait to the side for permission to interrupt, just like a server should. And don't stay too long unless it's obvious the customers want you to.

6. **Superficial Congeniality.** This term speaks volumes to the fact that service has to feel natural, warm and genuine to have true value for the customer. What does "superficial congeniality" look and feel like? Picture the flight attendants on any airline. If it's not a fake smile it's the inspiration-for-the-whiskey-sour-expression.

7. **Letting guests overhear managers and crew discuss the daily activities of running a restaurant.** Customers should never have to be within earshot of managers telling busers to wipe down a table, clean the bathroom, or bring more ice to a bartender. They should never, ever have to hear a manager reprimanding a server or greeter, or listen to a multi unit manager having a meeting at an adjoining table while complaining to a unit manager about pay or performance. You're always on stage. Make certain that your managers are pulling those conversations away from your customers, and do the same when you're meeting with them in your dining rooms.

8. **Not noticing a guest with a problem.** The most important real estate

"My customer is anyone who isn't me."

in a restaurant is the 18 inches or so between the top of the table and the top of the customers head. Managers must be taught to constantly scan the dining areas for guest's body language in every section. Look for patrons who appear to need something or seem unhappy with their food, beverage or experience. Managers should then direct the server to those guests or approach them herself to resolve the problem. Know what's even worse? See next point.

9. **Avoiding a guest with a problem.** This is much worse than not noticing a problem in the first place. Managers and servers must be vigilant in the dining room about resolving a small problem before it becomes a big one. The classic problem resolution formula follows the acronym BLAST: Believe the Customer, Listen to them, Act on the complaint, Satisfy them and Thank them for bringing it to your attention.

10. **A public work area that is not spotless.** Unless you're a grill cook in the middle of a dinner rush, there is no reason why your work area shouldn't be clean and neat, always and all ways. You serve better and sell more in a clean restaurant, (and to a clean table or counter top). Don't ever think that customers don't notice and talk about it.

> To give real service you must add something that cannot be bought or measured with money, and that is sincerity and integrity.
>
> – Douglas Adams

11. **Don't thank the cash register.** In too many foodservice operations that feature cashiers (which includes most fast casual, QSR and family tableside operations), they conclude the transaction with customers by handing back change and then looking downward while they mutter "thank you." Ouch. Eyes up, big smiles, sincere appreciation.

12. **Spending too much time with regulars and ignoring the "unknowns."** Teach your managers the importance of seeking out strangers every shift and touching *every* table. Ask guests if this is their first time with you, learn their names, and thank them for their patronage. Don't let managers spend all their time with familiar customer faces and miss opportunities to meet new ones.

The 7 Stages of Building High-Performing Partnerships and Teams

13. **Making pre-shift meetings optional not mandatory.** If you don't stage pre-shift meetings daily, how and where can your customer-facing staff practice their service and selling skills? You don't want them practicing on the customer do you? Visit our website archives at **Sullivision.com** and download the free article titled "The Art of the Pre-Shift Meeting" or invest in the *Jumpstart: How to Plan and Execute Effective Pre-Shift Meetings* DVD for your managers.

14. **Forgetting who the real competition is.** Again, that would be your customer, not another brand.

15. **Making lots of mistakes (but never learning from them).** Messing up is one thing, failing to recognize the mistake and learning to not make it again is what distinguishes average operators from great ones. At their weekly meetings, your managers should each bring in 3 service or operations-related challenges from the previous week to discuss and analyze together so that they don't happen again. It's all about continuous improvement. As the Japanese proverb says: "One hundred days to learn; one thousand to refine." Think like your guests and focus your managers first on what not to do. We're only as good as our last happy customer.

16. **Forgetting to say goodbye and thank you.** Keep it fresh, keep it focused, keep it fun, and remember to say thank you to every customer. (Note: cashiers often have the bad habit of "thanking" the cash register!)

Summary

A *Servant Leader* accomplishes goals through the performance of the people they supervise. If they work for you, you work for them. Always serve the team first, and then the customer. Leadership comes first, not the customer.

Defining what to do and letting go of telling your team how to do it is a hard-won skill of high-performing multi unit managers. Servant leadership in many ways means giving up power to get power, a Zen-like concept that may be best explained by author James Autry as the final word on this chapter.

"My customer is anyone who isn't me."

Here's his response the question *"How does one go about overcoming ego in a leadership position?"* (as seen on the Greenleaf.org website):

"Rather than make a statement, ask a question. Instead of saying 'Here's what you should do,' you ask, 'What do you think we should do?' That's a huge leap for a lot of people. It seems simple to say it, doesn't it? But it's difficult for us to fathom how challenging that is for some people who act out of ego. Because you are saying, 'Put my ego in the drawer and I'm going to ask how you think it should be done; you, who are layers down in the hierarchy from me.' And the next step is not doing that just as a technique, but to recognize that you're open to learning, and that the other person may have already figured out the thing to do. My attitude about this is, if an employee comes in and says, 'Jim, here's the situation and this is the problem and I'm laying it out and what do you think we ought to do?' Well, I know that person already knows what to do. They've got the situation surrounded, they have the problem defined and they know what to do…probably. If not, they've got a good first step. They know that I know. But as soon as I fulfill that expectation that I'm going to be 'Big Daddy'; you know, I'm going to make a pronouncement and they're going to do it. Then I've destroyed any possibility, one, to learn something from them, and two, to recognize their own power, which is their knowledge and their skill, and which is real empowerment. Empowerment is not about 'I take some of my power and give it to you'. That's the myth. Real empowerment is recognizing that you, by your skill, your knowledge, your commitment, already have power. What I'm trying to do is take off the leashes I've put on my own team."

We will explore this concept of collaborative decision-making in much more detail in the *Synergist* chapter. But how many MUMs "coach" by show-and-tell instead of thoughtful inquiry and collaboration? How many MUMs are content to execute their jobs as "compliance inspectors" instead of Servant Leaders? Texas retailer H.E. Butt once said: "He profits most who serves best."

The 7 Stages of Building High-Performing Partnerships and Teams

Bottom line? The essence of Servant Leadership is giving. Consider the classic advice of NCAA basketball coach John Wooden: "You cannot live a perfect day without doing something for someone who will never be able to repay you." Retired Disney executive Lee Cockerell suggests that supervisors "Fill up your tank everyday with the three types of fuel that drives performance: Recognition, Appreciation, and Encouragement. These three energy sources are self-renewing and self-replenishing. No matter how much you use them with your team your 'tank' will be full again 5 minutes later."

Self-assessment: **Servant Leader**

Review the list of core Servant Leader characteristics below. Assess your personal strengths and challenges relative to each of them in one of the boxes to the right. Review the boxes again in six months. Did you progress?

Competency	Good At	Average	Needs Work
I routinely thank and recognize team members			
I help my team collaborate (P2P sharing)			
I am an Expert Listener			
I'm a Thermostat not a Thermometer			
I connect with internal and external communities in my restaurants			
My team knows that "Everything Speaks"			
My team knows has the "Excellence Reflex"			
I see my stores through the customer lens first			
I'm an above-average public speaker			

"My customer is anyone who isn't me."

Expert Opinion: **Multi Unit Leadership and Franchisees**

Being a multi unit manager who works exclusively with franchisees (as opposed to company-owned stores) is a challenging role. Balancing brand standards, compliance issues and entrepreneurial spirit creates the need for a unique set of supervisory skills. Frank Steed, the CEO of The Steed Consultancy has been working with both franchisees and multi unit managers for many years as an executive with foodservice brands like T.G.I. Friday's, Country Inns by Carlson, Bennigan's, Country Kitchens, Bonanza, Ponderosa and Tony Roma's. I asked him to share his insight and perspective on the role of multi unit management and franchisee development.

Q: Why is Multi Unit Management important to franchisees?

Beyond the obvious education of a franchisee's own multi unit managers, most franchisees don't realize that from the opening of their own second unit they are now multi unit managers themselves. Many franchisees are terrific owners and entrepreneurs but may not have the inherent management skills required to oversee a multi unit business.

Q: Are there different skill sets for Franchise multi unit managers?

For the managers working within a franchise organization's company stores, no, but for the franchisor's multi unit supervisors the skill set required beyond the ability to oversee multiple locations are significant.

Q: For the franchisor, what are the additional talents needed to manage multi-franchise locations?

First, the franchisor does not "manage" the franchisees' locations. The multi unit person that works for the franchisor is much more of a business consultant than a manager. While still needing the required multi-tasking skills, the Franchise Business Consultant (FBC) must also possess the maturity and communication skills to work with both managers at the unit level and franchise owners who have their own needs, such as strategic and business planning and who actually own the businesses the FBC is critiquing.

Q: Tell me more about this.

The franchisee, unlike the GM at a company-owned unit, is not making a career decision when they tell the franchisor no. The FBC may have come from a company background where no one has ever been able to refuse to follow their direction. This takes some getting used to for many first-time FBCs who've worked only in company-run stores before. The franchisee will challenge the franchisor to prove their business plans make good sense and will result in successful and profitable operations. The FBC is often the first recipient of this discussion. The FBC must be able to explain instead of direct, to show over and over again and to restate the obvious many times without becoming frustrated. The maturity needed to work with both young managers (as a company supervisor might) and then to simultaneously interface with a multi-millionaire franchisee owner is a key to their success. The FBC may find themselves directing a shift or doing a quality audit one visit and then be in the Boardroom the next. This seldom happens to a company MUM in the comfort of the company support system.

Q: So there is a difference in span of control for a franchise multi unit operator?

Yes, very often their span is two to three times that of their multi unit manager counterpart on the company side of the business. Remember, while the FBC has the responsibility to help make the franchisee's units profitable, they usually don't have the day to day accountability for food and labor cost as a company Regional Manager or Area Director would.

Q: Is it easier to be a franchisee support person?

I think it is more different than "harder" or "easier." The maturity and communications skills replace those of a great numbers producer, but the FBC must still be able to pick apart a P&L and assist the franchisee's managers in meeting the return on investment hurdles expected by the franchise owner. As I mentioned earlier, the franchise multi unit owner must enjoy the relationship and the challenge of working with many different franchisee personalities and skill sets. The company operator's world is usually much the same, relatively speaking, from day to day.

Q: How can franchisors find, select or develop FBCs with these skill sets and what are some of the core competencies needed?

This should start when they are company operators, teaching them communications skills, negotiating techniques, developing planning skills and basic business management versus just the operating skills necessary to do the job. Standardized selection tools can be effective. Remember you are looking more for the right personality here than the numbers producing company manager. The key is to select someone who is flexible, has a great deal of empathy,

"My customer is anyone who isn't me."

is very bright (not just smart) and is passionate about the success of the brand. You can teach the mechanics of the company job but you must hire the personality and desire.

Q: *How can franchisors find, select or develop FBCs with these skill sets and what are some of the core competencies needed?*

This should start when they are company operators, teaching them communications skills, negotiating techniques, developing planning skills and basic business management versus just the operating skills necessary to do the job. Standardized selection tools can be effective. Remember you are looking more for the right personality here than the numbers producing company manager. The key is to select someone who is flexible, has a great deal of empathy, is very bright (not just smart) and is passionate about the success of the brand. You can teach the mechanics of the company job but you must hire the personality and desire.

Q: *What are the biggest mistakes a franchisee makes in selecting MUMs?*

No different than company operations, the usual error is taking the best General Manager and assuming he or she will be a good multi unit supervisor. The ability to communicate and manage without being on the scene and to teach versus tell is the key to success for the franchisee just as it is for company owned operations.

Q: *What does the Franchisee look for in their Franchise Business Consultant?*

The franchisee wants someone to consult, not direct. The franchisee and their managers understand how to run the operation. What they want is someone they can turn to for communication with the home office, who can help them find creative solutions to their issues and someone who will hold them accountable for performing to standard. The FBC must be a "jack of all trades", but also must be able to deliver assistance from all of the members of the restaurant support center. A successful franchisor realizes that most of the great new ideas for a system will come from the seasoned franchisees. These same franchisees will also present some of the dumbest ideas you have ever heard. The FBC's job is to help sort out these two and champion the causes that really make sense. It is always good to remember that in a system as great as McDonald's, ideas such as the Big Mac, Egg McMuffin and even Ronald McDonald were created by franchisees. And somebody also thought of the McLean Deluxe.

You can reach Frank Steed at www.thesteedconsultancy.com

STAGE FOUR
Head Coach™

Cautionary Tale

"When I asked him to describe my new Area Manager job to me, my Regional VP said 'I don't know what to tell you. I had to figure it out. You'll figure it out, too. It's pretty simple, if your managers aren't hitting their numbers, get rid of them and find managers who can.' Later on, about a year into my job as a new Area Manager, I figured out that if that if I'm not coaching my team every day, they'll never find the time to learn on their own. No train, no gain."

"The more you spend on training the less you spend on advertising."

The critical characteristics of a Head Coach include:

- Focuses on know why before know how
- Teaches everyone something new daily
- Brilliant at the Basics: works on fundamentals daily
- Team Builder
- Finds coach-able moments every day
- Makes tough calls
- Adapts coaching style to the learner
- Coaches to the career-path
- Makes the company money

Head Coach is the 4th growth stage of high-performing MUMs and it sits square in the middle of the Leadership Ladder, serving as a keystone for the other six. The job of the Leader is to make more Leaders, and I can think of no skill more relevant to this responsibility than *TLC: teaching, leading and coaching.* "Excellent companies don't believe in excellence—only in constant improvement, constant change and constant training."

The multi unit manager role is a *thinking*, not a "doing" job. As we discussed earlier, one of the first things a new MUM realizes is that he or she has just transitioned from *hands-on* leadership as a GM to a role which now requires the finesse and discipline of *indirect influence*. This

The 7 Stages of Building High-Performing Partnerships and Teams

Spectacular success is preceded by unspectacular preparation.

new role is both challenging and frustrating, because it brings with it a whole new mindset and skillset. The better you develop your team, the more you achieve, *but you can't do it for them*. If you preferred "doing it yourself" as a GM (as opposed to teaching others how to do it) you may find the MUM role to be extremely frustrating. Alas, some MUMs never learn the difference and become little more than "Super GMs"; a fatal flaw for any Area Manager. Ultimately, your people will do as much or as little as you teach them to do. You can show your team where to fish, how to bait the hook, when and where to cast the line, but you cannot catch the fish for them. Here's what to teach them, and do it in this order: 1) *why* to do it, then 2) *how* to do it, and finally 3) *what* to do. Now, get the heck out of their way.

The concept of **Head Coach** is a good analogy for understanding the MUMs role as a teacher, trainer, and motivator. In most organized sports played at the varsity and professional level, the head coach does not work alone. He or she will oversee a team of assistant coaches who focus on specific player roles and responsibilities. In NFL football the head coach supervises a team of assistant coaches that are responsible for a variety of specific disciplines which can include: strength and conditioning, offensive line, defensive line, quarterback, receiver, kicking, punter and special teams. In professional baseball the head coach is called a manager, but he too supervises a battery of coaches responsible for the team's hitting, running, fielding, pitching, base-stealing, and fitness. Each coach is then responsible for executing a focused part of the game plan. The Head Coach now aligns preparation and talent to strategy and tactics, setting the game plan in motion, while the assistant coaches ready their players to execute the parts that achieve the whole. During the game they

"The more you spend on training the less you spend on advertising."

make adjustments based on prevailing and changing conditions and competition. The analogy is apt; the multi unit manager is the **Head Coach** for the General Managers in the territory or market she or he leads.

Sing from the same page

MUMs get their direction from above (HQ) and execute their strategies below (unit level). There are 7 steps an excellent Head Coach/MUM will follow to implement and execute a winning game plan:

1. Clearly define and support headquarters' annual growth and financial goals.
2. Work with their supervisors (RVPs) to determine the appropriate and necessary strategies and tactics to achieve those goals by concentrating on the Key Result Areas (KRAs) or Key Performance Indicators (KPIs), for each unique market.
3. Assess the potential challenges of executing the plan, define strategies and tactics to overcome them, and know how to make the tactics scalable across each store.
4. Identify the training and development resources necessary for their teams to incrementally achieve the objectives in each quarter and each period.
5. Obtain buy-in and support from manager teams for quarterly and period objectives, execution, timetable and measurement.
6. Manage the clock.
7. Make adjustments to the game plan when necessary based on shifting resources, acts of God and competitive maneuvers.

Be a Coach not a Parent

Head Coach MUMs must interact as partners, not "parents" with their managers. Effective *Head Coach* MUMs are not high-strung, autocratic

The 7 Stages of Building High-Performing Partnerships and Teams

know-it-alls who consider teamwork to be "teaching everyone everything I know." First of all, that presumes they know everything, and they don't. This leadership style may enforce short-term compliance but will fail to generate long-term growth, awareness, self-assurance, and commitment in their teams. The autocratic MUM also treats their managers the way parents treat young children; in need of a lot direction from someone wiser. As a result, many MUMs tend to use what foodservice executive Toni Quist calls the "Inspect, Direct, Correct" approach to managing stores. These autocratic MUMs think: "I know what's best simply by visiting your store for a few hours and I'll tell you how to fix it". If this is your approach and you believe it works because that's the way you've always done it, then let me ask you this: why do the same problems keep re-occurring in your stores? And before you begin blaming the "quality of help these days," let me ask you: who hired these people or who is tolerating their continued employment? Look in the mirror before you point a finger at your managers.

Our research shows that the MUMs who get the best results from their 21st Century teams follow a distinctly more collaborative and investigative approach to store leadership and team-building. They focus on thoughtful inquiry, collaboration and patient development, not merely "show and tell." Development is not something you "do" to a team; development is a collaborative process. Your role and goal is support, development, and sustaining goal-oriented performance among your store managers. A coach is not a "handyman."

If you're constantly addressing the same operational challenges over and over in your stores, you have to question the effectiveness of your style and approach. It can't always be the "store's" fault. There must be other reasons. Perhaps we're treating symptoms instead of identifying the true

"The more you spend on training the less you spend on advertising."

cause. (See the "Iceberg Solution" in chapter 6). Maybe our leadership style is to blame, maybe we're asking the wrong questions, maybe we're focusing on the wrong problems, maybe we haven't considered that repeatedly solving the same problems is odd…because that's what we're hired to do, right? Wrong. Our job is to grow the team and climb the ladder, not to spin our wheels and call it progress.

> **The only enduring source of competitive advantage is an organization's ability to learn faster than its competition.**
>
> –Arie de Geus

The Coach Approach

Head Coaches start by assessing and clearly defining what their team already knows, what their team doesn't know, and what their team doesn't know that they don't know. Once these knowledge gaps are identified, they then assess the strengths, weaknesses, opportunities and threats of each of their competitors, stores, and managers. This analysis gives the *Head Coach* insight into where the team and territory are most vulnerable and how they may become vulnerable in areas where they are currently strong (for example, sudden high turnover or a robbery can destabilize any store that was confident by feeling safe or fully staffed). Sometimes even being strong and knowledgeable and good at what we do can make your stores more vulnerable simply because you believe you are not vulnerable. Author Jim Collins warns that "good can be the enemy of great."

MUMs begin preparing effective game plans for their teams three ways: 1) assess strengths (and how they both help and harm you), 2) detail vulnerabilities, and 3) identify dependencies. Exemplary *Head Coaches* closely examine the visible and hidden dependencies of their company, team and marketplace, and always consider contingency plans should any of those dependencies tip unexpectedly, affecting store or manager performance. Examples of dependencies could include vendor

The 7 Stages of Building High-Performing Partnerships and Teams

relationships (which could change by chance or choice), customer loyalty (which could turn quickly based on store leadership or food safety issues), lack of competitors (which can change when a new store opens down the street) and even the weather ("acts of God" are unpredictable and unconcerned with your planning calendar and budget forecasts). As you can see, *Head Coaches* must not only thoroughly plan their team's development, they must consider all the relevant marketplace vulnerabilities and dependencies in detail so that the unexpected never takes them by surprise.

The easy part is learning new things. The hard part is letting go of what used to work for you two years ago or five years ago that no longer applies. Once vulnerabilities and dependencies are assessed, and the team's intellectual/ operational expertise and gaps catalogued, the *Head Coach* multi unit manager can now realistically prioritize development needs and focus.

Assign and Rotate Subject Matter Expertise to Every Manager

Effective Head Coach MUMs make a concerted effort to teach their "assistant coaches" (GMs and junior managers) something new every day. This strategy is both smart and selfish, but selfish in a good way. Smart, because improving the intellectual capital of their managers is always a wise investment. Selfish, because when unit managers achieve their goals, multi unit managers achieve theirs, too. Investing TLC (teaching, leading and coaching) in their team today consistently pays huge dividends tomorrow. Doesn't it make sense to invest time upfront planting solutions in your team instead of wasting time on the back end constantly fixing problems? We call it Preventive Coaching and it's a concept and skill that is both overlooked and under-used in our industry.

It is better to know it and not need it than to need it and not know it.

"The more you spend on training the less you spend on advertising."

Since all your assistant coaches (store managers) have variable skill levels and expertise, the enlightened MUM has several coaching options to choose from:

1. Equally teach every GM all they need to know about everything,
2. Try to do everything yourself,
3. Teach one GM a lot about everything and then ask that GM to try and share the new-found expertise with one of their colleagues,
4. Assign each GM a key result area topic and ask them to become experts in that area. Twice a year (or three times a year if you have a team of fast learners) have them become experts at another key performance area. Rotate the expertise until the whole team is confident about the topic (and can teach everyone else).

Options 1 and 2 are impractical. Option 3 succeeds in making only one or two people better. Don't presume that everyone's "knowledge glass" is empty and that each manager needs equal and identical amounts of coaching and content. Every manager has differing levels of expertise and challenges and therefore different coaching needs. Managers don't get better in "general", they get better in specific. *Choose option 4*. Always. Our research with high-performers confirms its impact. Identify your critical KRAs (Key Result Areas) like hiring, retention, training, repair and maintenance, marketing, sales-building, or service. Now assign one of those areas to each of your GMs and ask them to become the "area expert" on the subject for the next 90 days.

The 5th Day Strategy

On the fifth day of each work week, have your managers set aside time (at least an hour) to work on the specific KRA (Key Result Area) you've assigned them to learn as Subject Matter Experts.

Make certain they research their topic area's best practices both inside

The 7 Stages of Building High-Performing Partnerships and Teams

and outside the company (don't forget to include what competitors and retail operators are doing). Share your expertise on the topic, but don't tell them what to know; expect them to dive deep and immerse themselves in the topic, researching best practices via the web and trade periodicals as well as gleaning all their fellow store managers know on the subject. This in effect will make them veritable subject matter experts (SMEs) on the topic. Have them keep detailed notes and relevant companion materials or website addresses. They should first present what they've learned *in writing* to you. Be sure the report is not just a collection of random ideas on "hiring" but is geared to suggest solutions to specific challenges related to hiring (or whatever the topic area is) in your stores. Add your thoughts or suggest any appropriate additional resources that they may have overlooked.

Then have them formally share their new-found expertise on the topic with you and their colleagues. If you have 6 stores, you have 6 GMs who can simultaneously become local subject matter experts on 6 different KRAs (Key Result Areas) every quarter. Every four to six months rotate the subject matter expertise topics, assigning hiring to the person well-versed in negotiation and sales-building to the marketing expert and so on. Be certain to archive the information and share it with junior managers and intra-company. General Managers are not by definition "specialists"; (hence the name "general" manager) so anything you can do to create and enhance their specialties improves your company. This style of pegged or building block learning can have tremendous payoffs. It not only saves time and travel, since you no longer have to be the resident "expert," but it can also measurably improve your team's collective knowledge and execution at each store. None of us is as smart as all of us.

> **A team that won't be beat can't be beat.**
>
> —John Keener

"The more you spend on training the less you spend on advertising."

If they work on their new expertise area one day a week, four days a month, 48 days a year, just think of what they'll know, what they'll share and where you'll be one year from now. Consider how much you'd improve their coaching ability and self-confidence by continuously rotating this expertise among your managers; each GM adding to the previous body of knowledge and sharing it with one another. This is how MUMs can transcend from "telling people what to do" into leadership development. It's the direct route to creating a roundtable of knowledge-sharing and growth that characterizes an each one teach one culture. The best way to learn something is to teach it to someone else because when you teach, you learn twice. Developmentally-driven MUMs gain more time, less turnover and better performance as a result. We'll discuss this topic further in Chapter 6.

Skills of Great Coaches revealed

Our research among high-performing MUMs has revealed a wide variety of competencies that reinforce the role of the Head Coach multi unit manager:

- **Informed intuition.** Experienced MUMs know through experience and training if "this" occurs, then "this" or "that" is likely to happen. Informed intuition is a skill that results more from cumulative experience than training alone. High-performing MUMs we interviewed learn to listen to their inner voice and gut about warning signs and déjà vu feelings. This is one more good reason to collect and share best practices from your MUMs so their shared experience can help their future leaders become more intuitive more quickly.

- **Faith in their team members.** Even the most consistent managers will occasionally falter or fail. Sometimes they start

The 7 Stages of Building High-Performing Partnerships and Teams

doubting their own abilities when they're challenged. It's important for MUMs to stay steadfast in their support and stand behind their high-performing GMs (and also our junior managers) during their temporary setbacks. How many of us owe our current success to someone who believed in us when we didn't believe in ourselves?

- **Understand the importance of unreasonableness.** "There are many qualities that make an effective multi unit manager: empathy, adaptability and the ability to organize and manage time, just to name a few. But the most important quality for us is 'unreasonableness'," says Joleen Flory Lundgren, Executive Vice President, HR and Training for Famous Dave's restaurants. "We want our multi unit managers to be thoughtfully unreasonable from time to time – to stretch everyone who works for them and *expect* them to succeed. Our founder Dave Anderson tells us that 'a lot of people have gone farther than they thought they could because *someone else* thought they could.' That 'someone' is the multi unit manager. That's how our managers develop, and that is how excellence occurs". So we suggest that you assign "stretch goals" (not too easy, not too hard) to everyone who works for you, and expect them to succeed. You'll find that their capacity for achievement will grow incrementally and proportionately, just like exercising muscles.

- **Don't confuse being a disciplined MUM with being a jerk.** As we stated earlier, be tough on standards but easy on people. A disciplined person never compromises the brand standards and non-negotiables of his or her company.

"The more you spend on training the less you spend on advertising."

- **Know the difference between training and mentoring.** Training means putting faith in the process, mentoring is putting faith in the person.

- **Spare some change?** Today's multi unit manager must keep one eye on the present and one on a crystal ball. They must be knowledgeable and insightful of not only company trends but also foodservice industry and retail industry trends. Author Jay Conger echoes the notion of leaders as change agents in an article we saw at *Strategy and Business* online:

  > *"Earlier conceptions of leadership were little more than descriptions of good managership. But the emphasis has changed and radically so. Because of the enormous competitive pressures felt by most organizations, we now think of leaders as change masters. As a result, leadership training has shifted toward teaching managers and executives how to anticipate what is on their industry horizon and how to mobilize their organization to shape the future. Any training program that fails to place an emphasis on this dynamic of change is probably antiquated."*

- **School is never out for the pro.** Being so busy at "busy-ness" that you have no time to learn can mean a death spiral for any organization's leaders. To keep leading, keep learning. And if you're not learning something new each day in this business, you're just not paying attention.

- **Define the symbols and rituals.** What does your company do to recognize achievement relative to hospitality, suggestive selling, teamwork, status, or education? Pins? Certificates? Different colored aprons or shirts or hats for certified trainers? Awards?

The 7 Stages of Building High-Performing Partnerships and Teams

What rituals do you follow when giving rewards or recognition in your company? Always make it a big deal. What you reinforce is what you get more of. Never underestimate the importance and value of rituals and symbols in your company when recognizing and rewarding performance.

- **Premise can control performance.** Nothing will affect how you supervise someone more than your belief system or premise about how they should—or are likely to—perform. If you have high hopes or dim hopes for your managers they are likely to perform either up to, or down to, your expectations.

- **Snap lethargic managers out of their routines.** If you have two GMs who seem to have stopped learning or are stuck in a rut, here's a suggestion: swap them between stores for a week or two. Fresh eyes in both units can rejuvenate leaders and jumpstart better performance in each of their stores. Celebrate any progress, don't wait to get "perfect."

- **Align communication to the mission.** The more layers there are in a company, the more challenging the communication tends to be from top to bottom. The vision/mission of the company must be reinforced and aligned with all communication at every level. With each new decision MUMs must ask: "Is this message or policy consistent with the mission and vision we're preaching?" Remember how important it is to align brand values to the behavior of the people in your company who are closest to the product and the customer.

- **Focus on strengths too.** While it's certainly important, we

"The more you spend on training the less you spend on advertising."

suggest you don't spend all your energy just trying to eliminate weaknesses in your managers. Spending just as much time enhancing their strengths is also a good use of your time. People will do what you encourage them to do, not what you nag them not to do.

- **Self-esteem and learning from mistakes**. "Building self-esteem and being patient with the learning process are two of the greatest resources you can offer Area Directors," says David DiBartolo, VP of Operations for Doherty Enterprises which operates a variety of concepts in the Northeastern US, including Panera Bread, Applebee's and Johnny Carino's. "Providing specific leadership training in areas of opportunity for the individual is key, but allowing them to make mistakes and helping them find the lesson learned in each challenge is critical, too."

- **Align the right skills to the position.** Dr. Lewis Hollweg, Ph.D is the co-founder of Batrus Hollweg International, (www.batrushollweg.com) a talent assessment and development consulting firm in Dallas, TX. Here's his take on how the skills of MUMS and GMs differ: "At first glance, some of the competencies for multi unit managers appear to be the same as those for general managers. This similarity results from the broader nature of competencies for business management positions. Critical differences can be seen looking at the specific tasks underlying the competencies and the measurable behaviors supporting the competencies. For example, *Business Planning/Financial Responsibilities* is a competency for both multi unit managers and general managers. The behaviors for the general managers include forecasting revenues/expenditures

The 7 Stages of Building High-Performing Partnerships and Teams

and analyzing financial profit & loss performance data. By contrast, the multi unit manager behaviors for this same competency include assisting managers in projecting appropriate resource requirements and advising general managers on ways to control spending without sacrificing quality or service. The focus for multi unit managers is to work with general managers by advising, assisting, and demonstrating which requires skills and behaviors on a much higher level of complexity. It is much harder to achieve results by managing through others rather than acting directly. Even greater differences between general managers and multi unit managers can be identified by analyzing the tested skills, abilities, and individual characteristics of those successfully employed in the two jobs. MUM's consistently show stronger intellectual capabilities than GM's and are more long-range and analytical in their thinking. The greater complexity of the MUM job demands higher levels of problem-solving skills. As leaders, MUM's are also more assertive and more direct in giving feedback while at the same time being more supportive in their expectations of subordinate performance. Conversely, GM's are more gregarious, structured, and more self-reliant in exhibiting the competencies that drive success within four walls of the restaurant."

- **No train, no gain.** If you're new to multi unit management, one of the best ways to improve your leadership perception among your managers is by improving your public speaking skills. The second best way to earn a reputation as a great trainer. Head Coaches study the principles of adult learning, and know there are as many as 7 or 8 different preferred-learning styles. This means not everyone prefers to learn the same way you do (and the way you like to learn is the way you're most likely to teach).

"The more you spend on training the less you spend on advertising."

A good *Head Coach* learns to sync their coaching style with the learning style of each player. After all, your house key won't start your car and your car key won't open your front door. And as far as team-learning dynamics go, remember it's the speed of the slowest many, not the fastest few that determines how quickly knowledge will be assimilated, spread, and executed among your managers and their hourly associates. That being said, let's discuss some basic creative training techniques *Head Coaches* can use to get the most out of their team and their team's potential.

Basic Creative Training Techniques

The very nature of multi unit Leadership is developmental, so nearly every communication they have with their team can be considered a training opportunity. MUMs have dozens of coach-able moments and opportunities to teach their team something new every day. In fact, multi unit managers are potentially training every time they:

- Leave a voice, text, or e-mail message
- Have a meeting, big or small
- Do a store visit
- Interact with their managers or manager's team
- Stop and talk with an hourly team member

How do we get better at these informal and formal training opportunities? The same way you "get to Carnegie Hall...practice, practice, practice." Let's begin with the assumption that you're hoping to improve your people, performance and profits over the next 12 months. And since "hope" is not a strategy, I will further presume that manager education plays a critical role in how you plan to achieve measurable performance growth in your stores this year. Then study these basic creative training techniques below. They're adapted from our

The 7 Stages of Building High-Performing Partnerships and Teams

Fundamentals book and are appropriate for both new MUMs and veterans who just want to get better.

1.   Excellence is a learned behavior. Consider the notion of an athlete's "muscle memory" as a metaphor for training excellence. A professional baseball player takes dozens or hundreds of perfect practice swings before every game, repeating key behaviors like "hips open, shoulders square, eyes on the ball." Through perfect practice, their muscles eventually memorize the habitual movement, and the response becomes automatic during the game. The same is true for MUMs and unit managers who train their crew how to be brilliant at the basics every day, via the pre-shift meeting and shift coaching. Eventually the crew's "muscle memory" is trained to respond with excellence, executing the "little" things correctly over and over again. This notion of habitual consistency by working on the fundamentals daily is the cornerstone of any effective training regime and curriculum. And it needs to be taught over and over again until it is a reflexive response on the part of your managers. After all, it's not what you know, but what you do with what you know. And that leads us to the next point.

2.   Know the great enemies of training in the classroom. The two biggest obstacles to effective training inside the "classroom" are preoccupation and distraction. If your team is *preoccupied* with tasks not done, calls to be returned, or e-mail yet to be answered, your chances of getting through to them during any meeting are slight. If they're *distracted* by lackluster preparation on the MUMs part, or by an excess of irrelevant information, or inappropriately timed or structured meeting room or agenda, your odds of getting through will decrease dramatically. Design any formal training session by first eliminating distraction.

"The more you spend on training the less you spend on advertising."

3. Know the greatest enemy of training outside the classroom. It's habit. If you expect significant behavior change as the result of just one meeting, you're living a pipe dream. Behavioral psychologists' research shows that it takes an average of 21 to 28 days of different behavior to change a habit. Meetings and speeches and handouts don't change things, *people change things*. And people don't change "things" until they change their way of *doing* things. And that starts by changing behavior that's inappropriate for your goals. "Habits," Mark Twain once famously said, "are not thrown out the window. They have to be coaxed down the stairs, one step at a time." That's not accomplished via one meeting. True, and lasting, behavior change is something that takes weeks of repetition, reinforcement, and recognition to accomplish. If you believe managers can realistically morph and alter their behavior after just one training session or meeting, remember: there's a huge difference between "belief" (wanting to change) and "behavior" (making the change). Here's two questions that provide a fitting example: 1) Do you believe that health is important? 2) Are you currently doing anything in your life right now that is not particularly healthy? Your honest response to those two questions should clearly illustrate the difference between belief and behavior. Use the meeting to propose the change, use daily coaching to effect the change. Now work on the new behaviors every day for the next month with your managers. We don't think ourselves into a new way of acting, we act ourselves into a new way of thinking.

THE PAOMNNEHAL PWEOR OF THE HMUAN MNID
Aoccdrnig to rscheearch at Cmabrigde Uinervtisy, it deosn't mttaer in waht oredr the ltteers in a wrod are, the olny iprmoatnt tihng is that the frist and lsat ltteer be in the rghit pclae. The rset can be a taotl mses and you can sitll raed it wouthit a porbelm. Tihs is bcuseae the huamn mnid deos not raed ervey lteter by istlef, but the wrod as a wlohe... Amaznig, huh?
(Moral: are your manuals over-telling and under-explaining?)

The 7 Stages of Building High-Performing Partnerships and Teams

4.   The Three-to-One Rule of Teaching. Sometimes training sessions are either too brief or one-dimensional to leave much chance of recall and execution in the real world. So when you're planning a training session, be sure to factor in a three-to-one learning ratio. This means for every specific objective you want to accomplish training-wise, attach three different activities which can help the learner execute on and accomplish that objective. For example, if you want to educate your managers on Financials 101, choose three different ways to educate them, perhaps by studying spreadsheets, physically doing inventory together, plus a written quiz. If you want managers to get better at conflict resolution, training options could include case studies, group discussion, and role-playing. Adding multi-sensory and groupthink opportunities also increase retention. This blended learning approach goes miles beyond lecture to educate and works better than a manual or a quiz alone will. Your mother was right: actions do speak louder than words. Remember: one training objective, three learning activities to support it.

5.   Retention's "rule of three." When it comes to retention, advertising people, film directors, coaches and even marksmen have long known the power of stringing together a trio of phrases or words to encourage recall. Consider these classics: "reduce, re-use, recycle," "the few, the proud, the Marines," "Lights! Camera! Action!," "Ready! Aim! Fire!," or "On your Mark! Get Set! Go!" It works for remembering key training points too. So when you're looking for a memorable catch phrase or memory peg for your training or coaching session, think three (i.e. Serve-Sell-Succeed, Think-Plan-Execute).

6.   Spaced repetition is the mother of all learning. Have you ever watched a stonecutter at work? He will hammer away methodically at a rock as many as a hundred times without a crack showing in it. Then, at

"The more you spend on training the less you spend on advertising."

the 101st blow, it will finally crack open. It is not the final blow alone that accomplished the result, but the100 others that preceded it as well. So it is with learning and retention as well. Teach key concepts repeatedly, but with enough space in between to allow for reflection, discussion, trial, error, understanding, guided practice, and eventually, alignment and assimilation. What would make you a better tennis player if you'd never played before? One five-hour lesson, or five one-hour lessons spread over five weeks with time to practice in between?

7.   Always teach WHY before how. 99% of MUM-to-manager and manager-to-crew training fails because we first tell our team *what* to do and *how* to do it, sometimes completely ignoring the most important step: *why to do it.* This is especially evident when your unit managers try to "coach" hourly team members. If you explain *why* something has to be done with enough conviction, rationale and passion that the trainee responds by asking you "how" to do it, you have just set a mind afire, and leapt a major training obstacle by creating a self-motivated learner. How many of us have the patience to teach "why" first, instead of the rapid-fire steps of "how," "what," "where," and "when"?   Frame every performance issue, new policy, or training discussion around why it will benefit our customers.

8.   Think KFD before any meeting. Whether you're meeting one-on-one with a manager for half an hour or addressing a group of 200 for two, every successful presentation starts with the KFD principle. The **K** means you should always plan the conversation or presentation by first asking yourself: What do my manager(s) need to **know**? Is it about changes, financials, promotions, problems, policies, coaching, marketing? Detail in writing what you're trying to say (and don't forget to begin with *why*). The **F** stands for how do we want the trainee to **feel** as a result of what you're

The 7 Stages of Building High-Performing Partnerships and Teams

teaching? Should they be excited? Motivated? Confident? Dissatisfied with their current behavior? How do we want them to react emotionally to the information presented? The ultimate goal of any training is a heightened emotional experience because people are self-motivated to change only when their emotions are engaged. Finally, the **D** stands for what do we want them to **do**? Always link learning to action. What specific actions do want those managers to take? Learning does not take place until behavior has changed. What they do as a result of what you say is much more important than what you "told" them. KFD: what do we want them to *know*, how do we want them to *feel*, what do we want them to *do*? Use the KFD principle for every training session, every voice mail, every letter and every e-mail, and you'll see better retention, more productive managers and even MCIYP: more cash in your pockets.

9.   Blended learning approach gets best results. This means combining live instruction with print materials, online learning, role-playing, case studies, feedback, and guided practice. The more senses you impact during the learning process the greater the retention rate.

10.   Make it fun. What we learn while having fun we rarely forget.

11.   Making meetings pay. What can I say about #@*%! meetings that hasn't been muttered and uttered by thousands of bored and frustrated managers under their breath a million times before? Not much. So let's talk about where and why meetings matter most: in the wallet. *Rule number one* regarding meeting planning: don't call a $1000 meeting to solve a $100 problem. Do you really need to have this meeting? If it's mostly about transferring information, is it better communicated via e-mail, voice mail, text message, fax or memo? Whenever you schedule a meeting with your managers, have you considered how expensive it is

"The more you spend on training the less you spend on advertising."

and how to get the greatest return on that investment? If a multi unit manager meets with six of their GMs, there's a minimum of $1200 an hour of collective time and expense sitting in that room…$20 a minute. (Every hour they meet with you is an hour they're not in their stores building business.) If you had to write a personal check for $1200 every hour you met with your team, would you plan your get-togethers any differently? Plan every meeting in detail, start and end on time, make it upbeat, concise, cost-effective and interactive.

12. Skinny the monologue, fatten the dialogue. A manager meeting should not be a series of one-way proclamations or monologues by MUMs. They should be interactive, energetic and experiential, built on spirited dialogues, engaging visuals and idea-sharing, not monologues and text-filled handouts. And by dialogues, I don't mean morale-killing "bitch" sessions, but rather focused feedback which encourages the team to share their individual and cumulative expertise to solve common problems and achieve common goals. For bigger meetings with lengthy agendas, perhaps focus first on smaller topics so that there's a sense of accomplishing much early on. This can quickly add momentum and value to any get-together.

> **Sometimes I get the feeling that the two biggest problems in America today are making ends meet and making meetings end.**
>
> – Robert Orben

13. Know the difference between information and communication. The two words "information" and "communication" are used interchangeably, but in fact they mean two different things: information is giving out, communication is getting through. Bottom line: keep it fresh, keep it focused, and keep it fun.

14. People never argue with their own data. As often as possible design your coaching and training so that your managers discover information for

The 7 Stages of Building High-Performing Partnerships and Teams

themselves, and as often as possible have them collectively brainstorm solutions to the challenges you need to overcome. The more involved your people are in the decision-making that affects their future, the more likely they are to support and drive the necessary change.

15. Agonize over handouts. If you're covering five different topics, put the key information relevant to each topic on five different colored sheets of paper so they're easy to refer to both during and after the meeting. Anything you design as a handout to aid or facilitate learning should mix text and graphics equally. Think *USA Today* not *Wall Street Journal*.

16. Know the 3 performance problem areas. Managers or hourly crew will not perform for one of three reasons. They either: *1) Don't Know, 2) Can't Do, or 3) Don't Care.* If they don't know how to do something, that's a training issue, and it's the MUMs responsibility to try and coach them through it. If they *can't do* it, that's usually indicative of a lack of resources; and that's also the MUMs responsibility to identify and provide the tools they need to fix it. If they *know how* and *can do*, but *don't care*, my experience is that apathy is difficult to reverse. If not caring is chronic behavior on the manager's part, I suggest you cut your losses and give them a job at the competition.

17. If you try to save money on training, you end spending twice as much on advertising. You'll be advertising for new managers, new crew, new customers, because what your team doesn't know *will* hurt you. Make team learning a line item on your daily to-do list. To teach, train and coach is to touch the future. "The only enduring source of competitive advantage," wrote Arie de Geus in the Harvard Business Review, "is an organization's relative ability to learn faster than its competition."

"The more you spend on training the less you spend on advertising."

18. Remember: "SWAWC". When does somebody finally "get it"? It all depends on how self-motivated they are to learn whatever it is you want them to "get." And despite what you may have heard in your last leadership seminar, you can't motivate anyone; everyone is *self-motivated.* Some people are self-motivated to listen or be on time, others are self-motivated to ignore you or be late. Knowing this, a smart way to begin planning any formal or informal training session is to first consider the five key words of self-motivated learning: "So What and Who Cares?" Be the Devil's Advocate for your own content, design and agenda before you get up in front of your team and you'll train better every time.

19. Make pre-shift meetings <u>mandatory</u> not optional for your managers. If your "assistant coaches" aren't taking the time to plan and execute pre-shift meetings with their crew daily, then every associate will have her or his own idea of what the shift should be. Plus, no pre-shift meeting means

> **Your people will do as much or as little as you lead them to do.**

the team will end up *practicing on the customer.* If you'd like to show your managers how to plan and deliver energetic and effective pre-shift meetings, check out our free online clips from our best-selling DVD called *Jumpstart: How to Plan and Execute Effective Pre-Shift Meetings* at **Sullivision.com**.

20. Always train learners FIRST on what causes them the most pain and frustration day and day out. When you are deciding what's most important to teach your team, prioritize the options based on what they wrestle most with day in and day out. A simple and consistent fact of human nature is that people will do more to avoid pain than to gain pleasure, so coach the team first on the things that will make their job easier.

21. Create "front porches." Learning is not doing. Learning is reflecting on doing. Allow yourself and your managers time to both digest and

The 7 Stages of Building High-Performing Partnerships and Teams

absorb the new information shared with them at your meetings or what they might have gotten at company conferences. Give them time to discuss how the knowledge relates to what they already know and how to apply it. This is the essence of what is called "Action Learning" and unfortunately it is the opposite of what happens in most "formal" training programs, especially at big company-wide franchise and manager conferences. More real learning and knowledge transfer occurs at the breaks and at the bar than in the "classroom". I can certainly understand the rationale for trying to get out as much information as possible; it's expensive to get everyone together. But by *firehosing* as much content as they can at the audience within the available budget and time frame will, more often than not, create a false belief among the executive team and training department that "learning has occurred" merely because content has been delivered. Allowing time for realistic and patient gestation/reflection/guided practice after presenting key content is critical for true learning to take place and measurable performance to improve. You must factor in this "front porch" reflection time in learners. Nag your executive team and trainers to follow suit in an effort to create effective learning environments and bridge the critical "learning-doing" gap. Likewise, whenever trainers develop new programs for the unit manager, they must also simultaneously develop an aligned facilitation program for that person's multi unit manager. It should clearly detail what will be taught, how the course enhances previous learning and specific steps the MUM can take to facilitate and enhance the learning transfer and process back at work through both sequential coaching and guided practice.*

22. Practice, practice, practice. The fundamental skills of training aren't hard to understand, they're just hard to do. The key naturally is not to practice on your managers. Practice coaching and training skills with your fellow MUMs, mentors or trainers. Who has time to be constantly fixing

*P.S.: Executives and trainers may no longer present and "sell" a new policy, program, or procedure by alleging that "it saves time." From now on whenever you introduce a new policy, program, or procedure that "saves time" you must simultaneously identify and remove a current a new policy, program, or procedure that wastes it.

"The more you spend on training the less you spend on advertising."

operational and management problems that training could have and would have prevented in the first place? Speaking of time, every successful *Head Coach* we've studied, either in professional sports or in multi unit leadership "manages the clock" exceedingly well. Time out?

Can't run away from Time

"They say you can't fight fate and time won't wait, you can't run away from time. Time is the Avenger." *–Ray Davies on the CD "Other People's Lives"*

The very names we ascribe to foodservice categories like "Quick Service" or "Fast Casual" speaks volumes about the important role that time plays in our daily operations and industry. What is "time"?

To some, it's money.

But time also goes by, flies, is shared, marches on, runs out, waits for no one, is of the essence, has come today, is fleeting, gets killed, is in a bottle, changes everything, is on my side, and you can't turn back the hands of it. No matter how you think of it, it's a fact that time is either your greatest ally or adversary. How we invest, spend or waste our time—and how we manage our timing—is perhaps the most critical task of the high-performing multi unit manager. Unlike other resources we have at our disposal, time can't be bought or sold, borrowed or stolen, stockpiled or saved, manufactured, reproduced, or modified. All we can do is *make use of it*. And whether or how or *if* we use it, time nevertheless slips away. We all get the same allotment: 24 hours in a day, 1,440 minutes between midnights, no less, no more.

The successful MUMs we researched realize time is intangible and that managing the intangible is impossible. Our research shows that they

The 7 Stages of Building High-Performing Partnerships and Teams

approach the notion of "time management" from a slightly contrarian point-of-view: you can't "manage" *time*, you can only manage *activities*. Others challenge the very notion that time is an enemy: "Lack of time is not an Area Coach's biggest challenge," said one multi unit manager we interviewed. "We have plenty of time, the same amount everyone else gets every day. We just need to learn how to use it better. Being focused, having an organized workspace, aligning plans to priorities, and 'just-saying-no' to distractions that pull you off task are skills that are chronically under-taught and sorely over-needed by area supervisors. When I hear my colleagues complain about time while their calendars are a complete disorganized mess I fear for their future." If you'd like a sample of an effective daily calendar planning template, you can download it free at **www.sullivision.com**.

> If I gave you $1,440 dollars and asked how you'd spend it in the next 24 hours, you'd probably think about it very carefully. Now how carefully do you consider how you'll spend tomorrow's daily dose of the 1440 minutes we're given each day? If every minute of your time is worth a dollar, how will you spend $525,600 in the next 12 months?

The way to go about making the most of your limited time is to first identify and then *prioritize* the activities that put the greatest demands on our time, not just "spending" time on your activities. (That's why a written Quarterly Business Plan tied to a weekly calendar is such a key and critical starting point for personal time-and-activity management in your area or territory; more on this in Chapter 6.) Some activities are less worthy of your time investment than other activities; the critical difference lies in knowing which is which. Stop, think, prioritize, and then act. Always "bank" and allot discretionary pockets of time into your daily and weekly schedule to deal with the unexpected fires and un-planned demands that can and will pop up. Every day something unexpected is going to happen. Count on it and don't forget to build *"what the hell??!"* time

"The more you spend on training the less you spend on advertising."

into your daily calendar. The routine nature of the unexpected emergency never surprises high-performers. Anticipate crises du jour, plan on them, act on them and then get back to the bigger objectives. Be like Smokey the Bear; prevent fires.

Plan your work, work your plan

Once you prepare a thorough Quartly Business Plan you can now begin building your daily and weekly calendar which is the key first step to time and activity management. Make both a to-do and a *to-don't* list but make sure that each item and the steps necessary to achieve it are assigned specific due dates and incorporated into your calendar. (Don't make "lists" that are not incorporated into your calendar...ever.) Detail and prioritize the activities that have either the greatest need or the greatest potential ROI each day. Then assign estimated time increments to each activity and the day you need to work on it, whether it's a store visit, data review, performance appraisal, marketing briefing, conference call, or vendor meeting. Your "to-don't list" should include things like "don't compromise brand standards, excellence, values, policies, ethics."

60 Second Time and Activity Management Tips

Awareness of the kinds of things that steal time from a well-planned day is the first step in becoming more productive and less stressed. Here are some common time traps along with suggestions on how to make them allies not adversaries.

Start here. Everyday begin by asking yourself three important questions: "What is truly important right now considering 1) what my time is worth and 2) what is *not getting done* while I'm busy doing this other thing? 3) what will happen (or not happen) if I fail to get this done?" Before you assess each task, consider who else may be waiting on your counsel or

The 7 Stages of Building High-Performing Partnerships and Teams

> **There is never enough time unless you're serving it.**
> —Malcolm Forbes

who else may be available in a supporting role to help you accomplish it. Determine the most urgent projects to complete each day and then get them done (or at least get them started), no matter what. Incorporate your list into your calendar. Start with the most important task and work down. If you accomplish nothing other than your number one priority, you're ahead of the day. Avoid the temptation to tackle fun or easy tasks first just because you like shorter lists. Make a little progress every day on bigger projects. How do you eat an elephant? One bite at a time.

You will always be managing competing priorities. So don't act surprised when they happen.

Know what your time is worth. Based on an 8 hour day (hah!), 244-day work year or 1,952 hours, here's what you or a team member's time is worth:

Annual Income	One Hour Is Worth	One Hour/Day Wasted per Year Costs You
$20,000	$10.24	$2,500.00
$25,000	$12.81	$3,125.00
$30,000	$15.37	$3,750.00
$50,000	$25.61	$6,250.00
$75,000	$38.42	$9,375.00
$100,000	$51.23	$12,500.00

Keep a log. In her book *Organize Your Office*, Ronni Eisenberg suggests: "If you don't know where your time goes, keep a log for a week. As you evaluate the tasks that consumed your time, ask yourself: Did I really need do this? Could someone else have done this? Could I have delayed this task to work on a task of higher priority?"

"The more you spend on training the less you spend on advertising."

Know your peak performance time. Always do priority work during your "peak performance" time. Take on the creative or complex projects when you are the sharpest and do the mundane stuff when you're least creative. For most people that's first thing in the morning, for others it's late in the afternoon. If you have recurring paperwork or reports set a specific time to do them weekly or monthly. You'll find you get more done in less time with greater efficiency. If you always complete—or at least start—your hardest task first each day, then the remaining tasks will seem that much easier. Use your energy in proportion to your personal peak times. Either way, don't put off until tomorrow what you can do today. Like Pappy Sullivan used to say: "If you do it then it's done."

Forget your ABCs. Coordinate and detail the activities you need to get done into your calendar and forget the old belief that you should assign A, B, and C priorities to each task (for instance, "A" priorities are the activities that are critical, "B" priorities are important but not as critical, "C" priorities would be nice to do if you get the time. How much time do you spend re-writing these lists day after day?) We suggest instead that you break each task down into the sequential subtasks necessary to complete the project and then assign those subtasks to a calendar day. The best book we've seen on the topic of time and activity management is David Allen's *Getting Things Done*.

Quick tip for processing workflow. When you're facing stuff in your in-box (a phone message, e-mail, package, report, mail, etc) here's the smart MUM's plan-of-attack: 1) first define what it is and then 2) ask yourself "is it actionable?" If the answer is "no" then trash it or reference it.

> If you've ever dropped loose change in a piggy bank, you were probably astonished to find how quickly those coins added up to 'real money'. Think of time the same way. Each of us has small 'coins' of time we spend waiting each day : for the elevator, at the doctor's office, in the bank line. You will be amazed to learn how much free time you can buy with this 'small change' of time.
>
> – Stephanie Winston

The 7 Stages of Building High-Performing Partnerships and Teams

If "yes", do it *if it takes two minutes or less*. If not, then either delegate it or defer it to your calendar or next actions. **Hot Tip**: Sometimes you can complete a whole bunch of two-minute-or-less items while you are waiting on hold.

OATS. My first Regional Manager taught me a simple three-step process years ago which still works wonders for weekly time management. He called it the "OATS" formula:

- **O**: Objectives. What results do you want to see by the end of the week? Write them down on your calendar and rank them.

- **A**: Activities. What do you have to do to achieve your weekly objectives? List the necessary activities--and this is the important part—always *put them in sequence*.

- **T**: Time. How much time will each activity require? To plan realistically, allow yourself more time than you think you will actually need. This will give you flexibility if unexpected problems develop.

- **S**: Schedule. Look at your calendar and decide when you can do each activity. Add it to that day's priorities. Oh, then be sure that you do it.

Clear the Clutter. What does your desk, office, car look like? How much time do you spend each day or week simply looking for things? An organized workspace at home and in transit saves time, and learning how to manage your in-box makes more time available. It's also wise to learn how to file properly and do it at the end of each day. It bears repeating: learn how to file properly and do it at the end of each day. Label a folder called "To Be Filed" and put relevant items in there as you progress through your workday. At the end of every day—no exceptions—file the

"The more you spend on training the less you spend on advertising."

items in that folder. Everything deserves a "home." Put things back in their place so you can easily find them next time. For desktop organization try this: if you're right-handed, make sure the landline phone or cellphone is located on the left side of your desk. Keep the right side of the desk (and your right hand) free to take notes. The opposite is true for left-handers.

Paper, E-Mail and Voice Mail. As you handle every piece of paper or e-mail (or voice mail) that crosses your desk, Blackberry, or laptop, first ask yourself *"How do I plan to use this?"* instead of *"Where should I put or keep this?"* If you don't plan to use it, toss it. This filtering question will save you time, space and effort. This tip takes extraordinary discipline but pays off with extra time and storage space. Master the power of Outlook if your company uses it for e-mail. Most multi unit managers we've worked with only know how to use about 10% of Outlook's ability to organize and prioritize e-mail.

OHIO. When it comes to in-box management and paper shuffling or e-mail archiving remember the acronym O.H.I.O., which means "Only Handle It Once." And what should you do with each in-box item you only handle once? Consider this follow-up acronym: T.R.A.F. (Trash it / Refer it / Act on it / or File it). Be strong and committed to these rules and you will considerably minimize the odds of being buried under mounds of paperwork. Just say no to pack-ratting! You have the time, most people just don't manage it properly.

> Things rarely get stuck because of lack of time. They get stuck because the doing of them has not been defined.
>
> –David Allen

Keep ideas and notes centrally located. I'd suggest buying a spiral-bound notebook and use it as your central depository for all of your random notes and ideas, rather than accumulating a thousand thoughts on a

The 7 Stages of Building High-Performing Partnerships and Teams

thousand random scraps of paper. Review this book weekly and transfer the best ideas to your daily calendar.

Breaking the e-mail leash. Check your e-mail on the half-hour, not every minute. Technology like Blackberries and Treos are intended to be enablers, not enslavers, but many a well-intentioned MUM becomes distracted and driven off task by the constant "ping" of e-mail. NEVER check your e-mail during a manager conversation unless you've told them ahead of time you need to check it for an important update *related to the conversation*.

Managing the magazines. You know those industry trade magazines which show up each week and month, creating a bigger pile every 30 days? You're reluctant to toss them because of the insight you might miss, yet they're stress-inducing just to look at. Here are three time-saving suggestions regarding periodicals:

1. *Take them along.* Grab 10 or 12 of those industry magazines from your stack and put them in your briefcase whenever you have to fly or drive somewhere. They make great airplane or hotel reading and the stack will shrink after every trip.

2. *Rip and read.* If you're not flying or staying overnight in a hotel anytime soon, take 15 minutes every Friday afternoon, choose ten back issues from the stack, quickly leaf through each one, and tear out all of the articles you *think* you would like to read. *Don't read them now.* Put them in a color file folder labeled "To Read", leave the folder next to your phone or in your briefcase, and then toss the bulk of the leftover magazines. Your stack is now much smaller and you can read the relevant articles at more appropriate times, like when you're stuck in traffic, on hold, or waiting in a doctor's office or at the airport.

"The more you spend on training the less you spend on advertising."

3. ***New Year's Eve Toss.*** On December 31 every year take a deep breath, close your eyes, and just toss that big stack of magazines and publications that you're "getting around to." Don't worry about missing them because 30 short days later that stack will magically replenish itself once the new issues begin arriving in your mailbox again.

Plan each day in advance. When you start work each morning, are you ready and raring to go? Or do you start your day with a "first-thing-that-comes-to-mind-I'll-do" mentality? A little time invested in advance planning always pays off in increased efficiency and productivity. Your plan doesn't need to be complex; in fact, a simple things-to-do list properly prioritized and added to the appropriate calendar day will work wonders for saving time. Some items to consider:

- At the end of each day—without fail—write down the three most important things in your calendar you need to do first the next day. Then do it.
- Tackle your most pressing or unpleasant task first. *If you do it then it's done.* List the phone calls you *have* to make, and the e-mail you *have* to respond to and do those first.
- If you're visiting stores tomorrow, or have a meeting scheduled in a place you're unfamiliar with, plan and prioritize the day's driving and routing electronically via MapQuest, Google search, etcetera.

During a lifetime, the average American will spend a total of seven months waiting at stoplights, four years doing housework, five years waiting in lines, six years online, and six years eating. But MUMs will spend an additional 7 more years doing paperwork and dealing with OPP (other people's problems).

Use Windshield Time as a mobile university. Have you ever considered how much time you spend on the road each year, and how much more you'd know if you applied that time to learning something new while driving (or waiting) in traffic? Here's a chart that will give you an idea of how much time that daily commute eats up annually:

The 7 Stages of Building High-Performing Partnerships and Teams

Daily Commute (round trip)	=	Hours per year in car
10 min	=	40 hr.
30 min.	=	120 hr.
60 min.	=	240 hr.
120 min.	=	480 hr.

Invest in motivational or instructional MP3s, CDs or podcasts for your car or iPod and listen and learn while you're working out, walking, or driving to and from appointments. If your management team uses MP3 players, consider sending them weekly podcasts from you with industry or company updates and progress reports, or post it on your company intranet or personal webpage for your team. Visit our website for a variety of free podcasts which can improve your management skills.

Leave yourself reminder voicemails. When you're driving and get a great idea, send yourself a voicemail while the idea is still fresh and top of mind. This saves you the time—and frustration—of trying to remember the brilliant idea later after a billion other distractions occur.

Save time when leaving voice mails. Leaving effective voice mail messages encourages people to return your phone calls faster. A few suggestions:

- Answer three questions before you reach the voicemail of the person you are calling—1) why you called, 2) what you need and 3) when you are available for callbacks. If you don't want to hear the entire voicemail intro message, press 1. Most of the time, you'll hear a beep and you can leave your message immediately. When returning calls from new customers or potential customers, note what time they called you and then call them back around the same time. Chances are, they'll be available then.

"The more you spend on training the less you spend on advertising."

- Keep your voice mail messages brief. Too short and the message may seem insignificant. Too long and you may irritate the other party.

- Talk slowly and always repeat your number twice. Pretend you're writing your phone number in the air as you recite it. Most callers speak much too fast, which forces the annoyed recipients to replay the message repeatedly, or worse, 86 it out of annoyance.

- Speak a little bit louder than usual, enunciating as you speak. The person retrieving your message may do so in a noisy place...like a busy kitchen or in an airport.

Fill up your car on the way home from work. Don't waste your prime morning time at the gas station.

Make the most out of Meetings. Make the person who arrives last for the meeting the person responsible for taking the minutes. Want to bet they will show up on time for the next meeting!? Want to shorten meetings? Have a stand-up session. Everyone will stay awake and will want to get to the point quickly. Want a really short meeting? Hold it in the walk-in cooler! Always have an agenda. Complete all of your agenda items before moving to unrelated topics. Capture important items not scheduled for the meeting that are brought up during discussions in a "parking lot" list for discussion later. The parking lot issues should be part of the minutes when they are distributed.

> If a cluttered desk is a sign of a cluttered mind, what is the significance of a clean desk?
>
> – Laurence J. Peter

Remember the 80/20 Rule. Statistically speaking, 80% of your results will come from 20% of your activities. Figure out the 20% of your activities that are the most important and get better at them so you have more time.

The 7 Stages of Building High-Performing Partnerships and Teams

Preserve Corporate Memory

"Between then and now, there is a chasm across which swings only the frayed-rope bridge of memory." *—Richard Seltzer*

Time management applies to the past as well as the present.

Most companies put a premium on preparing for the future, but many of them fail to put a similar value on capturing the lessons of the past. The mystery of history in your operation, once revealed, can teach both your present and future leaders valuable lessons about obstacles to anticipate and strategies to win. We're all familiar with the classic old saw warning that "those who fail to study history are doomed to repeat the past," and it's true, especially when you consider the rapid turnover and job-changing that characterizes our industry.

The best organizations have learned that actively collecting and archiving the past experience of its people (think of it as *knowledge capital*) is critical to a successful future. It's said that what you don't know won't hurt you. But what you don't know that your company has forgotten will cripple a successful business, because you will invest a lot of unproductive time making the same mistakes over and over again.

While many chain restaurants in the QSR arena have been around for 50 years or more, most successful casual theme restaurant chains are relatively young, having originated or grown in the 1980s or 1990s. Unlike current McDonald's or KFC executives who most likely never met Ray Kroc or Colonel Harlan Sanders, many of the current casual theme leaders may have worked directly with the company founders. And while founders may write memoirs, what experience did their second-tier associates (today's CEOs, COOs, and Area Directors) gain as they helped grow the concept? What did

"The more you spend on training the less you spend on advertising."

they learn as "second-generation Brand Ambassadors," and what cautionary tales do they have to share with future leaders? Most importantly, is someone collecting and sharing their stories?

Time is fleeting

Every year every company has a lot of experience, insight and culture going out the door, either by chance or by choice. Don't let this impending Brain Drain make your company vulnerable. Whether you're big or small, you're facing a serious knowledge gap unless you've made a concerted effort to capture, record, preserve and share this collective corporate memory on an ongoing (and outgoing) basis.

How to upload more memory

We've helped many companies, big and small, collect, archive and re-distribute knowledge capital to their next generation of leaders. (Visit us at **Sullivision.com** to learn more.) Here's a primer on how to extract key learnings from the past and present to help your future:

> Have you heard of the 9 Pregnant Women rule? It takes 9 months to have a baby, but you can't get the job done in one month with nine pregnant women. That rule applies to any project; as you think about managing time that you have available to complete a project, it's critical that you identify which steps you must complete sequentially.
>
> – Scott Mills

- Today, tomorrow and the next day, start taking lots of photos of team members, your dining rooms, kitchens, drive-throughs, signage, building exteriors, menus, uniforms and customers. File them, label each picture or menu with names, dates, locations. Five years from now, these will be "archive" photos, ten years from now they'll be "historical."

- Ask your senior executives to make a list of "The 10 Stupidest Things We've Done" (and just hope it doesn't include "hiring you"!). Then make sure you and your company don't do them again. Now ask your *current* MUMs and managers to make a list of "The 10 Stupidest Things We

The 7 Stages of Building High-Performing Partnerships and Teams

Do." Compare it with the list from the senior execs. Hopefully it doesn't look familiar. Either way, learn to stop making the same mistakes over and over again.

- Track down and archive every menu edition, employee manual and relevant photos from opening day to yesterday.

- Interview all key personnel who have been with you for more than 10 years. Record stories relevant to company milestones, anecdotes about the early days, especially growth challenges and how they were overcome, and insight gained from the experience. Who do they know who might have photos or memorabilia from the "early" days that you're missing? Video speeches at key executive retirement dinners and award ceremonies.

- Make sharing company history and values a critical component of any orientation programs for new franchisees or team members. "Without knowing history," says author Michael Crichton, "you're like a leaf that doesn't know it's part of a tree."

- Collect stories from current team members that may grow to be classic tales of selfless service, tireless teamwork or customer-centric behavior. A good way to start is to ask team members this question: "what story about work do you wish everybody here knew?" Of course not every shared story is valuable or appropriate, but the ones that are can be used as "training parables" in your manuals or videos or online learning to illustrate brand values much better than "steps" can.

Yesterday is history, tomorrow is a mystery, today is a gift. That's why we call it the "present." What we learn from the past helps us understand what is true today and possible tomorrow. Memory is the pilot light of the future. Keep it burning by capturing the light of knowledge and spreading the flame of learning. Don't procrastinate because both time and talent flies...two short days from now tomorrow will be yesterday.

"The more you spend on training the less you spend on advertising."

Summary: Head Coach™

Head Coaches are critical to keeping our learning alive and helping us stay on track in our stores and in our companies. Continuous improvement of people is as important as continuous improvement of systems. While the selection process (Talent Scout) aims at finding the right people, it is the development process (Head Coach) that helps those people do the right things, and do the right things right.

The primary goal and role of an outstanding **Head Coach** is to elevate the thinking of their people, develop deep smarts among the team, and to know the way, show the way, and go the way. Your team may not listen to what you say but they rarely fail to imitate what you do. Be committed to teaching your team something new everyday because most managers tend to under-learn and over-forget. Don't be a "compliance cop," be a committed coach.

Think about the maturation and development process that most GMs go through as they master their job. They had lots of time (years in most cases as they grew from assistant manager to GM) to mature, experiment, make mistakes, learn from those mistakes and then grow on and into the job. Eventually they became very good at leading one unit. Now they're promoted to the role of Multi Unit Manager and are expected to perform at a much higher level from Day One. Mentoring, guidance and coaching is critical at this stage if the new MUM is to be given a fair chance at excelling in her or his new role.

> **You can train people and they may wind up leaving. But if you don't train them and they wind up staying, you have bigger problems.**
>
> – Jim Koch

The 7 Stages of Building High-Performing Partnerships and Teams

Real transformation among your team is ultimately about performance, not merely "competence." So while we frame successful MUM behaviors as competencies, remember once again that "well done is better than well-said." If you don't study and use these ideas they're worthless; tools left in the toolbox never built anything. Re-think where your productivity and bonuses are born: in the brains and hearts of the people you supervise. Teach every manager how to coach each team member into position, through the position, and out of the position. Teach them to make every decision as if they owned the company.

Know where the game is being played (and it's not on a spreadsheet). The *Head Coach* MUM knows that the real game in our industry is not being played at the Home Office or headquarters or in meetings or planning sessions. The real game—where our company either wins or loses—is played out daily in the restaurants during The Shift. A successful business is the result of the endless repetition of perfect and near-perfect shifts.

If you are a baseball or football coach you begin every season planning to win, not to turn in an average performance. "Average" means you're either the best of the worst or the worst of the best. Begin every season—every quarter, every period, every day—focused on what it takes to develop and build a winning team in your stores. Despite what you've heard before, it <u>is</u> whether you win or lose, and not just how you "play" the game. And the game begins or starts over every time the customer walks in.

"The more you spend on training the less you spend on advertising."

Self-assessment: **Head Coach™**

Review the list below. Assess your personal strengths and challenges relative to each competency in one of the boxes to the right. Review the boxes again in six months.

Competency	Good At	Average	Needs Work
Do I rotate subject matter expertise among my managers every quarter?			
How would I assess my ability as a trainer?			
Do I teach everyone something new each day? What?			
How am I at time and activity management?			
Am I a good communicator?			
Am I a Thermometer or a Thermostat?			
Require my managers to collect and share best practices?			

STAGE FIVE
Marketing Guru™

Cautionary Tale

*"I had been a pretty good General Manager, especially at operations.
I loved hiring and training servers and cooks and interacting with customers at the
counter or in the dining room. I was extremely 'hands-on' and spent most of my time in
that store. The one thing I hadn't paid much attention to though was marketing. I kind
of presumed that advertising did that and it was somebody at the home office's job.
When I got promoted to area director I was stunned by three things: 1) how important
local store marketing was, 2) how little I knew about it, and 3) how
I couldn't change things by myself anymore, that other people were in charge of the
stores now. Those three realizations were humbling experiences and I stayed awake
many nights worrying about them. I was too afraid to ask my Regional Director for help
because he thought that was a sign of weakness. I figured it out and survived somehow.
I had to learn to influence and delegate rather than command and control. I figured out
how to connect the stores to the community. Mostly by trial-and-error.
I guess necessity really is the 'Mother of Invention'."*

"Marketing is a philosophy, not a department"

The key and critical characteristics of a Marketing Guru include:

- ABM (Always Be Marketing) mindset
- Equally adept at both external and internal marketing
- Views marketing as a philosophy not a "department"
- Learns the differences in each market
- Connects with the community (outside and inside the restaurant)
- SWOT analysis for every restaurant
- Connector: has both know how and know who
- Makes the company money

Goal-Getter™

Synergist™

Marketing Guru™

Head Coach™

Servant Leader

Talent Scout™

Brand Ambassador™

Bumpkins and Pumpkins

Two rural Oklahomans, Phil and Bill, hatched a dim-witted money-making plan. They arranged to buy pumpkins by the truckload from a local farmer for a dollar each and then re-sell them to customers in Kansas for…exactly a dollar each.

Every Friday in September and October they purchased all the pumpkins they could load into their pickup, and then drove 110 miles north where they sold the pumpkins along a Kansas road for the same price they paid for each one. They hand-painted big colorful signs and offered free hot apple cider. Business boomed. But every week they lost money though the reason why was puzzling the two slow friends. Going over the books one night, Phil turned to Bill and said "I just don't git it. We've sold 150 truckloads of punkins this month, but we ain't making a dime. " Bill solemnly nodded, stared out the window, thought for a while and then suddenly his face lit up: "I got it! We need a bigger truck!"

Moral? Marketing isn't just about generating "volume"; volume can hide a multitude of sins. Marketing is about aligning all systems and processes into attaining and retaining customers and being profitable along the way.

The 7 Stages of Building High-Performing Partnerships and Teams

Marketing Guru is a critical rung on our Leadership Ladder for a simple reason: *all restaurants are sales-controlled, but unfortunately, not all restaurants are sales-driven.* Marketing done well generates more customer traffic, sales, talent and profitability. Marketing is a core element of any successful team's DNA. It's what keeps you in business and the competition out of it. As foodservice executive Linda Allison puts it: "Our goal is to turn the competition into a non-profit organization... without the tax-exempt status!"

"Marketing" today has many names, many meanings and many forms: viral, direct, indirect, branding, advertising, promotion, "local store," guerrilla, and "e," to name just a few. Call it what you want to, you'd better be darn good at it if you expect to be successful as a multi unit manager in today's competitive world. Today, *everything* is marketing. Advertising is marketing, training is marketing, promotion is marketing, leadership is marketing, menus are marketing, public relations is marketing, QSC is marketing, quality is marketing, service is marketing, selling is marketing and every time you hire someone you are adding to your marketing team. Through experience, high-performing MUMs learn that marketing is a philosophy, not a department, and they transfer this mindset to their GMs and junior managers daily.

Strategies versus Tactics

Strategy without tactics is the slowest route to victory. Tactics without strategy is the noise before defeat. – <u>Sun Tzu</u> (Chinese General, circa 500 BC)

A basic starting point for all *Marketing Gurus* is to define—and understand the differences between–Strategies and Tactics for increasing market share and sales in their territory and stores. Consultant Craig Miyamoto, an expert in the area of public relations, explains it well:

> There is often confusion about the difference between a "strategy" and a "tactic." Occasionally, they are used interchangeably, and of course, this is a mistake.

"Marketing is a philosophy, not a department"

STRATEGY involves the "big picture" – the overall plan, how the campaign will achieve organizational goals and objectives. It involves deciding who the customers are and which of them will be the recipients of your messages (i.e., "target audiences"). Strategic planning helps determine how the organization will be positioned; it decides how target customers will learn about your company and how it can benefit them. Each strategy must be considered on its own merits, and must be a viable option to be judged on its own strengths – one that definitely will solve the problem. All of the pros and cons of each strategy should be considered, and in the process, options are more easily identified. Any approaches that will not solve the problem independently should be eliminated. If a combination of approaches can solve the problem, consider the combination as a strategic alternative. Don't shoot from the hip: you could end up with powder burns on your butt.

TACTICS are activities specifically created and selected to reach specific and measurable objectives. Tactics are the actual ways in which the strategies are executed. They include newsletters, publicity, seminars, trade shows, promotions, advertising, Internet presence, and any other tool that target audiences actually are exposed to. Look at each tactic from the standpoint of what it will do to achieve the objectives. Tactics include:

> • *Action Events:* Non-written tactics such as special events, demonstrations, exhibits, parades, community contributions (manpower, talent, advice, money) and other non-verbal activities.

> • *Communications Tactics:* Verbal tactics (oral and written) that use words or pictures. These include newsletters, flyers, news releases, brochures, direct mail, advertising, themes, slogans, the World Wide Web, and other initiatives that use words and language as their basis.

> • In both action events and communications tactics, separate the initiatives into message tactics (which will be used to get your message directly to the audience), and media tactics (how the news media will be utilized to publicize action events).

The 7 Stages of Building High-Performing Partnerships and Teams

5 Ways to Grow Your Business--Strategies

No matter what kind of business you operate, there are five basic **strategies** for growth:

1. *Increase Volume:* acquire more customers (of the type you want to have.)
2. *Increase Frequency:* maintain the customers you have and get them to come back more often.
3. *Improve the Process.* Streamline the efficiencies and lower the cost of systems and processes to positively affect margins.
4. *Increase Sales:* increase the average value of each transaction.
5. *Increase Price.* The least practical option, and not the best strategy, but an eventuality for any business. Not a brand-killer if done judiciously and infrequently.

A *Marketing Guru* MUM will carefully assess and define ways to use the first four as often as they can and the last one as little as possible.

Tactics

MUMs and General Managers should consider these three **tactics:** Preventive Marketing, External Marketing, Internal Marketing.

- **Preventive marketing.** What you do to keep the customers you already have.

- **External marketing.** What you do to "acquire" more customers or "generate trial use." Usually involves advertising, promotion, merchandising, and/or discounting. External marketing is designed to get customers in the door.

- **Internal Marketing**. What you do to keep the new customers you get, usually measured by how well we treat our customers once they're *inside* our four walls. Internal marketing involves tactics like service, hospitality, suggestive selling, and upselling.* Sometimes referred to as "soft skills" these behaviors produce more "hard cash" than many external marketing tactics.

*Definition: in a restaurant, suggestive selling means recommending an item the customer may have overlooked ("Fries or a soda with your burger?" "Save room for dessert!"). Upselling means suggesting a bigger size or value ("Would you like to try a large Coke?")

"Marketing is a philosophy, not a department"

A new customer will visit a restaurant for the first time by either chance or by choice. Effective external marketing (advertising) may get them to choose you once. But effective internal marketing (service) gets them to return. Smart MUMs combine external marketing with internal marketing to generate trial, not errors, and transform first-timers to frequent diners. Chisel this in stone and know the difference: The *function* of any business is not to "make money," the function is to acquire and maintain customers. The *goal* is to make money. The fact is that you can fill every seat in your restaurant through an effective promotion and still lose money because no one on the team is *selling* anything!

But before we discuss best practices relative to external and internal marketing, let's start in an area that most marketing plans overlook altogether; setting explicit targets for *retaining* customers.

Preventive Marketing

Nearly everyone is familiar with the term "Preventive Maintenance," the process of routinely inspecting and improving equipment and replacing worn or torn parts before the whole machine breaks down. The rationale is simple; routine inspection, repair and maintenance means that the equipment is likely to work better and last longer, the return on investment is greater, and that operations will run more efficiently. Plus, the selling process is not being impeded due to a faulty process (like no inventory) or broken equipment (like an ice machine, slicer or mixer). Knowing that routine R&M (repair and maintenance) improves service, sales, and efficiency of equipment, why is it that very few operators apply this same mindset to other key areas of operations like marketing (or training)? They should, and they must, and here's how. Let's discuss the basics tactics of preventive marketing.

The 7 Stages of Building High-Performing Partnerships and Teams

All customers are at risk. The first step of an effective marketing plan is not to project the customer traffic you desire, but rather protect the customer traffic that you already have. How many operations have you seen over the years that put all their marketing efforts into advertising and promotion, then fail to invest similar resources and training to show their customer-facing associates how to maintain the customers they already have through better service? Job one of any effective marketing plan is to draw a line around your current customers and protect erosion or defection of this foundation due to preventable problems like sloppy fundamentals or poor service. Invest in routine and creative "mind maintenance" of your customer-facing crew via training so that they connect with customers, transforming "satisfied" patrons into loyal ones.

Be Self-Competitive. Smart restaurant operators or managers are not sitting around waiting for the competition to kick their butt; *they own their communities.* They pro-actively protect themselves from competitive intrusion by thinking like a rival would. They begin by asking themselves this question: *If I were the competition, how would I put me out of business?*

The answer to this question is to perform a thorough written S.W.O.T. analysis for each of your stores. Detail each unit's Strengths, Weaknesses, Opportunities and Threats. Every manager and multi unit manager should be involved in the process. Discuss what you need to do to shore up the weaknesses, block the threats, enhance the strengths and expand the opportunities in each store. Use the following questions to jumpstart your Preventive Marketing mindset:

- What do competitors fear about our concept, products and services?
- What do competitors (or customers) claim is our major weakness?
- How do competitors try to differentiate themselves from us?

"Marketing is a philosophy, not a department"

- What common complaints do our customers raise?
- What do our customers like best about us?
- Which customers have gotten the greatest value from us?
- What distinguishes those customers from others?
- What customers did we lose most recently? Why?
- When we criticize ourselves, what problems do we identify?
- What are we doing to improve?
- What intangibles – accuracy, service, quality, value – are our toughest sell?
- What demographic or industry trends could affect our profitability next year?
- How about two/three/five years from now? What do we need to do today and tomorrow to prepare for that?

The foundation of any successful marketing plan is training. Protect and enhance your relationships with current customers before you try to drive more traffic, because "great" marketing can kill a "bad" business. If an effective external marketing campaign successfully drives in lots of new customers, but then your team can't retain them because of your poor internal marketing skills (due to lack of training), you will lose money and market share every time. "Everybody wants to build," says author Kurt Vonnegut, "but nobody wants to do maintenance."

Stay abreast of change. Read trade publications and websites each week to stay up-to-date with industry trends, issues and solutions. Stay current on technology trends like web-enabled POS systems, payment and payroll systems, employee recruiting, energy-saving equipment, e-learning, and sale-leaseback options that add new capital for food/ re-modeling/ new-unit expansion, etcetera.

The 7 Stages of Building High-Performing Partnerships and Teams

Be the first to know. Learn about proposed or pending government decisions that may affect your store or market area. A store manager or restaurant operator should never be surprised about planned new road construction, office or housing developments, building permits for competitors, or proposed new regulations and tax hikes that will affect your trading area. You should never learn about it by reading a newspaper article. Work and expand your social network monthly and show your store managers how to do the same thing. Find out who has applied for building permits in your trade area; ask your vendors, contractors and distributor sales reps (DSRs) who they know that are opening new businesses (or competition) near yours. They know long before you do.

External Marketing

Now that we know how to protect the hard-won business we have, let's discuss ways to move from preventive marketing to External Marketing. Being pro-active about developing relationships within the community is mandatory not optional and the benefits are not just "more business" for you; every customer who spends money with you is also <u>not</u> spending money at the competition. The tactic of External Marketing is built on relationship-building.

The size of the idea matters more than the size of the budget.
– Pat Fallon

Most MUMs consider external marketing to be more visible and "sexy" than internal marketing since it involves activities like radio, print, TV or Internet advertising, billboards, promotions, direct mail, signage, e-mail campaigns, printed flyers, radio ads, coupons, fishbowls, collecting business cards, instant messaging, electronic databases, and Limited Time Offers (LTO's).

Driving more traffic to your stores via media buying and advertising is expensive and difficult to measure. This book is not about how to get the most out of mass media, but we can share a few of the best practices high-performers

"Marketing is a philosophy, not a department"

shared with us for building more business without spending a bundle. Grass roots marketing that forces managers to better connect with the community is the first step in any realistic and revenue-generating marketing plan. External marketing is not just about "advertising or promotion" it's about connecting to your community and all the groups and individuals that define it.

Checklist: Connecting to the Community

Within a 3-5 mile radius of every store or restaurant there are dozens of other businesses, hundreds of homes and thousands of potential new customers. High-performing MUMs know that a prime objective for their unit managers is to canvass and contact those local businesses and neighborhoods, building rapport with receptionists, sales people, sales managers, workers, and executives to generate more patronage. Do the businesses have employee meetings or sales meetings that present takeout or delivery opportunities? Banquets? Business dinners? When? How often? What can you do to get them to try you? Samples, deals, coupons, hospitality? You have to start with a weekly plan for making contact and then work that plan every week, with patience, persistence and without fail.

Connect with community "influentials." One American in every ten tells the other nine where to eat, what to buy and how to vote. They are called "influentials." Identify these community "influentials" with your managers and devise a plan to get them to patronize you and talk about your business to the customers and co-workers they interact with on a daily basis. Hairdressers, hotel bartenders, receptionists, concierges, religious and civic leaders are a few community influentials who come to mind. But there are many others to consider as well. Get to know the key contacts and influentials in local government, clubs, schools, and fraternal organizations, too. Become friendly and familiar with key players in the mayoral, police, fire, health, city

The 7 Stages of Building High-Performing Partnerships and Teams

council and planning or zoning departments (as well as the reporters who cover those areas for the local media). It's been said that the best-advertising in the world is a happy customer with a Big Mouth.

"We have a program called 'Crossroads' that teaches our managers how to take the initiative to build strong, mutually beneficial relationships with the 'movers and shakers' in our communities," says Mike Stout, Regional Vice President for Buffets, Inc in Minneapolis, MN. "As a result of building those relationships, the 'movers and shakers' tend to hold more events or gatherings in our restaurants as opposed to the competition. The people who attend these gatherings then go out into the community and encourage other people or organizations to eat and meet in our restaurants. Our stores become intersections of frequently traveled 'crossroads' for the people in our communities. These operations become the talk of the town."

How good are you and your team at pro-actively identifying, encouraging and engaging city, school, business, religious and civic leaders to be involved with and patronize your business? Who's who in your marketing area? Here's a checklist that both MUMs and managers alike can use to critique their marketing savvy relative to connecting to the community influentials that live or work within a 5 to 10 mile radius of your store:

Demographics
- Population (growing or declining?)
- Median Age/Family-to-singles ratio
- Average household income
- Major ethnic groups in area (growing or declining?)
- Are there any special holidays that these groups may celebrate? List the name and dates.

"Marketing is a philosophy, not a department"

Government

- Mayor or City Manager's name
- Names of your city/town/village council members
- Chief of Police
- Fire Department chief
- Names/Dates of major festivals, street fairs, fundraisers, etc.
- Who coordinates special events (parades, festivals, fairs) for the city?

Businesses and Organizations

- Name the local leaders and executive committees for five local charitable organizations and/or non-profit groups
- List the names of five local religious leaders and their congregation names
- Name of local sport complexes or health clubs in the area and their manager's name (i.e., YMCA)
- Name of area funeral homes and their owners (a lot of hungry friends and families might use your delivery or takeout services)
- Names of five best-selling realtors in your trading area
- List three hotels in your area and the name of their managers
- List five businesses with 50 employees or more that operate within 3 miles of your store
- Within 5 miles, list the malls/shopping centers/major office complexes/ hospitals/ major libraries/movie theaters /local performing arts centers
- Name five major tour group or charter travel companies/ travel agents/ florists/hair stylists/ meeting-wedding-event planners in your area
- Do you have a local small business owners group in the area? If yes, have you spoken to them about having the meetings at your restaurant? Do you attend the meetings?
- What are the 5 key charities within your community? Who are the contact people?

The 7 Stages of Building High-Performing Partnerships and Teams

- Who are the executives and key committee members of the local:
  - Tourist and convention bureau
  - Chamber of Commerce/Junior League/Women's Club/Knights of Columbus American Legion/VFW/ Elks/Kiwanis/Red Hat Society/Optimists
  - Political parties
  - Boy Scouts-Cub Scouts-Girl Scouts
  - Better Business Bureau
  - Local pro/semi-pro sports teams
- List any other groups, people, or businesses you think could positively impact your business by developing a relationship with them

Schools

- List three local high school, middle school and college coaches or athletic department heads and their team names
- Name the Principals from your local High School, Middle School, and Elementary Schools. How about their PTA committees?
- List major colleges and/or technical schools in the area
- Names of the "R.A.'s" (Residence Advisors) who are in charge of the dormitories
- List major clubs or organizations with which students are involved in these colleges, and the president/organizer's name

Seasonality

- Is your operation affected by changes in seasons? How much?
- When is your "Busy Season"? Why?
- When is your "Slow Season"? Why?
- How can we merchandise and sell more gift cards year-round?
- Detail your sales history: estimate your average monthly sales (or customer counts) for every month

"Marketing is a philosophy, not a department"

Shoe Leather Marketing:
Low-Cost/No-Cost Ways to Build Guest Traffic

The best product must be sold. People won't come to you and take it away from you. You must go to them. *–Edna Newman*

Smart operators have learned that investing time and effort into "guerilla-style" local store marketing can produce significant results with little or no cost. This hands-on marketing takes both time and focus, but it's measurable, cost-effective and puts the power back in the manager's hands via results.

Review the list below with your managers. Add to it from your own experiences. I don't suggest that you (or they) try every idea; instead think of it as a cafeteria-style approach to marketing; pick and choose what you want, leave the rest here. Call it local store marketing or guerilla marketing, but whatever you call it, it's a big payoff in exchange for putting a little wear and tear on your manager's soles...

1. **ABM (Always Be Marketing).** This is rule number one, always and all ways. Marketing is a philosophy, not a department.

2. **Use all 3 doors to build sales.** Too many foodservice operations focus their external marketing (advertising and promotion) and internal marketing (service and selling) on their two primary doors, the front door and the "side" door. The front door is your walk-in business, either sit down or take out; the side door is your drive-through. But don't forget the 3rd door—the "back door," that frequently untapped market of off-site banquets and catering business. Every week, MUMs and their managers should discuss opportunities to maximize volume and traffic via these three portals.

3. **IM and E-marketing.** Get permission from your customers to periodically send them e-mails or instant messaging (IM) text messages that feature

special offers and/or relevant information about your menu, promotions or services. This can be a great tool for reaching customers on the go about special deals, promotions, discounts, or daily features and specials.

4.   **Sell Gift Cards as school fundraisers.** Get students and faculty at local schools to promote and sell gift cards from your operation to parents, relatives, teachers and friends. Give a percentage of the sales to the school or organization.

5.   **Sell Gift Cards year round.** Most operators think of gift cards or gift certificates only at year's end. But your customers have plenty of other reasons to celebrate throughout the year with birthdays, anniversaries, promotions, sales contests, employees-of-the-month, weddings, etcetera. Don't slack off promoting and selling your gift cards and certificates in <u>every</u> other season or holiday too. Gift cards are relevant and appropriate for virtually any type of business. Consider reloadable-style gift cards to encourage re-use, and be sure to promote their sale with your servers and managers every single day. Display gift card point-of-sale near the front door, drive-through reader boards, cashiers, bathrooms, at the counter, on table tents, on any newsletters, and at the bar if you have one. Offer your gift cards to local businesses as sales incentives for their employees. Consider doing some kind of value-added promotion to kick start the gift card promotion. Maybe you can buy a $25 gift card for $20, or get a $25 card free with the purchase of a $200 card. You may even see some unexpected ROI; recent studies indicate that gift certificate redemption rates are only about 80 percent to 90 percent. If that's accurate, those unredeemed cards may pay for your printing and promotion.

> They're only puttin' in a quarter, but they want a dollar song.

6.   **Silent Auction Gift Baskets.** Choose to participate in fundraising charity events that attract the kind of customers you want more of. Participate with attractive gift baskets that feature your menu, a gift card and any appropriate signature-item retail merchandise you sell.

"Marketing is a philosophy, not a department"

7.   **Parade of Homes.** Have your gift baskets or menus featured on the kitchen counters of the Parade of Homes in your area.

8.   **Train your team how to read the newspaper.** Many of your managers and crew miss opportunities to build incremental traffic in your restaurants every day when reading the newspaper. Teach them how to read beyond the headlines to see the potential business opportunities that lie underneath. At your next meeting hand out a copy of the local paper to each manager. Ask them to review it for ten minutes and highlight anything that might generate more business. News of engagements, weddings, parties, local heroes, business awards, birth announcements, honor rolls, scout awards, meetings, arts groups, groundbreakings, business profiles, anniversaries, company expansions, etcetera can fuel ideas for business-building opportunities they may have routinely overlooked when perusing the daily news. See who can find the most leads. The idea is to train your managers to read the daily paper with a "marketing eye" everyday. Now ask them to teach their hourly team to do the same.

9.   **Follow the driver.** An enterprising pizza concept MUM we know spent her night off following the delivery vehicles of her nearest competitor, jotting down addresses that she then sent coupons and letters to in an effort to convert the business.

10. **Banquet Halls.** Visit your local banquet halls, even if they already have a kitchen, and introduce yourself and your company. Talk about what you do, and how you can help them provide what they may not be able to offer their customers (like use of your extra dining room or meeting room on nights they get double-booked).

11. **Bus Tours.** Can your company build additional business by marketing your store or restaurant to bus companies that operate charter trips and tours for schools, athletic departments, organizations or seniors? If so, then

The 7 Stages of Building High-Performing Partnerships and Teams

contact your local athletic department head, school bus operators or Google "bus tours" or "coach tours" and contact the companies that organize specialized group excursions in your area. Find out the specific criteria for being able to handle these large groups (volume, timing, and special needs are just part of the considerations; it's not a simple task) and then decide if your restaurants can handle it.

12. **Get help in the mail.** In this cluttered world we live in, it helps to know what kind of point-of-sale materials will catch the eye and which ones won't. If you or your company use direct mail to attract new business, consider using the Postal Service as your primary research tool to analyze what works. For the next six weeks, save every piece of promotional and advertising material you receive in the mail. Then make two stacks—one for material that appeals to you visually, and one for pieces that don't. Note what specifically caught your eye in the mail; then evaluate the ones you didn't choose, and ask yourself what they lacked. Keep those visual and copy elements in mind when you sit down to design your next menu and marketing, catering, or large group brochure.

13. **Post Cards for direct mail.** If you choose to use direct mail, I recommend postcards over letters for three reasons: 1) they're more cost-effective, 2) they're already opened, and 3) the postal sorter and carrier may read and be influenced by them too! But make them both eye-catching and thoroughly proof-read before you mail.

14. **Car Dealerships.** Every weekend automobile salespeople face their busiest days and never leave the lot or showroom. They get hungry. Do you deliver? Could they pick up food to go from you? Then what are you waiting for?

15. **Build a Playground.** A great way to build business is by building social capital (goodwill) in your community and pride among your team members. Find a needy older school or park playground and invest money for equipment

"Marketing is a philosophy, not a department"

and sweat equity from staff volunteers to make the play area new again. "Adopt" the school to help with projects or needs. Promote the event with a photo collage in your restaurant, and a call to the local TV, radio and newspaper reporters and photographers. No greatness without goodness.

16. **Funeral Homes.** Get to know your local funeral directors. When unfortunate circumstances cause families to suddenly gather from far away, they're often unprepared meal-wise for all the people. Offer your operation as an alternative to cooking for the houseful of grieving friends and family who've gathered.

17. **Invisible Customers.** Every week scores of vendors glide through your operation and you see them so often that you may have stopped seeing them at all. FedEx drivers, vendor and distributor salespeople and delivery people, postal employees, repair and maintenance people, for instance. Here's a question: do they ever get hungry or thirsty? Do they have friends, families, meetings, banquets, get-togethers? Here's another question: wouldn't your restaurant be ideal to host those occasions?

18. **Kids.** Families dine out earlier, bringing revenue to traditionally slower meal periods. Families are decision-driven and you influence their decision-making when you impress their kids. Kids may not always choose the restaurant the family's going to, but one thing's for sure: they always have the veto vote of where they're not going.

19. **Pharmaceutical reps.** Five days a week these salespeople bring lunch to doctor's offices while they pitch new drugs, supplies or services. Bring key doctor office employees lunch (like physician assistants or receptionists-- they're the real decision-makers), or at least bring samples of your food and beverage and menus and ask them to suggest and request your food and beverage from their pharmaceutical salespeople.

The 7 Stages of Building High-Performing Partnerships and Teams

20.   **Yellow Pages.** Take out your local Yellow Pages phone book and open it to any section at random. Let's say it's "Veterinarians." Now brainstorm with your managers all of the related occupations, clubs, organizations or businesses in your local marketplace that relate to this profession. A partial list might include:

Dog Breeders • Pet groomers • Riding clubs • Pet trainers • Kennels • Dog/Horse tracks • ASPCA • Pet stores Dog/Cat/Horse clubs/Dude ranches

That's at least ten areas of customer opportunity to which you can now market breakfast, lunch, dinner, drinks, banquets or catering to. Ask your assembled employee task force the following questions: Do the local dog clubs, riding clubs, or groomers go out to eat and drink individually and as a group? Do they have meetings? Awards banquets? Who's the contact person? When are the meetings? The next step is to assign two employees as team leaders to contact the decision-makers in each group and solicit their business for your restaurant. Send a letter of invitation filled with free appetizer coupons (good only on one of your slower nights so you can pay special attention to the group), or better still, invite these groups into your restaurants between 5 pm and 7 pm on a slower night for an after-work Happy Hour. Set up a free appetizer buffet exclusively for them with their group's name on it in an area near the bar. You provide finger food, they pay for their own beverages, and you get a lot of new business out of it. The key is to have the managers and staff really work the party hard with exceptional hospitality, friendliness and good cheer to earn the repeat business of these "new" people you've worked so hard to bring in for the first time.

21.   **Tap your team to market to their acquaintances.** Studies show that the average 21 year old in North America knows nearly 250 people either directly or indirectly. What if we could inspire or motivate each of our employees and managers to bring in just three of their 250 acquaintances as new customers each month? If you employ 30 people, that's another 90 new customers monthly. If your average transaction is $10 per person, and customers tend to

"Marketing is a philosophy, not a department"

patronize you, say, 10 times a year, that's another $9,000 in higher annual gross sales from a referral of just three people from each employee. What if you have 100 employees, and they each bring in three new customers? That's $30,000 in new annual revenue. And if each of these new customers just told one of their friends...well, I think you get my drift. Ask your team members who they know that's celebrating a birthday, anniversary or special occasion. Get them to recommend your restaurant for any celebratory occasion. Don't presume they naturally think of you when a special occasion occurs in their circle of family or friends. Think of this as creating your own personal marketing task force.

22.   **Create an in-house event for the Chamber of Commerce.** Talk about "influentials"! Think of all the diverse people and professions who are members of your local Chamber of Commerce: concierges, florists, meeting planners, realtors, elected officials, architects, small and large business owners. They probably all have meetings, business meals, banquets and parties throughout the year. And maybe your place is the best place of all to host their functions. Like we suggested above for pet fanciers and the Yellow Pages, throw a party for C of C members at your restaurant with free appetizers and soft drinks, giving them a flavor and flair for your hospitality, food, beverages, and community commitment. Be sure that you and all your managers are there to work the crowd.

23.   **"Try-vertising"**. Let guests (and servers in pre-shift meetings) sample bite-sized portions of new appetizers, entrees, desserts, or beverages. Be sure your managers enthusiastically describe the items to your servers in detail and that servers practice the descriptions with each other first in the pre-shift meeting so that they don't practice on the customer.

24.   **Watch for good ideas elsewhere.** Encourage your crew to notice good marketing ideas at the other restaurants, bars, nightclubs, or stores that they frequent and ask them to *share those ideas* with your managers. Preach what you practice and practice what you preach.

The 7 Stages of Building High-Performing Partnerships and Teams

25. **Chalk the walk.** Many restaurants will take color chalk and inscribe a fun message on their sidewalk to their guests in general or to a particular customer who may be coming in to celebrate a special occasion in the restaurant during the lunch or dinner period. It's an inexpensive way to add flair and fun to any occasion.

26. **Bridal Shows.** Participate in these semi-annual events and promote your restaurant as the ideal catering or dinner host for the bridal party and their friends and relatives.

27. **Shop the competition.** Have you shopped or eaten at one of your competitors in the last 30 days? Have you made notes of the experience? What are they doing to keep customers coming back? Can we use their tactics?

28. **Focus and energy.** For your managers and servers it may be just another meal but for every customer it's always a special occasion. Don't overlook how important energy and spirit is for both the internal and external customer's experience. Keep it fresh, keep it focused and keep it fun for your customers and give them a "new" and fresh experience every time they visit.

29. **Consistency in operations.** Make certain that your internal marketing efforts (great service, quality food, and cleanliness) get as much attention and focus as your external marketing efforts. The number one way to drive more business is to take care of the customers you have and encourage them to tell their friends and family about your operation. The best way to do that is via habitual consistency in your external marketing and internal marketing efforts. As retailer John Wanamaker once said: "make sure that the story isn't better than the store!"

30. **Training is marketing.** The more you invest in training, the less you spend on advertising. The more you invest in training, the better service your team gives the customer (and one another) and the more the customer returns.

"Marketing is a philosophy, not a department"

Remember our ultimate goal is not necessarily that the customer buys more but that they buy more often!

31.   **Hire right.** Every time you hire someone, you're adding to your marketing team.

32.   **Retention is marketing.** The best way to keep good people is to give them a good reason to come to work. When you have low turnover and "A" players in place having fun daily, it inspires better customer service and more customer traffic. Customers are attracted to energy like moths to a flame.

33.   **Service is marketing.** Happy customers buy more.

34.   **Moving is marketing.** Befriend realtors and moving company drivers and supervisors. They know when potential new customers are moving into your market before anyone else does.

35.   **Cleanliness is marketing.** Servers and managers must be taught to be adept at pre-busing and keeping facilities spotless. You sell more in a clean restaurant. On smaller scale, the cleaner the counter-top or table-top, the more you will sell. In QSR restaurants, the cleanliness of the kitchen floor is a critical factor for customers at the counter.

36.   **Teamwork is marketing.** The better your team is at working in sync together, the less time you and your managers spend managing crew relationships and the more time they (and you) have to improve customer relationships.

The fundamental skills of guerilla-style marketing aren't hard to understand, but they are harder to do. Every successful "shoe leather" marketing plan has more moves than U-Haul, because every market is different and different strokes attract different folks. All of your potential customers are not standing in one spot waiting for you to invite them in. There are dozens and dozens more ways to build traffic without mass media advertising, so which one works? Like a diet, *the one you stick to*. Marketing success results more from persistence than creativity alone.

The goal of external marketing is acquiring new customers. And if you're going to spend all that time and effort acquiring new customers though external marketing, you'd best spend an equal amount of time and effort *keeping them* through internal marketing.

Internal Marketing

Internal Marketing is based on the twin towers of better service and higher sales.

Wise MUMs (and managers) know that an expensive advertising campaign or promotion can fill your restaurant with customers and you can still lose money because of poor training, poor service, no focus, and no menu merchandising. In other words, you can spend a lot of money attaining new customers through external marketing (advertising) and then fail to capitalize on it by not retaining these new customers via internal marketing (service and selling). A *Marketing Guru* is always looking for opportunities to not just generate more volume but to also transform that new volume into more revenue. What good is a marketing campaign that generates new traffic you can't convert into repeat business?

The Brand is Crew and the Brand is You

Our company has the privilege of working with some great brands, including *Applebee's, Wendy's, Hershey's, Marriott, Anheuser-Busch, the Cheesecake Factory, Coca-Cola, Walt Disney Company, Panera Bread, Pizza Hut, Sam's Club, Target Stores, Rich's, Sodexho, McDonald's,* and *American Express*. We've helped them design and execute a variety of operational programs, including brand line extensions, sales & marketing plans, customer service programs, leadership courses, and Nintendo-Generation training materials for their teams. I'm also privileged to address their managers and MUMs via live seminars at

"Marketing is a philosophy, not a department"

their conferences. One thing I've learned by working with these great companies is what advertising portrays is not as important as what the customer experiences when they interact with the company's people, products and processes. From assistant cashier to Area Director, repeat business is earned by how well the customer connects emotionally with your people and therefore your brand. Your brand is defined by the collective behavior of everyone whose actions affect the guest's experience, from the dishwasher to the board member. Since the store is where your company meets your customers, the interaction with the greeter, sales associate or drive-through cashier is more important to customer loyalty than the 30 second TV spot. That's why we say that every time you hire someone you're adding to your marketing team.

Since "service" continues to grow as a brand value and brand differentiator, we can't forget that service is a by-product of people, not ads. As mentioned earlier, the word "quality" is so over-used that it has now become a commodity-like term in the customer's mind. So if quality has become a commodity, where does the battleground now shift? To our people. Greeters, servers, cashiers, drive-through order-takers, assistant managers, kitchen crew and even delivery people can exert as much, if not more, influence on repeat business than the MUM, restaurant owner, VP of Operations or even Director of Marketing. So we dang well better be selecting the right people and then training them better than the competition. "You must realize that any contact today defines a brand," says advertising executive Douglas Atkin. "A brand isn't just what the customer experiences, it's everything that a company's vendors, employees and board members touch. Companies need to rethink who defines their brand." The emotional feeling the ad creates and the in-store experience should be seamless. The notion that marketing, training and operations are managed as different departments makes as much sense as throwing eggs, butter, flour, baking soda and milk on a table and calling it

The 7 Stages of Building High-Performing Partnerships and Teams

"cake." The brand experience is not segmented in the eyes of your customers, so why should the management of that experience be?

Internal marketing is built on better service and suggestive selling

The two key *tactics* of Internal Marketing are service and selling.

What if we invested in crew training that resulted in measurably better service (generating positive word-of-mouth) and we were able to bring in a mere 25 more customers per week? And what if that same training resulted in our cashiers, associates, servers or bartenders now being able to "upsell" more food, beverage or merchandise to our customers, raising the "guest check average" (GCA) a mere 50 cents per person? Presuming that you currently serve 100,000 customers per year and your current check average is $10, the ROI on the training would look something like this:

If We Increase Traffic 100 Customers per Month and Boosted Sales 50¢ per Person...

Annual Customers	Check Average	Annual Gross Sales
100,000	$10	$1,000,000
101,200 Gain 25 Customers per Week	$10	$1,012,000 (+ $12,000) ← Nice Bonus!
101,200	$10.50 (50¢ PPA Bump)	$1,062,600 (+$62,600) ❋ per UNIT!

Nice payback from service and sales training, wouldn't you say? But just as there's clear opportunity investing in frontline staff training, there's also a cost associated with <u>not</u> investing in training. Let's look at the same scenario, but this time let's

"Marketing is a philosophy, not a department"

presume that service has slipped and sales have slumped. Look at how quickly your P&L moves from champ to chump status if your customer count slips by 25 patrons per week and your average check drops fifty cents per person...

What if Poor Service Causes us to Lose Both 100 Customers per month and 50¢ per Person?

Annual Customers	Check Average	Annual Gross Sales
100,000	$10	$1,000,000
98,800 Lose 25 Customers per Week	$10	$988,000 (- $12,000)
98,800	$9.50 (50¢ PPA Loss)	$938,600 (-$61,400) ◀— That was quick!

Tips for Better Service and Higher Sales

These two graphs can offer either hope or despair depending on your team's ability to perform and your manager's skill at training. How swiftly we can rise or fall depending on whether we choose to sharpen the focus or take our eyes off the ball. Here are a few things to consider regarding the issues of service-giving and sales-building that can help you build traffic and revenue at the same time:

Rethink what service means today. Repetition is the mother of all learning, so allow me to repeat what I suggested earlier: *Eliminate "Dissatisfaction" First*. Anticipate their needs and eliminate the things that dissatisfy them. Every 12 months re-identify and re-define the Top 10 Expectations and the Top 10 Complaints of your customers. Now 1) exceed their expectations and 2) stop doing whatever you were doing that made them complain.

The 7 Stages of Building High-Performing Partnerships and Teams

Know the difference between service and hospitality. Service fulfills a need. Hospitality fulfills people. You can get "service" from an ATM. Not so with hospitality. Service fulfills expectations, hospitality exceeds them.

Manage the architecture of the Shift. How well do your managers understand the duties associated with opening, running and closing a profitable Shift?

- Do they conduct daily ready-for-revenue walkabouts both outside and inside the building before every shift?
- Do they do 100% table visits with customers? Do they know how? Do they know why?
- Do they know the names of the most frequent customers?
- How good are they at preparing and executing pre-shift meetings with their teams? Your pre-shift meeting or "Jumpstart" is the key to setting up and delivering high-level internal marketing every shift. View clips of our pre-shift meeting DVD *Jumpstart: How to Plan and Execute Effective Pre-Shift Meetings* at Sullivision.com.

Connect with your internal customers first. How well do your managers connect with their internal customers (team members) daily? It's wise to remember that the way we treat our associates will determine how they'll treat our customers.

Think big act small. Bring focus to your Service Strategy with this question: *"What do we want to be famous for with customers?"* Define all the little things that add up to famous-ness.

Manage Your "Moments-of-Truth"

The ultimate key to effective Internal Marketing is teaching your team to re-discover and manage each interaction through the eyes of your customers.

"Marketing is a philosophy, not a department"

Jan Carlzon wrote a groundbreaking book years ago called *Moments of Truth*. He defined a moment of truth as anytime that a customer comes in contact with a company's brand, people, or services and forms an impression of the quality of service they provide. List the chronological steps that customers go through when they visit and who they interact with during those steps. Examples of moments-of-truth in a restaurant might include:

1. Initial Contact: telephone, curb appeal, parking lot, signage, advertising.
2. Entrance: landscape, front door or drive-through.
3. Greeting: at host stand or counter or reader board speaker.
4. Ambience: cleanliness, neatness, freshness.
5. Ordering: at table, counter, drive-through, phone or bar. Crew should be helpful and suggesting add-ons, large sizes, combos, etc.
6. Food and beverage quality: hot food hot and cold food cold, and drive-through or delivery speed, accuracy, quality.
7. Follow-through: management presence, table visits, follow-up phone call if delivery or takeout.
8. Restrooms: clean, well-stocked, appropriate music levels, pleasant smell.
9. Repeat Business: farewell, website, customer 1-800 service line, etc.

Your moments-of-truth may be strikingly similar or radically different from the nine above depending on the type of operation you have (for instance a bar would be a separate moment-of-truth.) Whatever they are in your operations, determine which employees and what processes are involved in each moment-of-truth and define how to make the outcome a positive experience for every customer. Internal marketing is always focused on service and selling and they are not static concepts. If you or your managers think "service is service", think again: the meaning of customer service is always changing because the customer is always changing.

The 7 Stages of Building High-Performing Partnerships and Teams

The customer is why

Everything that you will ever have is currently in the hands of someone else: the customer. That's why internal marketing is so important. And you can etch this in stone: *If you're not serving the customer directly, you'd better be serving someone who is!* This book is not the place to discuss all the nuances of great service-giving and the art of suggestive selling because of space limitations, but if you'd like to learn detailed strategies and tactics surrounding successful service execution and teaching Generation Next how to sell, check out our website at Sullivision.com.

Summary

Remember, the function of every business is to acquire and maintain customers. We've outlined five strategies for growth and three basic tactics for attaining and retaining those customers and get them to come back more often and spend more each time they do. In the big scheme of things, you might think of Internal Marketing as the engine, External Marketing as the steering wheel, and Preventive Marketing as the period oil change. The end-game of the effective *Marketing Guru* is customer loyalty, not merely customer "satisfaction." A "satisfied" customer is simply "satisfied," a state of being that makes them targets for the competition as well. Focus on building loyal customers—"raving Fans"–not satisfied ones. As writer Jeffrey Gitomer says: "Satisfaction is useless, loyalty is priceless."

"Marketing is a philosophy, not a department"

Self-asessment: **Marketing Guru™**

Review the list of core Marketing Guru competencies below. Assess your personal strengths and challenges relative to each competency in one of the boxes to the right. Review the boxes again in six months.

Competency	Good At	Average	Needs Work
I've an ABM (Always Be Marketing) mindset			
I'm equally adept at external and internal marketing			
I'm a Customer advocate/customer lens			
I'm a Connector: know how and know who			
I view marketing as a philosophy not a "department"			
I help my team connect with the community outside and inside the store			
I do a SWOT analysis for every restaurant			
I know the differences in each market			

STAGE SIX
Synergist™

Cautionary Tale

"The first visit I ever had from my boss after I took over my restaurants as an Area Director was on Friday at noon when we were getting slammed big time at one of the busier units. I was helping out in the kitchen because of the rush. He came up to me on the line while I was expediting and said: 'I came here today to chew gum and kick ass. And unfortunately for you my friend, I'm all out of gum'. Nice timing, memorable opening line, and loud enough so that the manager, servers and cooks all heard him. I had read the One-Minute Manager but this guy was a Full-Time Jerk. I quit 3 months into it. So did two other area directors. Now I'm with a company that values servant leadership and the ability to synergize and then execute a variety of leadership skills depending on the situation. And they teach us how to get better in seminars every six months instead of leaving their MUMs to figure it out on their own. And there's no more important place to synergize learning and leadership than during the store visit."

"Running an organization is easy when you don't know how, but very difficult when you do."

The characteristics of a Synergist include:

- Weaves together all 7 competency rungs of the Leadership Ladder
- Can design and execute effective Annual or Quarterly Business Plans
- Can design and execute results-driven Store Visits
- Connects the dots between the Quarterly Business Plan, Period Goals and Shift Execution
- Strategic Thinker
- Matches strategy to situation

Goal-Getter™
Synergist™
Marketing Guru™
Head Coach™
Servant Leader
Talent Scout™
Brand Ambassador™

Synergy is defined as "the working together of two or more things, people, or organizations, especially when the result is greater than the sum of their individual efforts or capabilities." A slightly stuffy definition to say the least, so let's consider a different interpretation: a **Synergist** recognizes that the whole is greater than the sum of the parts. *Synergists* increase the effectiveness of their managers as they interact, coach, and share knowledge daily. They weave together diverse strategies, tactics, timing, talent, financial responsibility, forecasting, technology, business planning, resource allocation, reality and intuition to help their teams achieve company, franchise and personal goals. *Synergists* are Performance Environmentalists who assess and consider how the team's internal and external resources will affect short-term success and long-term growth and profitability. They "think globally, act locally" and know that well-done is better than well-said. The *Synergist* unifies, aligns, integrates,

The 7 Stages of Building High-Performing Partnerships and Teams

maintains, improves and appreciates the complex systems, processes, talents and goals of the company, crew and customers they serve. This most-critical rung of the Leadership Ladder is the make-or-break competency to master for new multi unit managers.

Here's what high-performing MUMs should be *synergizing*:

- The Company to the Customer.
- Employees to training.
- Training to performance.
- Diversity in skills and opinion to unity of purpose.
- Specialized knowledge to shared integration.
- Tools and resources to execution.
- All five previous competencies (Brand Ambassador, Talent Scout, Servant Leader, Head Coach, Marketing Guru) into a leadership mindset and demeanor.
- Goals to strategy.
- Strategy to *execution*.

The Art of Strategic Thinking

Strategic thinking is a challenging skill and mindset for the new MUM who—as a successful GM—was encouraged to think tactically (how to do it) more often than strategically (why it's important and what needs to be done.)

Consider all of the data and information an effective MUM must assimilate, assess and act on everyday in order to successfully compete. The list includes—but is not limited to—customer and market knowledge, financial reports, resource allocation, aligning company or franchisee goals with brand standards, staffing, customer complaints, applying team

*"Running an organization is easy when you don't know how,
but very difficult when you do."*

strengths and processes to goals, developing managers across varying degrees of expertise and understanding, and the wild-card variables of daily operations that range from climate to crime. Can "strategic thinking" realistically be taught in the midst of this daily tsunami of data, development and decision-making? A key place to start seeking the answer is by understanding the strategic thought process that differentiates "managers" from leaders.

The Strategic Mindset In Leadership by Charles Albano

- The leader scopes outwards to capture the larger context, to see how the pieces fit together.

- Is adaptive to realities and flexible in choice of tactics. Recognizes that once action begins the "game board" is fluid, offering both new threats and new opportunities.

- Where possible, tries to achieve multiple objectives through singular actions. Has the discipline to remain composed when the unexpected occurs.

- Stays future-focused. Acts decisively when the time to act has come. Is able to scrap or alter plans when information indicates actions are not attaining their intended results.

- Learns opponent's strengths and weaknesses.

- Assures that everyone knows their roles and are equipped with the resources to contribute.

- Uses "what if" speculation to stretch thinking in the direction of opportunities and possibilities.

- Studies the logic of the opponent's tactics with an eye toward determining what their ultimate end purposes may be.

- Has a clear sense of desired outcomes before acting. Develops a plan capable of delivering outcomes that will add significant value to a state of affairs.

The 7 Stages of Building High-Performing Partnerships and Teams

- Anticipates opponent's actions and mentally rehearses next responses should those contingencies arise.
- Has the discipline to remain composed when the unexpected occurs.

As you peruse the list above, consider your current thought process and how it might need to evolve.

How to Synergize Strategy with Execution

Strategic thinking is all about outcome-based visualization, but it needs to be coupled with action to have relevance. My experience and our research confirms that the best way to begin thinking strategically is to first picture the desired result, or "begin with the end in mind." Here are three questions to ask yourself (and then answer in detail):

- What is the <u>best thing</u> that can happen to my stores in the next 12 months?
- What is the <u>worst thing</u> that can happen to my stores in the next 12 months?
- What kind of development and coaching is necessary, today, tomorrow, and the days after that to make certain that the best things happen and the worst things don't?

It's all about anticipating ways to create more value for anyone and everyone involved with the brand. The strategic-thinking *Synergist* recognizes that stellar store performance is the result of stellar store development and leadership. They know that the store is the most important playing field in the company's universe *because the store is where the company meets the customer.* Corporate support is important, but "corporate support" can't keep hot food hot, cold food cold, hire the right people, develop store managers or build relationships with customers and the community. Weaving together **tools and talent** to execute success at the store level is both the starting and end point of any successful MUM strategy. MUMs know they are rewarded not for what they do but for what their people do.

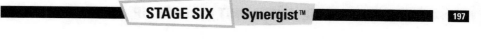

*"Running an organization is easy when you don't know how,
but very difficult when you do."*

Synergizing your role to your goal begins by assessing the tools and resources you need on your journey to greatness. The list would include:

1. Applying the competencies of the 7 stages of the Leadership Ladder
2. The Quarterly Business Plan or QBP (the resource that connects annual goals to period execution and period goals to Shift Execution)
3. Manager Meetings
4. Linking quarterly goals to period goals
5. Assigning period goals to shift execution (which includes leading effective Power Shifts and Pre-Shift meetings).
6. Revenue-generating Store Visits

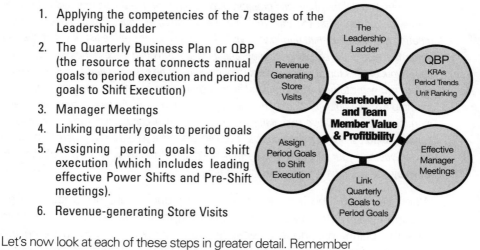

Let's now look at each of these steps in greater detail. Remember that managing the process is all about Alignment, Integration, Linkage, Resource Management and Consistency. It all starts with the written QBP (Quarterly Business Plan).

QBP: The 90 Day Plan

"Prescription before diagnosis is malpractice."

If you knew a month ago that you had to fly to Cincinnati today for an 8 a.m. meeting what would you do? Would you just wake up whenever and head out to the airport to buy a ticket and catch a flight? Of course not. You'd never make it to Cincinnati. Instead, you'd catch the flight by managing your time and activities backwards to achieve the desired outcome. Here's what you'd do:

The 7 Stages of Building High-Performing Partnerships and Teams

You'd have bought tickets at least two weeks or more ago because the fare's cheaper. Then you'd book a hotel room. You'd set up your meetings, appointments, and dinners in Cincinnati. You'd think about and probably make a list of all the things that had to be done before, during and after the trip. You'd have a list of what needed to be covered in the meeting and accomplished during your visit. Then you'd prioritize the list. If you're leaving tomorrow, you'd be choosing clothes and packing traveling accessories and relevant paperwork or files tonight. You'd work through your phone calls and voice mail and e-mail before you went to bed. You'd remember to recharge the cell phone and set an alarm or arrange a wake-up call. You'd thoroughly consider all the factors surrounding early morning variables relative to making your flight: weather conditions, traffic flow, airport parking, airport security, airport delays. If you need a ride it would be arranged, if you were driving yourself your gas tank will be full. You'd know exactly what time you'd have to leave by and you'll be up and gone by that time.

When you think about it, that's quite a thorough planning process to go through for something as routine as getting to the airport on time. Yet we take the planning seriously because we're working against a perceived absolute; a fixed deadline set by the airline that you can't alter. The flight is scheduled to take off at 8 am (well, in theory anyway) and it leaves with you or without you. So we think through and then manage a complex backward timetable to make sure we get there before our flight leaves without us. Give yourself credit, you did all that without hardly thinking.

So the big question is: do you invest at least as much time, effort, and planning to develop your team and improve your stores each week as you would to simply catch a flight? If not, why not, and what could your operations look like if you did?

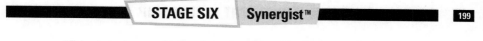

*"Running an organization is easy when you don't know how,
but very difficult when you do."*

QBP Me ASAP

Plan your work and then work the plan. You need a detailed and comprehensive written plan every 90 days and the plan needs to be communicated and the plan needs to be executed. Quarterly improvement tied to period (and shift) execution in your restaurants does not occur merely because you "hope" it will. *Hope is not a strategy.*

A QBP (quarterly business plan), as the name implies, is written in advance of every 90 day period. Its purpose is to detail, align and prioritize key company financial and operational goals with execution strategies for the market, for the managers, and for each store or unit in your territory. I'm sure you've heard the phrase "if you don't know where you're going, any path will get you there." Everything you do both strategically and tactically as a MUM starts with the QBP. A written quarterly business plan is the Road Map that shape priorities, defines progress, and stimulates growth.

No one single document or resource can help you more than the QBP. The best possible use of a MUMs time is not "full-speed ahead in all directions." They must pause, assess, analyze relevant data, review the near-term and long-term targets, and then prioritize the activities, people, systems, guidance, and coaching tasks necessary to meet or exceed those goals. This is strategic thinking tied to tactical execution, a target goal for any high-performing MUM.

Every successful MUM we interviewed used some type of written quarterly plan for their area. There are many different names we've heard applied to the document including: quarterly plan, QAR, (quarterly assessment review), Q-View, 90 day roundup, Balanced Scorecard, etc, but Quarterly Business Plan or QBP is the most common term we heard in our research across companies so it's the one we'll use.

The 7 Stages of Building High-Performing Partnerships and Teams

What's in it for me?

A well-planned and well-executed QBP benefits MUMs in many ways. Here's a brief list of what a QBP will do for you:

1. A QBP paints a broad picture of the state of the territory and helps set and prioritize goals that balance people, quality and profits.

2. Details gaps between "performance should be" and "performance is" in each restaurant.

3. Insures effective schedule-making that allows the people you report to (and the people who report to you) to use their time more effectively.

4. Helps you understand what your top performing and bottom performing restaurants have in common.

5. Lets you better manage competing priorities.

6. Allows for better ROI and more strategic scheduling of time, money and resources.

7. Aligns annual goals to quarterly execution.

8. Aligns quarterly goals to period execution.

9. Keeps important goals in focus.

10. Sets priorities relative to coaching and development needs.

11. Helps you prioritize the specific shifts that need attention.

12. Identifies restaurants requiring more visit time.

13. Helps identify high-potential GMs, a key component of career-pathing and bench-strength in the organization.

14. Creates more value for your managers by knowing specifically what you're focusing on each quarter.

15. Highlights and helps evaluate all areas of the business.

16. Gives insight to continuity (or lack of it) across your market.

17. Translates data into coaching opportunities.

"Running an organization is easy when you don't know how, but very difficult when you do."

18. Helps insure you'll do the right things and do the right things right.
19. Allows you to work smarter not harder and clearly aim at financial targets.
20. Helps you plan and develop an effective daily, weekly, monthly calendar.
21. Creates more value for your company, your people, and yourself.

A thorough and comprehensive QBP not only allows you to build a rational and realistic calendar for the next 90 days, it creates a template where you can analyze performance and allot resources (time and money) to prioritize and resolve new or recurring challenges. A written 90 day plan minimizes the danger of overlooking important tasks and aligns and integrates company goals to quarterly, period and shift execution. A QBP gives you the precious gift of time by pairing up projects and processes to priorities, so that you can work smarter not harder. The fact is that compiling and executing effective Quarterly Business Plans allows smart MUMs to get twice as much done, often in the time that other MUMs waste while trying to decide what to do.

Measure what matters: KRAs

You get what you inspect not what you expect, so naturally every organization measures its MUM's performance against targeted goals related to growth, profitability and leadership. Most companies refer to these as either "KRAs" (key result areas), "KPIs" (key performance indicators), "SBIs" (strategic business initiatives) or the "Balanced Score Card." We'll use KRAs in this text. An effective quarterly business plan focuses on how to attain key result areas (and how they will be measured) in each store over the next 90 days. Examples of Key Result Areas that should be accounted for on the QBP would include:

> **If you don't measure it, you can't manage it.**
>
> –Brett Gosse

- Food safety and cleanliness.
- Product quality.

The 7 Stages of Building High-Performing Partnerships and Teams

- Staffing levels, development, diversity.
- Customer service scores.
- Marketing and events/activities that drive business.
- Customer traffic (actual versus projected).
- Comp (Same) Store Sales and crew salesmanship.
- Profitability.
- R&M (facility or equipment repair and maintenance).
- Systems and processes: dining room, drive-through, takeout/carside/to-go.
- Training and development needs for managers and crew.
- Company turnover and tenure goals versus territory goals and results, both in the hourly and management team.

Components of the QBP

The purpose of an effective QBP is not to create a 90 day "Super Calendar on Steroids"; the purpose is to create a living road map that serves as a daily compass and guide that links quarterly goals to daily execution, aligns activity to results, transforms theory into reality, and helps your territory transform from "potential" to profitability.

Every company plans differently for each quarter, so whichever performance or result areas your company deems most important to evaluate, account for them in your QBP. We've learned that effective QBPs should include the following line items, each of which we'll discuss in more detail over the following pages.*

- *Previous Quarter Summary (including Key Result Areas and Period Trends)*
- *Next quarter's KRA goals*
- *People: tenure, turnover, development and training*
- *Marketing: Activities, Events, LTOs*

*To get a sample QBP planning form, visit us at **www.sullivision.com**

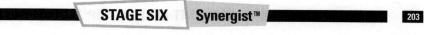
*"Running an organization is easy when you don't know how,
but very difficult when you do."*

- *Facilities/Operations*
- *Profitability and Productivity*
- *Store Visits*

Now let's look more closely at each of these areas...

Previous Quarter Summary: what to include

- Analyze the previous 13 periods and project relevant trends.
- Assess the KRA (key result area) targets you need to focus on, especially in the financial areas.
- What were the sales and margin trends for the quarter in your area?
- What were the underlying internal and external causes of those trends? Be specific, store-by-store.
- Detail the best practices and key learnings from the last quarter and share with GMs and junior managers.
- Detail what was accomplished, what's in progress, what hasn't been started but still needs to be done.

Next Quarter's Key Result Areas

- Briefly summarize the KRAs you will focus on like food safety, quality, staffing levels, sales, service, retention, marketing, profitability, teamwork, training, turnover, cleanliness, R&M, etc. Assess and prioritize them based on last quarter's results and each manager's current goals and input.
- Review the results of your S.W.O.T. analysis.
- Get input from General Managers on all KRAs and what they need to do to achieve them. Their input and pre-buy-in is key to team success. Show them which reports to use to assess their strengths and areas for improvement. What are their Top 3 operational challenges? What changes may occur in the marketplace over the next 90 days that could affect operations (e.g. construction)?

The 7 Stages of Building High-Performing Partnerships and Teams

People: Training and Development

- ***Leadership:*** For each store manager, discuss the specific actions that each Manager will take to achieve the targeted business results in each unit.

- ***Crew staffing and training:*** Define the steps or tactics that managers need to accomplish to insure prime staffing levels, minimized turnover, and team growth. This includes development plans, training needs, turnover issues, staffing levels/needs, retention targets (company versus area progress), succession planning for all key hourly employees, and labor pool trends in the marketplace. Are we approaching a busy or slow season relative to hiring? What impact will that have on manager's time and priorities?

- ***Manager development:*** Review and detail each store's manager development needs, resources, and bench strength/succession plans. Do you anticipate manager status changes in any store? Who is being groomed from hourly rank to manager status? What kind of timetable do you anticipate? How will that affect staffing, hiring, training, leadership? Who is promotable? Who could you lose? Why?

- ***Training and knowledge capital:*** What are the learning gaps among managers and crew? What barriers to learning are in place? What training is scheduled with whom? How will we measure its effectiveness? How well are your managers executing pre-shift meetings? How well do they understand the Architecture of the Shift? Are they talking each team member into position, through the position and out of the position every shift? What LTOs are rolling out this quarter and what kind of training is necessary to support them? How—specifically--will we improve sales and service via crew training this quarter?

- ***Recognition:*** Who among crew and managers is being honored this quarter for performance and achievement? Who is celebrating a hiring anniversary? Which GMs family or spouse should be sent an email, letter or small gift to thank them for their support after a particularly busy/successful period?

Bottom Line: At the end of the next 90 days what do you expect your management team to be better at?

*"Running an organization is easy when you don't know how,
but very difficult when you do."*

Marketing: Events, Activities, Competition

- ***Marketing and promotions:*** What events will be occurring in the immediate trading area over the next 90 days that are likely to affect business? Include both external activities and events (i.e. construction, concerts, conventions) and internal events (i.e. promotions, fundraisers, Limited Time Offers). Include rollout dates, potential impact, and preparation resources needed.

- ***Marketing Strategy:*** Develop a local store marketing (LSM) plan with each store manager that details strategies and tactics for building traffic from the business and residential communities within a 1-3 mile radius of the store. Discuss specific ways to acquire and maintain more customers in the next 90 days through retention, service, selling, training, awareness, and internal marketing tactics. Pay attention to what the competition is doing in the marketplace over the next 90 days. Visit their websites and stores; ask employees who work there what's coming up.

Facilities and Operations

- ***Facility and systems evaluation:*** Determine and prioritize the readiness state of the physical plant of each store and its equipment. What's old, what's new, what's likely to need replacing, what cosmetic changes may be necessary? Is the store scheduled for re-model or retro-fit? If so, how might that affect volume projections in the next quarter?

- ***Costs Assessment:*** Have each GM assess, prioritize, and estimate costs for specific R&M issues, new equipment or upgrades/improvements to their stores. Ask them to prioritize it from a "need-to-have" versus "nice-to-have" perspective. Review and assess each store's request and rank them relative to urgency and budget.

- ***Throughput Review:*** Assess and review the throughput (the speed, efficiency, and accuracy of the people, processes and systems) and operations of each unit. Are there bottlenecks or barriers? What's causing the problems? Is it people, equipment, leadership or process? How do you know that for sure? Is the store's team aware of it? What's their plan for improvement? What are they doing well that can and should be shared with other units?

The 7 Stages of Building High-Performing Partnerships and Teams

Profitability and productivity

- Is the store making money? Could they be doing better? How?

- Which units are doing the best job with sales and service? Why? How do you know that for sure? How can that expertise be shared with the other units you oversee?

- Set specific revenue and profitability goals for each unit in conjunction with store managers. Ask each GM to break down these quarterly revenue goals into period goals and then assign specific revenue targets *for each shift*. The QBP is not an abstract "paper"; its 90-day targets should be broken down into 30 day period goals and then further delineated to daily shift execution. By the inch it's a cinch, by the yard, it's hard.

- Review goal-versus-actual financials at the conclusion of each period with GMs. Then review and adjust each of the next quarter's period goals where necessary.

Assess and Schedule Store Visits

- Which stores need my attention the most? *Why?*

- After assessing *Previous Quarter Summary, Key Result Areas, Period Trends, People, Marketing, Facilities, Operations,* and *Profitability* now ask yourself:

- Which stores will I visit on which days? Why?

- What are the focus areas I will concentrate on? Why?

- What pre-work will be assigned to that GM?

- What are the top three areas of concern for the GM?

- What KRAs are strong, which are weakest in that store?

- Draw this information from the QBP and add it to your calendar. For a closer look at the process, see the detailed section on Store Visits later in this chapter.

"Running an organization is easy when you don't know how, but very difficult when you do."

Collaborate with Managers on targeted goals

- Send each GM a copy of a blank business plan to complete for their unit. Have them gather relevant data and self-evaluate how to achieve the KRAs that your QBP will focus on. Each store's KRA should be aligned with and compared to the brand or company goals for that specific performance area. For instance if the company goal for hourly turnover is 110%, then each store's KRA turnover target should be pegged to the percentage of achievement above or below the targeted company-wide goal of 110%.

- Schedule meetings with each GM to review their individual business plans. Discuss how to align the QBP to period goals and shift execution. Work as a team to create the plan, and collectively determine and agree on how the QBP (broken down into period and then shift goals) will help shape your priorities and achieve your goals.

- Follow your company's specific policies, but we suggest that MUMs complete and submit the QBP to their regional director or VP within seven days after the end of the quarter and then both the MUM and the MUM's supervisor should sign-off on the QBP draft.

- Finally you may want to consider compiling a simple S.W.O.T. analysis from your QBP for your stores or units. Ask your GMs to do the same. No two restaurants are alike. Each has its own identity, personality and challenges. An effective QBP consists of compiling a thorough forensic examination of the strengths, weaknesses, opportunities and threats facing your markets, managers and units in the next 90 days. The following page has a sample S.W.O.T. analysis.

The 7 Stages of Building High-Performing Partnerships and Teams

Location	Strengths	Weaknesses	Opportunities	Threats
Fairview 117	- New re-model - New GM - Location - Service	- Kitchen crew - Asst Mgr - Takeout execution - Customer count	- LSM (Marketing) - Training: Kitchen crew and Servers - Re-orientation	- New competition across street - GM progress
Carson 118	- Kitchen team - Bar - Sales - Leadership	- Equipment - Older store - Cleanliness - Food Slow	- R&M - Server Training - QSC - Ticket time training	- Old equipment - Competition
Grover 119	- Cleanliness	- "C" players - R&M	- Recruiting talk - "A" Players - Costs	- Mgt bench strength - Turnover
Branson 120	- Low turnover - Strong Mgrs - High Sales	- Greeters - Kitchen crew and KDS	- Seating during rush - KDS training	- Complacency - Maintaining excellence

You probably oversee more than 4 stores, but you get the idea; having the S.W.O.T. analysis at-a-glance for each store helps you compile a more effective QBP. Now you're ready for the most important job of all...

Planning and Executing Revenue-Generating Store Visits

Now that we've discussed the importance of pre-planning and designing an effective QBP let's discuss the most misunderstood (and greatest) opportunity high-performing MUMs face: the art of planning and executing revenue-generating Store Visits.

Store visit time is IMPACT TIME. Accomplishing an effective and strategic store visit is not merely a matter of "going to" the store. The nature of all store visits is developmental; you are visiting people, not stores. The revenue-generating store visit is a complex *process* (not a "project") that involves thoughtful pre-planning, careful execution and thorough de-briefing with the GM to get desirable results.

"Running an organization is easy when you don't know how,
but very difficult when you do."

Despite what many MUMs have been taught, store visits are not about "inspection", "direction", or "correction", they're about coaching, collaboration and development. Effective store visits are characterized by these specific steps:

1. Review the Quarterly Business Plan (QBP) and current progress on goals and objectives. Review your top 3 concerns and the GMs top 3 concerns. Note overlap if any.

2. KRA Analysis: review the unit rank, period trends from last calendar year, key result areas progress and goal-versus-actual for each store.

3. Determine visit focus and inform the GM of your visit (unless the visit is purposely unannounced.)

4. Conduct Outdoor facilities and systems "walkabout" first without—and then with—the GM or managers.

5. Conduct Indoor facilities, people and systems "walkabout" first without—and then with—the GM or managers.

6. Meet with GM or managers after visit to review, assess and coach.

7. Assess the visit and determine ways to make it more effective next time. Always leave the restaurant better than you found it.

Steps of Effective Store Visits

1. Assess Progress on the Top 5 Key Result Areas
2. Review the Quarterly Business Plan
3. Determine Visit Focus and Inform GM
4. Outdoor Ready for Revenue Walkabout alone & with Mgr
5. Indoor Ready for Revenue Walkabout alone & with Mgr
6. One on One with Manager after Walkabout
7. Assess Visit, Improve the Process

Our research shows that there are very few materials and resources that define how to plan and execute a meaningful store visit. The hodgepodge of store visit styles we witnessed (unfortunately characterized by little or no thoughtful/ thorough pre-planning) means that the MUM ends up *practicing on the GM each time*, a time-gobbling and dangerous role for both leaders. The *Synergist* knows that to transform store visits from careless/chaotic to disciplined and developmental, takes patience, practice, and preparation. Your objective is to be in the stores as often as possible, doing TLC: teaching, leading and coaching. Revenue-generating restaurant visits are not an "interruption" of your job; *it is* your job.

The 7 Stages of Building High-Performing Partnerships and Teams

Remote Control coaching is ineffective

Despite common belief and practice among most MUMs, you cannot effectively coach and develop your management teams via the phone, voice mail, text messaging or e-mail. Nor can you improve revenue and performance by merely (or exclusively) reviewing financial reports and suggesting corrective behavior based on numbers alone. This is patently absurd. Using that same logic, that means that I could beat the best tennis player in the world by watching the scoreboard while they watched the ball. The degree to which your managers improve is directly proportional to how much time you spend in your restaurants seeing what they see (and don't see) and then coaching and steering their performance. Our research has shown that the best MUMs spend at least 70% of their time in their stores and each has a disciplined approach to how they plan and execute their store visits for maximum results.

Why store visits are important

Why do MUMs need to visit their stores weekly? The number one reason is simply because *the store or restaurant is where the company meets the customer.* Where else is your time better spent given that fact? Effective store visits also create opportunities to find out what the managers know (or don't know) and how well they use what they know. Store visits also shed light on tier talent and bench strength, and how well the GM is developing and growing their teams. And finally store visits are important because *the store is where the company makes money.*

Time out?

Most MUMs will identify their two greatest enemies as Time and Geography; they have many duties multiplied by many stores across a wide area divided by a mere 24 hours in a day. In addition, MUMs complain that their companies saddle them with so much paperwork that store visits become theoretical, not

"Running an organization is easy when you don't know how,
but very difficult when you do."

practical, because of the data overload. MUMs are clearly frustrated by this perceived reality, asking "where the heck do we find time for people work under those mounds of paper work?" Let's look closer at how MUM's time constraints integrate with the necessity of purposeful store visits.

"It doesn't surprise me that Area Directors complain about the time they have available to spend in their stores, I mean, do the math!" says foodservice executive Sam Rothschild. He points out the following MUM calendar-year time constraints:

Reality Check: Available Time vs. Store Visits

- There are 365 days in a year.
- If you work for an enlightened company that gives you two days off per week, subtract 104 days. That leaves 261 available days to work.
- Subtract six annual Holidays: 255 days now available to work.
- Subtract 70 random meeting days or admin days per year: 185 days left.
- Subtract 36 days travel time/windshield time per year: 147 days left.
- Subtract 2 days per week of unexpected new paperwork, voice mails, e-mails, crises du jour per week(or 104 total days): you've got 43 days left.
- Finally, subtract 3 sick days per year (as if you can afford to be ill).
- That leaves you 40 days per year or a TOTAL of 3.3 days per month to spend meaningful time in ALL of your stores.
- If you oversee 6 restaurants, that's only **4 HOURS per MONTH** you could possibly spend in each store.
- If you supervise 8 stores that's **3 HOURS per MONTH** you'd have available to visit each store.
- If you supervise 10 stores…you've got a little more than **1 HOUR per month** per store!

Given the time constraints detailed above the big question becomes: how much thoughtful evaluation, focused supervision, and effective coaching

The 7 Stages of Building High-Performing Partnerships and Teams

can you realistically accomplish in 90 minutes, 3 hours, or even one-half day per store *per month*, especially since high-performing MUMs recommend a minimum of *weekly* visits to every store you supervise?*

With the time-and-geography barriers they're saddled with, many MUMs are forced to default to one of the following "supervisory" techniques:

Seagull Visits: Fly in to one store unannounced, screech about everything that's wrong, poop on 'em all, and fly off. If they have a little more time—but not much more—the time-stressed MUM does the...

Swoop, Snoop, and Loop Visit: Quickly visit 6 stores in 3 hours in 1 market and either yank their chains or praise their gains...in *general*. Then off they go. This ineffective method at least gets you face time with your people as opposed to the...

Virtual Visit: This option is characterized by rarely visiting but constantly threatening to. These absentee MUMs make announcements, pronouncements, and/or threats via voice mail, e-mail or IM: *"I'm coming in sometime this week, I'm not telling you when, but you dang well better be prepared! Heck, I might even be in your parking lot right now; you don't know!"* That's how losers, not leaders, act.

Our research shows that few MUMs have a clear understanding of what a truly revenue-generating store visit looks like. Most could not articulate the necessary behavior that results in a successful store visit, from pre-visit planning through post-visit recaps. On the other hand, the high-performers clearly knew their role and goal, and shared their insights for purposeful store visits with us. Let's examine the principles and behaviors of revenue-generating store visits in greater detail.

---

* And a bigger question: if they were freed from the paperwork they feel is extraneous, would most MUMs even know why, when and how to execute a meaningful store visit that had measurable results?

*"Running an organization is easy when you don't know how,
but very difficult when you do."*

Store visits are a process, not a project

Meaningful store visits must be managed as a process, not a project. Processes are *cyclical*, they don't end, they have specific steps, desired outcomes, and can continuously improve, but there is no finish line. Projects on the other hand are *linear* with a clear beginning and end. For example, a store visit is a process; hiring a kitchen manager would be a project. Consultant Gene Baldwin explains the differences this way in *Franchise Times*:

> *A process is a series of steps that have to be repeated over an extended period of time. A project also requires a series of steps but the work culminates when the project is completed. Managers who manage their business as a project seem to be putting out fires constantly because they view each issue they encounter as a unique project rather than a systemic problem in the continuum of business. This difference is best shown when something goes wrong. If managers view their business as a project, they typically enter the situation in crisis mode.*

Just "visiting" a store without being process-oriented with clear goals and collaborative intent can be just as ineffective as not visiting the store at all!

Maybe the Process is broken...

Our MUM research with high-performers relative to conducting meaningful store visits has led to us to some troubling conclusions. Not only do most multi unit managers *not* know how to conduct revenue-generating store visits, but many of the ones who do think they're doing a great job are not, and we know that because the same problems re-occur week after week, period after period, quarter after quarter, year after year, in their units. Why is this? Who's to blame? Do we have the wrong store managers in place, wrong style of leadership, or is it the store visit process that's broken? Our research indicates it's the leadership and process that needs attention.

The 7 Stages of Building High-Performing Partnerships and Teams

Most MUMs ineffectively conduct store visits using what foodservice executive Toni Quist refers to as "the classic inspect-correct-direct" model. She explains that this means the ineffective multi unit manager rushes into the unit, hurriedly *inspects* the operations, crew, and leadership, over a multi-hour, half-day or full-day timeframe. They walk through acting like a custodian, not a coach, making notes, checklisting their way through the front-of-the-house, then the back-of-the-house as "Inspector MUM." This is done from a rationale of efficiency when in fact it does just the opposite. The MUM-to-manager discussion typically ends with the MUM telling the manager what's wrong and what's right, directing the GM to do "these things" to improve the situation, getting a piece of paper signed between them, concluding with the manager giving tacit approval to the MUMs suggestions, agreeing to "watch for these things in the future" and then the MUM moves on to another store to do the same thing, acting more like a compliance cop than a leader and coach.

> **If you always tell people how to do something, they will stop learning for themselves.**

We have the following concerns with this autocratic "leadership" style of store visits:

1.   It presumes that MUMs have all the answers. They don't.

2.   What the MUM is measuring is compliance, not growth. The MUM is acting as an auditor, not a coach. Think of how a health inspector operates; do they provide leadership or just evaluate compliance? How much do you look forward to a health inspector visits? How much does a GM look forward to "Inspector MUM" versus "Coach MUM"?

3.   The store visit is being managed as a project instead of a process.

4.   Very little collaboration---and therefore collaborative learning--is taking place. The best questioning many MUMs can muster collaboration-wise is a weak "What could you do to fix this problem?" This is not really collaboration if it's just a pause mechanism until the MUM delivers their own solution.

*"Running an organization is easy when you don't know how,
but very difficult when you do."*

5.   The MUM is acting as a *de facto* store manager; a "super-GM."

6.   The MUM relates parent-to-child, not partner-to-partner.

7.   Underlying *causes* of the observed problems are not being addressed, therefore long-term solutions related to performance (especially team development/progress) are not identified or solved.

8.   You're inspecting a "store" instead of the people, performance and processes.

9.   This method presumes that you can force compliance, accountability or performance. You cannot. *

10.   It is ineffective. It creates a dynamic of dependency between manager and MUM. The same problems tend to re-occur. A MUMs job is to get things done through other people. You are paid to develop and lead, not merely to tell others what to do. Coach more, direct less.

The assumption is that if people are taught, told or shown what to do they will do their job right and the problems will be eliminated. This may be true for simple tasks like plating an entrée, washing dishes or making change, but it is ineffective for the complex task of developing high-performing teams, high-performing stores, and effecting real long-term change.

| It is a commitment, not authority, that produces results.

Developmental disconnect

In our research we closely observed high-performing multi unit managers during store visits, literally audio and videotaping their conversations and observations (we fitted 41 different MUMs with tiny microphones and recorders, tailing them through four different store visits at the same unit over a 30 day period). We compiled verbatim transcripts of their conversations and then discussed it with them in detail after their visit, comparing notes from their last visit as well. We wanted to know their specific intentions and thought processes behind their questions,

*What if the MUMs directions are followed to the letter by the GM but then those suggestions fail to produce results? Who then is "accountable"...the GM or the MUM?

The 7 Stages of Building High-Performing Partnerships and Teams

comments, observations and conversations. Surprisingly, we found significant communication gaps between MUMs belief and the GMs perception. Many MUMs *think* they are executing effective visits when their managers often disagree. The disconnect between MUM belief ("That was a good visit") and GM belief ("What good did that do?") was a common occurrence. The disparity seemed centered around two post-visit results: first, the GM felt that they had actually learned *very little* but were "told" a lot after each visit and second, the same operational problems re-occurred after being "identified" by the MUM and "fixed" by the GM.

The problems weren't new, the people weren't new, the store wasn't new, so why wasn't "good" performance and long-term problem resolution sustainable? This recurring challenge prompted several questions: 1) are MUMs investing in detailed prep time to thoroughly assess and analyze each store before the visit? 2) Are MUMs possibly focusing on the wrong problems? 3) Are they conducting store visits in a way that may have worked 20 years ago but is ineffective today? 4) Is there a proven process for effective store visits that generates long-term results and the greatest ROI relative to time and profitability? The short answers to these four questions: no, yes, yes, and yes.

The successful MUMs we interviewed took a more collaborative approach to store visits. Rather than the "inspect, direct and correct" approach that Toni Quist warned us about earlier, the high-performers took a different approach; they'd invest a good deal of time in the pre-visit evaluation; reviewing past visit reports in conjunction with current period and quarterly goals. While at the restaurant they'd *observe* (a subset of patience), not "inspect" (a subset of impatience), what was happening–and what was not happening–outside, inside, and with the customers and team. They know that in management as well as medicine,

*"Running an organization is easy when you don't know how,
but very difficult when you do."*

prescription before diagnosis is malpractice, so they resisted the temptation to hastily jump to conclusions. Instead they reflect on and assess the potential root causes of every challenge they saw, both good and bad, focusing on how it relates to deeper deficiencies or failures in team and management perception or development. They consider which *underlying processes* or systems may have failed. If a toaster isn't working check first to see if it's plugged in before you call a repair man. If all the lights in your house go out, for instance, changing a light bulb won't resolve the problem. You may need to reset a breaker, or maybe the electrical system needs repair. Approach the visit as "Coach MUM", seeking root causes, not "Mr. Fix-It" solving only surface challenges.

Example: *A traditional full-service restaurant store visit might reveal a "compliance issue" of food taking too long to get to the tables. "Inspector MUM" identifies the problem during a busy lunch, citing the foodrunner and server as the problems and points it out to the GM in a follow-up chat. He suggests either training them or getting rid of them. But slow service in the dining room is not the result of a "bad" foodrunner or waitress, or even training. The problem has deeper roots: it's because the manager did not stick to standards of hiring "A" players, coaching them daily, pruning low performers, staffing properly, delivering results–driven pre-shift meetings, and having each department rush-ready and focused. The "inspection" method would reveal only that "Mary was bad" and so we might fire her and hire Sally. The person performing the role has now changed and we may see short-term results but ultimately the problem surrounding the performance persists. A viable and long-lasting solution is much more complex than hiring someone new or training someone old. The "inspection" method doesn't reveal that, however, so the real issue is not addressed and the problem persists. The autocratic MUM then accuses the GM of not fixing the problem.*

The 7 Stages of Building High-Performing Partnerships and Teams

Beware the Iceberg.

When spotting an operations challenge, the tendency for most multi unit managers is to identify the problem, tell the store manager to fix it and complete the conversation by telling them how. But if you don't take the time to first reflect and connect the dots from the observed problem to the possible root causes of the problem, you're applying a bandage to a broken leg. It may be short-term-smart (because you think you're saving "time") but it's long-term-stupid since the problem will persist and you'll double or triple your time investment working on the same dang problem over and over. Stop treating symptoms during store visits. Seek and treat the root causes of poor performance. For instance, the solution to a chronically dirty store is not to merely "start cleaning", it's also about deeper failings in systems, standards and processes like culture, pride, service, signage, marketing, training and collaboration. Its root cause lies not with under-application of elbow grease (although that's a start), but rather with who was hired, what was taught and how they're supervised.

Think of an iceberg; the visible part represents the problem you see; but the unseen mass of ice under the water (an average of four times the mass of the above-water ice), could sink the Titanic, and in fact, did. So when you spot an obvious operational problem in one of your stores, think deeper to what's causing and supporting the "visible" problem. Which root team, management, process or system problems may be "under the water" causing the operational problem to "float" and become visible? The root causes must be identified and solved first or the problem will bounce back quicker than a bad check. ***Note:*** *not all operation challenges are deep-rooted, many are quick fixes, but be sure you know which is which before you apply solutions.*

You can get at and mutually identify root causes of operational challenges by adopting open-ended questioning to determine if the managers see what you see and if they understand "why" before you ask them to detail "how." Questions in

"Running an organization is easy when you don't know how, but very difficult when you do."

our example might include: "Why do you think this cleanliness challenge is happening? How do you know? What evidence is there to support that? What should we do? Why? What will happen if we do that? Why? How do we know and what are we assuming?" Admittedly, this process takes more time than the "show-and-tell" approach that most MUMs call "coaching", but what are you really teaching them when you merely "inspect-direct-correct" and tell them what to do? *You're teaching co-dependency, not collaborative problem-solving and leadership development.* Worst of all, the problem always seems to return. This "command-and-control" store-visit-style is the most common barrier to effective long-term team development and one of the hardest habits high-performing MUMs learn to break. The reason that most MUMs prefer "show and tell" over leadership-by-development-and-collaboration is that the latter method is incorrectly perceived as being time-consuming and/or "wimpy," and as long as we're being honest here, the "Mr Know-It-All" role accentuates the dual desires of job security and feeling needed. But if we're fixing the same problems over and over again, doesn't this suggest that a different approach might be warranted? Otherwise where does the fault lie; with your managers? (Well who's responsible for them?) When MUMs visit the store in the role of "Inspector" versus

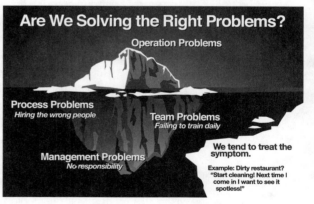

Are We Solving the Right Problems?

Operation Problems

Process Problems
Hiring the wrong people

Team Problems
Failing to train daily

Management Problems
No responsibility

We tend to treat the symptom.

Example: Dirty restaurant?
"Start cleaning! Next time I come in I want to see it spotless!"

Coach their lens is finely tuned to the forest, not the trees; they are spotting and fixing surface problems instead of identifying "icebergs" and true team development. It's true: an ounce of prevention is worth a pound of cure.

The 7 Stages of Building High-Performing Partnerships and Teams

A fresher approach

One definition of insanity is to keep doing the same things over and over again and expect different results. It's time to re-consider what a purposeful store visit should look like and how to get better results by focusing on collaborative coachable moments versus checklisting compliance violations.

Developmentally-driven MUMs opt for a more patient and methodical approach that results in both their team growing and their chronic problems being resolved. First evaluate each problem with a keen eye, determine if there are underlying causes for the problem, and then identify which internal processes are relevant and applicable to the problem area. Assess if those processes are actually in place in the store, if people are trained in the processes and if the processes are ineffective or outdated.

> Aim high; it is no harder on your gun to shoot the feathers off an eagle than to shoot the fur off a skunk.
>
> – Tim Cole

Direction and correction without context and collaboration is negligent, not enlightened leadership. After observation and reflection, smart MUMs ask their managers open-ended (not leading) questions that helps them understand how the GM views their performance and team development. They challenge assumptions by routinely asking "how do we know that?" Truth and progress can often be buried under deeply entrenched habits and routines. Last, they have a collaborative discussion with the GM regarding what kind of development would be most effective to get the store and the team and the KRAs to a higher level.

Let's review the action steps associated with each phase: 1) pre-visit planning, 2) during the visit, 3) after the visit, (including the visit recap with the store manager), and finally, 4) continuous improvement.*

---

* If you'd like to get a template to use when planning and executing your store visits, please go to www.sullivision.com

*"Running an organization is easy when you don't know how,
but very difficult when you do."*

① Pre-Visit Planning

Spectacular success is always preceded by unspectacular preparation.

Evaluate and Prepare

Remember the Seven P's: "Proper prior planning prevents pitifully poor performance."

The primary focus of any store visit from a MUMs perspective is not what the operation looks like but what actions or inactions of the team are causing it. *You are not visiting restaurants, you are visiting restaurant managers.*

Be clear on your visit expectations and the desired outcome of the visit. Ask yourself: what specifically am I intending to accomplish and what should the team be doing differently as a result of my visit?

Visualize the desired outcome by asking and answering these questions:

1. If this store was "ideal," what would it look like? *(Specify how associates would behave, how customers would feel, how sales would grow, how managers would be leading)*

2. How would we know when we got there? *(The restaurant should be busy every minute you're open, turnover low, performance high. "A" players only, deep bench strength)*

3. What training, coaching or development is necessary today, tomorrow, and the day after that to achieve that ideal? *(Identify what the managers need development-wise and what they need to reinforce daily to their team to achieve question #1)*

Remember that every store has its own collective personality and has to be managed accordingly. Determine the coaching style and direction most appropriate for each restaurant's unique character and market.

The 7 Stages of Building High-Performing Partnerships and Teams

Do your homework: Analyze relevant reports and data, especially the most recent period numbers and the current Quarterly Business Plan. Bring and review your evaluation from your last visit. Assess the *Top 5* performance areas (all of which should already be in your QBP):

- **Rank.** Assess how each unit merits performance-wise in your territory.
- **KRAs.** Detail progress relative to KRAs (key result areas) or KPIs (key performance indicators).
- **Historical trends.** Track the financial/performance trends of each unit over the last 13 periods.
- **Review** goal-versus-actual achievements.
- **Assess major marketplace trends and challenges.** Consider things like competitive intrusion/growth or road construction.

If an "announced" visit, communicate areas of concern to the GM prior to your visit. Note the unit manager's goals, achievements, growth, team development, where they're stuck, where they excel. Discuss how this visit differs from the last ones, and review previous key learnings and the results of the last visit. What was covered? Any outstanding issues from then?

What should the GM do to prepare for the visit? (Not running the shift while you're there for instance?) Identify and assign their pre-work. Ask them to detail the top 3 operational problems they have, or development challenges they're facing with their fellow managers or crew. Share your top 3 operational or developmental concerns too. Ask if they have any questions. Use your company's checklist of what to look for, but don't use it to merely "inspect, correct, direct" after the visit with the GM.

Set aside time for a one-on-one coaching session with the GM after the visit with no interruptions.

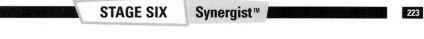
"Running an organization is easy when you don't know how, but very difficult when you do."

Finally, manage the schedule and you manage success. Many companies and most MUMs underestimate the power of a thoughtful schedule, but the bottom line is that you won't get anything worthwhile accomplished if you don't first prioritize and then schedule the time to do it. Use our online planning template to determine which of your stores require what specific kind of focus and development. How much time will that take? Schedule it and stick to it.

Determine the *TYPE* of visit

- **Announced Visit:** Most visits should not be surprises. Let managers know to schedule time to meet, before, during, and after the visit, with no shift-running responsibilities.

- **Unannounced Visit:** Only for operations that are chronic under-performers or feature inconsistent management. Hot Tip: well-run restaurants have no performance gaps between announced and unannounced visits.

- **Daypart Visit:** Prioritize the shifts--breakfast, lunch, dinner, peak volume, slow volume, weekends, or a combination of some or all of these--that will provide the appropriate and maximum input for effective analysis and decision-making.

Determine the *FOCUS* of the visit

- **Financial:** Sales? Profits? Labor? Costs? R&M?

- **Morale:** assess turnover, espirit de corps of crew or junior managers.

- **Leadership:** how well does the place run when the GM isn't there?

- **Systems/Processes:** observe behaviors and analyze purchasing, inventory, scheduling and throughput efficiencies.

- **Safety and Security:** use your company checklists.

The 7 Stages of Building High-Performing Partnerships and Teams

The Top 5 Complaints GMs have about MUMs

1. Too little face time.

2. Working positions during store visits instead of giving counsel.

3. Not focused during visits or recaps.

4. Stresses only the negative.

5. Too much "show-and-tell" too little guided learning.

- **Marketing:** POP, menus, signage, suggestive selling.

- **Performance evaluation:** Good or bad? Who? Managers? Staff? Both?

- **Communication and Training:** Observe pre-shift meetings, shift change, manager-to-manager / manager-to-staff communication, etcetera.

- **Major operations turnaround:** This challenge requires multiple consecutive day visits, a minimum of two. Think it through in detail and review recent progress or regress. Assess root causes of the apparent problems, analyze systems and processes first, then people (remember the iceberg).

- **Customer-centric:** Assess service delivery systems, service scores, volume, flow, table visits, customer complaint issues, potential bottlenecks on the line, at drive-through, takeout, host stand, etcetera.

- **Information-gathering:** For this type of visit, you may just want to take a friend out for lunch to the restaurant.

- **Training/recognition:** Perhaps you are visiting to observe or attend a manager meeting, an employee tenure or recognition ceremony or in-store training session or pre-shift meeting. Maybe you're visiting to facilitate new manager orientation or certification.

Determine the *TIME FRAME* of visit

- **Full Day Visits:** Give a truer picture of what's happening in the store since managers and team members can successfully hide or modify their behavior for only about three hours at a time. Full day visits make it easier to see what they've accomplished or are challenged by

"Running an organization is easy when you don't know how, but very difficult when you do."

since this gives you time to observe the arc and flow of each shift.

- **Half Day Visits:** Normally staged as a follow up to a recent full-day visit, but can also be effective for high-performing restaurants that need less coaching.

- **One-to-Three Hour Visits:** Most often a waste of time at an under-performing unit if you're looking for a true gauge of performance and under-lying causes. These brief visits are normally most effective only if you're looking for an answer to a specific question. *Hot Tip*: if the behavior, mood, appearance, and activities in the restaurant surprises you, your prior visits have been too short or you had blinders on.

> **Hot Tip: Know what your top performing stores and your bottom performing stores have in common so you can repeat the things that create high-performance and avoid the things that do not.**

- **Compile a Balanced Scorecard:** Goal should be to visit each store at least 4 times per period before making major decisions relative to people and performance issues. Here are some frequency-of-visits suggestions based on our research:

  -Friday is usually the most critical day to visit to assess the team's ability to perform in the storm. Tuesday, Wednesday, and Thursday are often the best training and project days. Weekend visits are usually the best information collecting days.

  -Two of your visits should be closing shifts.

  -One shift per month should be a Saturday or Sunday night.

  -Be there for at least one transition/changeover shift.

  -The goal is to spend 70% of your time in restaurants.

If you wonder about it check it. The restaurant that you least want visit is the first one you need to go to. Our research shows that the best MUMs will visit a high-performing restaurant first to get a keen sense of what to look for later in the low-performing store. *

---

* After the visit to a low-performer, visit another high-performing store to cheer yourself up.

The 7 Stages of Building High-Performing Partnerships and Teams

② During the Visit

Once you've done your preparation work, now you're ready to visit the store. Smart MUMs train themselves to never forget that they are visiting managers, not stores, and their role and goal during the visit is developmental and not as a compliance cop. Start with an outside-looking-in perspective.

Outside the store

First assess the "lay of the land" on your own without a manager; conduct a Ready-for-Revenue walkabout outside the facility and parking lot. Use your company's checklist of what to look for outside of the store tied to your KRAs.

Look first through the customer lens. Start with "curb appeal." Conduct an informal moments-of-truth or customer touchpoints audit (signage, parking lot, building, back door, dumpster, drive-through, cleanliness, etcetera). If you're evaluating a restaurant with a drive-through, order food. What impressions are the customers likely to form as they drive up and see what you see? Note what's aligned with and what's different from brand standards and expectations.

Now view the outside again, this time through your MUM lens. Make certain that systems, standards, people and POS are in place. Look for both the right things and the red flags (like company standards and non-negotiables that may be violated or overlooked.)

What to do you need to compliment the managers on?

What do you want the managers to notice that they may have been missing?

Make bullet point written notes of all you observe and sense or use a company checklist if provided. Checklists are like compasses, they

"Running an organization is easy when you don't know how, but very difficult when you do."

provide detail and direction, but true progress is never made just by recounting the bullet points to a manager. Like the medical school instructor told his students: "I'm going to spend a month showing you how to do abdominal surgery. Then I'm going to spend the next 3 1/2 years showing what to do if there's a problem." *

Now walk the exterior again, <u>with the GM</u>. See what they see.

Inside the store

One of the biggest challenges that many foodservice GMs and their assistant managers face is the art of effective dining room management. Many managers-on-duty prefer to work in the kitchen, on the expo line, or at the drive-though window instead of being in the dining room (or at the counter) directing the interactions of the crew and customers. This is a recurring challenge for MUMs and owners; how to make their managers feel confident on the floor and with their guests. Your store visits can provide key insight into your manager's ability or inability to "work a room", connect with customers, make the experience memorable, and get the guest to return. We'll look more closely at the art of dining room management at the end of this section. Here's what to do inside the store.

- Review and use your company's checklist of what to look for related to KRAs or operational concerns.

- Stay focused on the performance you came to assess. If you see another major focus area that needs attention, write it down and address it later, or on a different visit, don't give in to distraction from your core focus area (unless it's an emergency).

- There are two ways to evaluate progress in the store: walk it with or without the manager. If you choose to go solo, walk it again later, this time with the manager after you note what you're there to observe.

* Never underestimate the power of checklists, a 747 airline pilot may have flown that plane 1000 times before it, but isn't it comforting to know that they are going through that checklist one more time before you takeoff?

The 7 Stages of Building High-Performing Partnerships and Teams

- Purpose-driven MUM in-store walkabouts uncover and evaluate performance issues over three key areas:

    1. How well your unit managers walkabout-and-work the "rooms" (including kitchen, dining area, host areas, drive-through, carside/to-go). What do they see, what do they miss, how well do they interact with their teams and customers? Are they seeking out and delivering "coachable moments" with team members? If so are they coaching positively? Are they interacting equally and comfortably with both crew and customers or do they prefer hanging out in the kitchen or on the expo line? Are they "people persons?" What do they need to learn and what do they need to "unlearn?"

    2. What approach do they use as they walk through the operation relative to impacting key result areas like: Quality, Cleanliness, Ticket Times, Kitchen Display Systems, Service, Atmosphere, Hospitality, Speed, Accuracy, Suggestive Selling, Teamwork, Efficiency, Labor, Marketing, Signage, Safety, Execution, Communication, Pre-Shift Meeting, Energy, Table Visits, To-Go/ Drive-through efficiencies, Staffing Levels, Bench Strength, or Fun. Note what's there and what's not there.

    3. Try to get a sense of what they understand and if there are limits to their understanding or ability to connect process problems to performance issues. Are they able to identify and solve critical operation challenges or their deep-root causes? Are they only treating symptoms? Do they know the difference? Do the managers make notes as they go and transfer key learnings to the log book or personal calendars in detail for follow-up and continuous improvement?

- Evaluate status of furniture, glassware, beverage stations, restrooms, equipment, lighting, walk-ins, and storage areas. Review the preventive maintenance program, budget/goals with the GM.

"Running an organization is easy when you don't know how, but very difficult when you do."

- Observe line check, quality and food safety review.

- Observe employee food handling and hand washing behaviors.

- Observe pre-shift meeting. Is the staff engaged, the manager energetic and focused? Is everyone completely clear on what the shift goal(s) are? Is anyone learning? How do you know?

- Observe manager and employee behaviors. Are the managers finding and executing coach-able moments with their staff during the shift? *Is anyone having fun?*

- If applicable, observe and note the bartender's service, selling, drink-making behaviors and overall efficiency.

- If applicable, observe and note the behavior and efficiencies of the greeters and bussers.

- Are managers and crew executing the fundamentals in the kitchen and dining room and/or drive-through or carside/to-go? Are they being brilliant at the basics?

- Detail and note progress/regress since last visit. Be certain to note what's right. What should you be complimenting your managers on? What gets recognized gets repeated.

- Review the daily manager logbook; note if entries are up-to-date, relevant, succinct, clear, legal and include detailed key learnings from each shift. This process is one of the most overlooked and undervalued learning skills (and resources) in the industry. Teach your managers how to get better at Log Book detail and knowledge-capture daily.

- What systems or processes might be underlying the problems you observed?

- *Create stations of innovation.* MUMs should watch closely for innovation in their operations, and find out the why as well as the how of the idea. One of the MUM's key roles after spotting innovation in a store is to note it and then consider the scalability of the idea...can it be

The 7 Stages of Building High-Performing Partnerships and Teams

cost-effectively replicated? If so, let's try it out on other stores and then if it works, roll it out to another district or region. Franchise MUMs have great opportunities in this arena since franchisees are often the sources of new ideas.

- Be Coach MUM not Inspector MUM. Try to help your GM see what you see and note if they see it first. Don't "tell" her what to look for, see what she knows already, and how she interacts with the team and customers during the "walkabouts". Your job is not to walk ahead merely pointing at "things-that-need-fixing," your job is to walk along side—or behind-- and observe only; get a sense of what the GM sees or doesn't see, knows or doesn't know. You will have a chance to discuss this awareness afterwards during the one-to-one debrief.

- Finally, ask the GM to evaluate the walk-through not vice-versa. This patient system of observation and development not only gauges awareness, readiness, and talent, but will build a successful team much quicker than the autocratic (and broken) "inspect/direct/correct" approach that most MUMs take. Assess all KRA's and use a checklist so nothing is overlooked, but don't forget that your primary objective is to build a team, not merely comply to a checklist...you're visiting managers, not stores. Let go of "telling how to do it" and pick up on guided learning so they can get better at spotting and solving problems and developing team members on their own.

- Use all six senses when visiting your stores: sight, sound, smell, touch, taste and *common*.

- Spend one-on-one time with second-level managers and also the crew during the visit. This helps build the bench, spread energy, engender brand values and develop tomorrow's leaders.

- Don't compete with managers for team member affection. When you visit the store treat the managers like the stars, and refrain from the "when I was a GM" stories as much as possible.

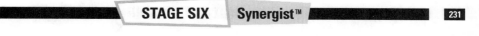

"Running an organization is easy when you don't know how,
but very difficult when you do."

- Bring positive energy to every restaurant visit, don't take it away.
- Finally, when you're inside the store observing the behaviors of your managers in the dining room or at the drive-through window, it is a non-negotiable behavior that they are positively impacting the experience of each customer. So allow me to suggest...

A Few Thoughts on the Lost Art of Dining Room Management...

"How you guys doing, OK?"
"Kara taking good care of you tonite?"
"How is everything folks? Good?"

How many times have you—or your customers—been interrupted in mid-bite or mid-conversation by a manager who pops in and tosses those trite comments at the table? How many of your managers confuse the inhospitable act of intrusion with the hospitable act of interaction? How many of your managers mistake the process of "checking on tables" with the art of "working the room?" The answer is "too many", and the question is: *why?*

For too long we've focused our unit leaders solely around managing margins, systems, throughput, labor, speed, hiring, sanitation, crew development and financial acumen. While those are all critical skills, the result is dining room managers who know how to checklist a process but are clueless about how to build repeat business or please an unhappy guest. Here are some best practices relative to a manager's priorities in our dining rooms:

First things first. A manager's five priorities when leading a shift:

1 Safety and sanitation
2 Driving revenue and repeat business (service and selling)
3 Delivering on the brand promise
4 Conflict resolution and prevention (among both guests and team)
5 Connecting with—not merely "interacting" with—every customer

The 7 Stages of Building High-Performing Partnerships and Teams

Be brilliant at the basics. Most of what is called good service is a combination of a hundred little things that the customer never notices…until you don't do them. When moving through the dining area, a primary responsibility of effective managers is to make sure all the little things are being executed before trying to "add" value to the guest's experience. The goal of successful operators is to first to meet the expectations of your customers, and second, to exceed them.

Purposed motion trumps walking around. One thing great managers have in common is continuous and "purposed motion" during the shift. They move in synchronicity from the back of the house to the front, spreading energy, confidence, direction, coaching and assistance. They move continually between kitchen, storeroom, back door, expo line, dining room (or drive-through window), greeter area and front door, assessing and directing flow, focus, food and fun. (We attached a pedometer to a casual theme manager who logged nearly 7 miles during one lunch shift!) The best managers get more focused the busier it gets and rarely get "stuck" in any one area (except temporarily, helping in the kitchen or at the host area during the rush for example). If you witnessed their movements from a "bird's eye view" it would resemble a Figure 8.

Touch *every* table. Many managers connect comfortably with "regulars" but often avoid making contact (or only make peripheral contact) with unfamiliar diners when walking through the dining room. The great dining room managers seek out a stranger every shift. They learn to become comfortable with—and actually enjoy–meeting and connecting with strangers. They wait for the right time to introduce themselves and always begin with an apology for the interruption. They ask about the food, the experience, what they can do to enhance it, and always, always, identify first time guests. After all, these people have driven past 30, 40, 50 other restaurants to come to yours, so be certain to recognize this effort, and possibly reward them for first time visits

"Running an organization is easy when you don't know how, but very difficult when you do."

by buying a dessert or appetizer for these potential future regulars.

Beware the Rush. The two most challenging times for a positive guest experience is when the restaurant is either slammed or slow. The busier it gets, the sharper the manager-on-duty must focus or the further they will get behind. The outcome depends largely on the manager's ability to lead under pressure. Stay in control. The team expects and respects a steady hand on the tiller. The best managers act like a Mayor, not a Firefighter, when it's busy in the dining room. Press the flesh, please the voters (restaurant customers vote with their feet), and make things right that may go wrong. Oh, and if things do go wrong? Don't go with them.

Beware the Hush. During slower times (after the rush, right after opening, right before closing, or all day during bad weather), is when the best managers are *most* vigilant and focused relative to the guest experience. They make certain their servers are focused on the customers in the dining room, not lollygagging in the kitchen, and that someone is vigilantly covering each section during transitions. Sometimes the worst service occurs when it's most preventable: during the slower parts of the day. And poor or inattentive service when it's slow is magnified in the eyes of the guest because they can't see any excuse for it. Every guest deserves attentive service no matter when they visit.

> Shared knowledge is power and power is the key to changing things.

Know the 55 to 5 Rule. You can positively impact a customer's experience perfectly for 55 minutes and ruin it all through 5 minutes of neglect or inattention.

The power of 1. Most managers struggle with the right question to ask each table to assess the customer's experience. That's why we hear a lot of "How is everything, folks?" and "How are you guys doing, OK?" Even if their meal did not meet or exceed their expectations, most guests clam up, avoid

The 7 Stages of Building High-Performing Partnerships and Teams

confrontation, and reply "Fine, thanks." Remember the question a manager can ask that always elicits ideas for improvement, even from happy customers: *"What's one thing we could have done better?"*

There are literally dozens of more ways that managers can enhance and influence a diner's experience and we discuss them further in our *Fundamentals* book. But here's what to remember for now: your managers can't "checklist" a guest to return with his or her friends, but you and they can ensure a positive experience and repeat business through focused interaction, caring behavior, and genuine connection with the crew and your customers. Study what the dining room managers at the best 4-Star restaurants do, discuss ways to improve manager-guest interaction at your weekly manager meetings, and smother the guest with appropriate hospitality, timely interaction and seamless service from the greeting to seating to serving and leaving. Service is free. Pile it on and teach your manager's the importance of being that *Brand Ambassador* in the dining room, kitchen and drive-through.

③ After the Visit

This is a very important stage of your visit, presuming you preplanned properly and observed correctly. This is where you de-brief, recap and coach the GM to future success. The learnings shared at this phase should be fed back into the QBP to adjust goals and focus for the next 90 days.

- Excuse yourself and explain to the manager you'd like a few minutes to record your thoughts and observations of the past few hours.

- Adjust your expectations to reality after concluding the store visit. Identify and rate/rank the gaps between "performance should be" and "performance is" in each store you visited.

- Select a quiet corner of the restaurant, label and date your visit report, and

*"Running an organization is easy when you don't know how,
but very difficult when you do."*

record as much detail as possible. Sort bullet points and actionable items keyed to KRAs. Next to each challenge area assess whether it's a surface problem easily corrected or a deeper-rooted challenge that involves more detailed examination and forensic work.

- As you identify the problems you observed, reflect on the root causes by asking yourself these questions:

  1. *Is this problem new or a recurring one? If recurring, for how many prior visits?*

  2. *Is it a team or management performance problem? How do you know? What assumptions are you basing that on? Are those assumptions still valid?*

  3. *If manager, is it the result of skill deficiencies, ignorance or attitude?*

  4. *Does the GM see it as a problem, and if so do they know how to fix it?*

  5. *What process or system may have failed as the underlying cause? How do you know? Did the GM see that too?*

- Create a "difference" list: what would be different if you were the unit manager? When you're done, remember three things: 1) the list is never finished, 2) expect it to be done, and 3) don't expect it to be done your way. The difference list is how you might approach the problem, but your goal is to be a coach not a custodian. Understand how your managers might likely approach the problem by asking them about what they saw, what they think they'll do, and why they think that method would produce the results they're looking for.

The One-on-One Manager Discussion after the Store Visit.

Sit down with your GM and debrief the visit and recap the key learnings. The conversation depends on the type of visit, what you observed, and what you expect to be accomplished before the next visit.

- Stay focused and eliminate distractions (put the Crackberry on stun and turn off the cell phone.) Give the manager your undivided attention.

- Briefly review and recap key points of prior visit reports. Discuss you and your manager's Top 3 Concerns.

The 7 Stages of Building High-Performing Partnerships and Teams

- Complete and review your current visit written report. Give the manager his/her copy.

- Share and discuss your impressions with the Manager. Read the report together, elaborate on key points. This conversation should be a dialogue not a monologue.

- Remember that your goal at this juncture is to develop performance, not direct it, and the key to doing so is to ask questions that dig deep to gain mutual understanding of where the root problems lie. Examples of such questions would include:

  - *What do you need to accomplish? Why is that important?*
  - *What do you think might be getting in the way of your success? How do you know?*
  - *How would you know when you were successful? What would it look like?*
  - *Why do you think this is a problem? Have you noticed it before? If so, for how long?*
  - *How have you addressed the problem? What happened? Why do you think that occurred?*
  - *How could you approach the problem differently to attain a different outcome? What are we assuming?*
  - *What don't you know that might be helpful to resolve the problem(s)?*
  - *What do you need from me to help you?*
  - *What do your junior managers need? Why?*

- Listen more than you speak.

- Balance discussion between personal development and restaurant or store performance.

- Be certain to compliment them on progress and celebrate relevant accomplishments. Ask them if they know what they did that made them succeed. Ask also if they'd do something different to improve in their challenge areas. Even if progress is spotty, or slow, be sure to recognize the small victories.

*"Running an organization is easy when you don't know how,
but very difficult when you do."*

- Ask what they might need from you to help them achieve their goals. Recommend additional resources; books, seminars, DVDs, articles, etc. Don't forget to follow-up. Discuss how to apply the new skills incrementally to improve the performance.

- Help them help themselves; encourage your managers to be responsible for their own development. Ask them to share their developmental goals with their peers to help them be more accountable and to get feedback on their progress. Be sure to follow up after the person has applied and practiced the new knowledge/skills. Give them the opportunity to celebrate successes.

- Link all suggestions and direction to period goals and then shift execution. Always explain how each observation you share or follow-up task you agree to after the visit connects to the manager (and territory's) period or quarterly goals. Alignment and integration is critical to manager buy-in, brand values, and execution. Managers should also be encouraged to discuss how they can then link those suggestions to shift execution.

- Agree on an action plan and next steps with timetable. Write it down on paper or capture on your smartphone, latop, or Blackberry. Either way, always leave a record, either written or electronic.

- Know and use the 5 steps of effective one-on-one manager communication. When discussing strategy, behavior, changes or performance issues after a store visit with your managers, consider the following discussion template to get the most from the conversation:

    1   *Identify the Opportunity ("This is what we can accomplish.")*

    2   *Connect it to the Big Picture ("This is why it will benefit the customer and us.")*

    3   *Define the Necessary Actions ("This is what we've agreed to do.")*

    4   *Specify the Behavior ("This is how we agreed you will proceed and what the other managers and team members will need to do.")*

    5   *Outline the Consequences ("This is what we'll get as a result.")*

The 7 Stages of Building High-Performing Partnerships and Teams

After following this 5-step process, you're not quite done yet. In between assignment and execution, the necessary glue is clarity and commitment. It's wise to recognize that truth and perception are not absolutes. You may perceive an assignment one way—that's your truth. Your manager may hear your words and perceive or interpret the same assignment differently. And that's also true—for them. Make sure the communication is clear and in sync by always clarifying and verifying the summary points. Ask these questions: 1) What are you going to do? 2) Why are we doing it? 3) How are you going to do it? 4) Who do you need to share it with? 5) When are you going to do it? Clearly confirming the agreed-upon plan and timetable minimizes the likelihood for wrongful interpretation or misunderstanding.

- If you have to be critical, criticize the behavior not the person. People can repeat or change behavior, easier than "attitude". Be tough but fair, and build trust in your team so that they're willing to discuss challenges and obstacles openly and are not afraid to make mistakes.

- In addition to the personal, verbal feedback, give Feedback before leaving either in writing or electronically (don't forget to insert these notes into the QBP also). The notes should be easily understood bullet points with actionable items. This creates a log of performance, communication and time use. A short report might be a page or less, a longer visit could be 3-4 pages. The purpose of these written visit reports is to improve the MUMs effectiveness and maintain management accountability for improvement and completing directed assignments.

- After completing the review, make a copy for the manager and keep the original for your files (or whatever your company policy mandates). Have manager sign your copy to verify the joint review. Integrate the report into the QBP. Review and use the report prior to your next visit.

- Schedule the next store visit. Don't leave until you know what you accomplished and you could explain to a stranger what you did while there. End with recognition and encouragement. Always.

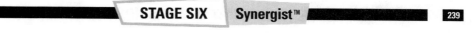
"Running an organization is easy when you don't know how, but very difficult when you do."

④ Back in Your Office

This key step is often overlooked by average MUMs. High-performers never overlook a detailed personal assessment after each store visit.

- Question the process: What are 3 things I can do to improve my store visits? What are 3 things I can do to improve my one-on-one conversations with my managers? Did I achieve my store visit goals including: 1) knowledge transfer, 2) goal-setting, 3) collaborative development, 4) alignment to period goals and company objectives, 5) real improvement not band-aids, 6) energy-transfer, and 7) re-direction to company resources they can use to get better. Great MUMs focus on continuous improvement and feed the lessons learned back into the planning process.

- Before entering the unit on your next visit, a review of this last report will refresh and re-focus your memory on the key issues from the previous visit. The key impact issue is always consistency. Consistency in operations is the measure of your impact as a MUM; that which is variable from visit to visit is the manager's impact, that which is the same is the MUMs impact.

- Reality check on Change 101: a MUM's impact via store visits is always temporary. Real change is a process, not a project. It takes time, re-focus, repetition, and it won't stick forever. It takes 21-28 days of different behavior to change a personal habit and approximately 120 shifts in a row to change an entire restaurant crew's behavior. It's never a quick fix. So don't believe and act like it is.

- To see a sample post-visit evaluation form visit us at **Sullivision.com**

Tie Annual and Period Goals to Successful Shift Execution

We've discussed 1) how to develop, assign, and execute goals via the QBP and 2) examined the nuances and behavior of high-stakes results-driven Store Visits. The final step of a *Synergist* MUM is learning how to integrate quarterly

The 7 Stages of Building High-Performing Partnerships and Teams

and period goals into Shift execution with your managers. Planning and strategy happens away from the "battlefield" in meetings. Execution and performance happens on the Shift. The QBP is only a piece of paper if it's not applied to Shift execution.

The last few years have grooved subtle yet seismic shifts in the systems, design, and processes of the foodservice and retail industries. Back-of-the-house technology integration, energy-saving kitchen equipment design, service auditing via interactive voice response, throughput analysis, cost-based and revenue-driven labor scheduling, drive-through speed improvements, and payment systems (moving from counter to kiosk) have affected our industry dramatically. These new-found technology-enabled efficiencies are mining incremental profits from a historically inefficient industry. But improving systems, design, throughput and processes does not mean that you automatically also improve people and performance; after all, anthropology will always trump technology in our industry. So I find it puzzling that little—if any—time, money, or resources have been put into understanding and improving the efficiencies of the most critical aspect of "operations": managing and leading The Shift.

Your building, systems, menu and equipment make up the physical plant and body in which you "do" business. The Shift combines people, leadership and execution to bring both your business to life and life to your business. Every critical strategy or tactic related to running a profitable foodservice operation— service, selling, hiring, retention, scheduling, purchasing, marketing, training, food safety, teamwork—evolves from abstraction to action (or inaction) during The Shift. The greatest food and beverage menu in the world is nothing more than paper if it isn't assembled, merchandised and consumed during The Shift. The best-conceived systems, policies and procedures are merely words in a training manual if not executed during The Shift. Your current Limited Time

"Running an organization is easy when you don't know how,
but very difficult when you do."

Offer (LTO) evolves from purchasing and planning to success or failure during The Shift. Even our common financial barometer—the P&L—reflects Shift execution. "Success isn't measured by reading a Profit & Loss statement," says Scott Roekle, Director of Operations for the Supple Restaurant Group in Oshkosh, Wis. "That's a history document. You make or lose money by what happens—or doesn't happen—during the Shift."

Every shift our managers oversee in their units is different and challenging in its own way. Each one has its own rhythm, tempo, and character and each shift requires a different management mindset and approach. The 3 basic Shift formats–Opening, Mid, or Closing—require a distinctly different style of preparation, focus and adaptability; there's a lot of play-calling at the line of scrimmage. Many MUMs and GMs never consider the architecture of the revenue-generating shift and how managers need to vary their approach and style to effectively get the most out of each. It's time our managers stop "running" shifts...and begin leading them.

> **If you don't do it excellently, don't do it at all. It won't be profitable or fun, and if you're not in business for fun or profit, what the hell are you doing there?**
>
> –Robert Townsend

How do your managers approach each shift? Do they let it happen, or plan it through? Do they leave it to chance or lead it by choice? Do they even know what a great shift looks like beforehand, or is it something they recognize only after it's over, when it's too late? How much time do you spend at manager meetings dissecting the architecture of a revenue-generating Shift? Do you exchange best practices weekly relative to how to coach the hourly team members into position, through the position and out of position? Your answer may well explain why your customer counts and sales or up, down, or flat in this competitive world. Smart operators are beginning to keenly assess and document how their best unit managers approach and lead a profitable Shift.

The 7 Stages of Building High-Performing Partnerships and Teams

As part of this book's research, we conducted detailed video, audio and written interviews with 102 high-performing General Managers from a wide cross section of chain and independent foodservice operations. We supplied 25 of them with recordable MP3 players and asked them to keep an audio diary of seven days of shifts, detailing what they did before, during and after both successful and unsuccessful ones.* Here's what we learned:

An opening, mid or closing Shift is composed of three distinct linear stages; before, during and after. The stages are simple, but the variables within each stage are complex. Things like rookie-to-vet ratio, labor dollars, no-shows, weather, marketing, customer traffic, safety, sanitation, equipment repair and maintenance, deliveries, etcetera all add up to potential chaos and revenue loss if not anticipated and managed properly. So when should GMs and their multi unit managers begin preparing for a successful shift? While most managers plan their shift about a half-hour before it starts (if they plan it at all), high-performers get their ducks in a row a little bit further out...

What to do a year before the Shift

A profitable shift has a dual platform rooted in both past preparation and present execution. It's the cumulative result of what your managers did (or failed to do) months, weeks, days, hours and minutes before it begins. For example, we'd all probably agree that a key element of a shift's success is having the right people in the right places doing the right things. But that scenario—having your "aces in their places"–is a pre-condition entirely contingent on past discipline. Did the multi unit manager supply the proper support and resources to help the GM select the right people? Were the unit managers patient in the selection process, or did they "panic hire"? Did they prune their "deadwood"? Did they invest the time and tools to properly train every day? The connective tissue between preparation and a profitable shift begins weeks, months, or even years before the shift. As one Area Director put it: "Spectacular success is always preceded by unspectacular preparation."

---

*To see some great free video clips of these all-star GMs sharing some of their insights, visit our home page at **www.sullivision.com** and click on **The Shift DVD** icon.

"Running an organization is easy when you don't know how, but very difficult when you do."

What to do 30 days before the Shift

Review, align, and integrate the period goals into Shift focus. Determine the subject of pre-shift meetings that will support the Shift goals. At their monthly manager meetings MUMs usually discuss topics like repair and maintenance issues, performance ratings updates, and critical data like same store sales, profitability, staffing needs, food safety, diversity, marketing, etcetera. What they don't do–but should do–at these meetings is break period financial targets down to the lowest common denominator: individual shift goals. For instance, let's say your period financial goal is to raise gross sales at each unit by $4000. That sounds daunting at first blush, but the savvy multi unit manager knows how to inspire their team to hit that goal every time: *sell it by the cut, not the cow.* In other words, focus on $63 more per shift, not $4000 more per period. Example: if you're open for lunch and dinner, you run 14 shifts a week. That's 64 shifts a month, and if you divide that into the $4000 goal, it means that you'd only have to raise sales $62.55 per shift to exceed your period sales goal. Now here's the best part: break that $62.55 down into the menu items your store's team would collectively have to sell to hit that target. Just 4 more appetizers, 5 more desserts, and 6 more sodas sold each shift would hit or exceed the $63 target, and beat the $4000 monthly goal. (If you're open for breakfast too, that means 21 total shifts each week, 84 shifts per month or only $47.63 more sales per shift to exceed your targeted $4000 period sales goal.) Don't let managers scramble to hit their goals in the last week of the period when they could easily make their numbers via incremental gains every shift. Managers should then share these incremental goals (4 more apps, 5 more desserts, 6 more sodas) with your server, kitchen, greeter and/or drive-through team in your pre-shift meeting. Not sharing your goals with the team at pre-shift meetings is like winking at a pretty person in the dark; you may know what you're doing but nobody else will. What's that? **You don't do pre-shift meetings???**

The 7 Stages of Building High-Performing Partnerships and Teams

What to do 10 Minutes before the Shift

Have unit managers gather each department together before the shift begins and detail their specific focus, goals and objectives for that shift. Specify the behaviors necessary to achieve the shift goal (or better still ask the team to). If your focus is that $63 incremental sales bump, you might begin by reminding both the front and the back-of-the-house teams that the servers' goal is to sell all the kitchen can make and that the kitchen's goal is to make all the servers can sell. Pre-shift meetings can also focus on dozens of other topics, too, but whatever you focus on, tell them why, show them how and reinforce WIIFM (what's in it for me?). Pump them up, and spread some energy. The pre-shift jumpstart meeting is the critical bridge between goal-setting and goal-achieving. Without this meeting it's extremely difficult to parlay twelve prior months of hiring right and training well into shift execution and success. Let's dig deeper into the art of planning and staging effective pre-shift meetings.

> **If you coast you're going downhill.**
> – Christopher O'Donnell

The Art of the Pre-Shift Meeting

Make Pre-Shift Meetings mandatory not optional. Can you imagine a sports team at any level–pro, college, high school, middle school, Little League— getting ready for a game without any communication from the coach relative to the game plan? Can you picture the looks on the team's faces if the coach shows up just before the game, strides onto the field or court and says nothing, praises no one, and begins chatting with the fans without any direction for the players? Can you have a winning season with a coach like that? Can you keep and recruit "A" players with that kind of leadership? What kind of fan base would you keep? Many restaurant owners and operators must think so, because they demonstrate a similar absence of leadership when they fail to prepare and execute pre-shift meetings for their staff on a daily basis.

"Running an organization is easy when you don't know how, but very difficult when you do."

Research reveals a key learning. Each of the managers we interviewed in our research for this book led units that were among the top 10 highest–grossing restaurants in their companies; these are dream-teamers. We identified scores of core competencies they exhibited, but the one behavior they all shared—bar none—is this: *they make daily pre-shift meetings mandatory, not optional* for their managers and staff.

Relate every Pre-Shift meeting to a bigger goal and strategy. As mentioned above, when managers meet each week, they should plan their daily pre-shift meeting topics for the week by first reviewing period goals and then aligning the pre-shift topics to support and execute on those big picture objectives. Daily pre-shift meetings achieve three goals:

1) energize, educate and focus the crew,
2) improve our people, performance and profits,
3) insures that every guest or customer leaves happy.

As a MUM, aren't those three topics key and critical to your personal and team growth, tenure and bonus?

Pre-shifts are for every department. Everyone affects the customer's experience, so everyone benefits from effective pre-shift meetings. Most companies focus on doing pre-shift meetings for servers, but it's just as important to have pre-shift meetings for all of your team members and departments; kitchen crew, bussers, greeters, and bar staff. They all impact the guest, so why shouldn't they all be informed and energized before each shift? Besides, without guidance and focus from the manager before the shift begins, every employee will have his/her own opinion of what the shift should be. If I'm upset or hungover or unhappy, for instance, I want a shift in which customers stay home or don't bother me. Is that what you want the customer to experience?

The 7 Stages of Building High-Performing Partnerships and Teams

One meeting, one topic. Focus is key. Pick one area to spotlight during each shift: service, selling, cost control, promotions, safety, recipes, marketing, teamwork, portion control, whatever. Don't try to cover everything because you end up covering nothing.

Be prepared and eliminate distractions. Turn off pagers and cellphones, hold the calls, and make sure you have the team's attention. "Pre-meal meetings should be upbeat and full of energy, but there also has to be discipline and organization," says Tim Weaver, an award-winning General Manager with O'Charley's in Cookeville, TN. "Allowing co-workers to eat, drink, smoke or have side conversations during pre-meals creates an atmosphere of apathy which blocks both listening and learning. Managers must keep the team focused and enforce standards where everyone is paying attention."

Bring energy, don't take it away. An effective pre-shift is part pep rally, part information, part training, all energy. Don't focus on the negatives. Charge them up, don't bring them down.

Keep it interactive. Effective pre-shifts should not be long-winded Manager Monologues or boring Data Dumps. Skinny the monologue and fatten the dialogue. The agenda for revenue-generating pre-shifts include energy transfer, recognizing yesterday's performers, anticipated volume, goal-setting (and how we'll attain them), and then asking the team to review what you just told them. "Karl, can you tell us our two goals for this shift?" After Karl reviews it for you, ask Rosa to do the same, then Michael. Now you ask Karl what he's going to do to achieve those shift goals, then Rosa, then Michael. Perhaps offer small team or individual rewards if the goals are accomplished. The key here is perfect practice with spaced repetition. (See a 30 second clip of how this works at our website at the **Jumpstart** DVD icon.)

"Running an organization is easy when you don't know how,
but very difficult when you do."

Keep it short and sweet. You know how long the pre-shift meetings of our high-performing full-service GMs lasted? An average of three minutes! And at QSR operations the top performers executed their pre-shift meetings in under two minutes. Get to the point and do it interactively. Only fine dining restaurants that feature lots of daily specials can really justify pre-shift meetings that last longer than 5 minutes. If you tend to run on and on do your next meeting in the walk-in cooler.

Don't neglect team members who come in later. Most operators don't have their whole staff in together before the shift at the same time. To minimize labor costs, we stagger their arrival. So do these team members miss the pre-shift meeting? Absolutely not! The best managers do thirty-second one-on-one pre-shift meetings with every staggered-shift crew member as they arrive. Write down your shift goals and post them in a common area; the same place every day, perhaps the walk-in cooler door. Have team members who come in at staggered times review the shift objectives and add their initials and personal goals to the sheet. Now have them find the manager who then conducts a 30 second one-on-one Shift Goal Review with the crew member.

Coach during—and follow up after—each shift. If you don't measure it you can't manage it. Don't set shift goals if you aren't coaching performance *during* the shift to help the team achieve those goals. And after the shift, keep the energy high, thank each crew member for their efforts, and teach your managers to clearly communicate what they learned in the manager log book so that improvement is continuously fed into your district and company. *

Have Fun. What we learn with fun we rarely forget.

This ain't "improv", folks. A whitewater rafting guide in northern Wisconsin offered this advice before we plunged down some scary Class IV Rapids: "Just

---

*Our best-selling DVD called **The Shift: How to Plan It, Lead It, Make It Pay** details how to design and execute revenue-generating shifts no matter what kind of operation you lead. Learn dozens of best practices your managers can use to improve their people, performance and profits each shift. Check out the sample video clips at **Sullivision.com**

The 7 Stages of Building High-Performing Partnerships and Teams

put your feet up and go with the flow." Great advice for rapids-riding, not so good for shift-leading. Know what you want to accomplish, communicate it to your team in a way they understand and measure success by whether or not you won the Shift. For every Shift you win, you're one step closer to hitting your quarterly and period goals, for every shift you lose, you're two steps back. If it was my bonus, I know I'd want to walk forward every shift. Because in this business, if you're standing still, you're walking backwards.

Like a Broadway play, a successful shift is the cumulative result of hiring the right talent, rehearsing endlessly, and focusing on bringing excellence to every performance. Never practice on the customer. It starts with the multi unit manager's guidance and leadership and ends with the unit manager's shift focus and execution. A successful restaurant is the result of never-ending repetition of perfect and near-perfect shifts, day-in and day-out. As I've said before: by the inch it's a cinch, by the yard it's hard. Little and often make much.

Summary: Synergist™

This chapter, the longest in the book, is challenging to summarize because of all the detailed strategies and tactics that comprise it. But I'd suggest that you consider these steps:

1 Very carefully assess the way you go about preparing your QBP (quarterly business plan) and determine if there's a better way.

2 Be certain to factor in period goals and daily shift execution as sub-tactics and goals of your QBP.

3 Question the mode and methods you employ during store visits and try to evolve from "Captain Compliance" to Head Coach.

4 Look for root causes of problems in your stores. Don't treat symptoms only.

5 Make pre-shift huddles mandatory, not optional, for all your stores.

"Running an organization is easy when you don't know how, but very difficult when you do."

Self-asessment: **Synergist™**

Review the list of core Synergist characteristics below. Assess your personal strengths and challenges relative to each competency in one of the boxes to the right. Review the boxes again in six months to chart your progress.

Competency	Good At	Average	Needs Work
I execute effective Quarterly Business Plans			
I prepare and execute effective Store Visits			
I connect the Quarterly Business Plan to Period Goals and Shift Execution			
I help managers understand Shift Architecture			
My managers execute effective Pre-Shift Meetings			
Self-Competitive (S.W.O.T. analysis for managers and stores)			
I'm Coach MUM not "Inspector MUM" when visiting stores			
Meets financial goals			

STAGE SEVEN
Goal-Getter™

Cautionary Tale

*"I've been a Multi Unit Manager for over ten years now, and one thing
I've learned for certain is that well-done is better than well-said.
To become great and stay great you have to make a difference every day.
Set goals, hit goals, win even small victories, and show others how to do
the same. Some of those goals are planned, some are thrust upon you
unexpectedly. Do your best and win as much as you can everyday, because
a sense of daily accomplishment is at the heart of self-leadership.
Don't wait until you get to the 'top' to learn to lead."*

"Well done is better than well said."

The critical characteristics of a Goal Getter include:

- In it to Win it
- Throws the cap over the wall
- Plays to win instead of playing not to lose
- Knows School is never out for the Pro
- "The Buck Stops Here" Mentality
- Makes the company money

Goal-Getter™
Synergist™
Marketing Guru™
Head Coach™
Servant Leader
Talent Scout™
Brand Ambassador™

The world does not pay for what a person knows, but it pays for what a person does with what they know. Execution is everything. So the 7th and final growth stage on our Leadership Ladder is **Goal Getter.** In the real world, *results*, not "effort" calls for rewards. Only in Little League do they reward effort for its own sake. So the *Goal Getter* competency focuses on bridging the knowing-to-doing gap by getting incrementally better every day.

What will motivate most MUMs to change? The question is relative. Psychologists tell us that most people will do more to avoid pain (learning new behaviors) than to gain pleasure | **All work is teamwork.**
(successful leadership), so the question is predicated on how much you think the perceived pain of change will be offset by the potential rewards of leadership. A smart way to transition from the emotional side of fear to the practical side of better performance is by setting and attaining realistic goals.

The 7 Stages of Building High-Performing Partnerships and Teams

> To bring out the best in others, leadership must match the development level of the person being led. Giving people too much or too little direction has a negative impact on people's development. Situational leadership is based on the belief that people can and want to develop, and there is no best leadership style to encourage that development. You should tailor leadership to the situation.
>
> – Ken Blanchard

Leadership is always situational

While we have thoroughly and scientifically researched and relayed the best practices and competencies of over 280 MUMs for this book, merely "studying" these 7 Stages of Multi Unit Leadership is not enough. Ideas are easy, execution is hard. Careful, appropriate and incremental *application* of new behavior is the bedrock of meaningful change and measurable results. Well done is better than well said.

A company—any company—has a lifecycle that apes a human's: infant, youth, young adult, young married, middle age, mature elder. And each stage of this cycle brings with it different leadership needs and knowledge capital based on the company's maturity and progress. Your company could be anywhere in this arc of growth. How MUMs lead their teams and territories at each stage of your company's lifecycle is critical to growing to the next. A different leadership style (or combination of styles) is necessary for every store, every team and every challenge. A different growth stage on our Leadership Ladder—*Brand Ambassador, Talent Scout, Servant Leader, Head Coach, Marketing Guru, Synergist*—might need to be emphasized depending on the personal development needs, the store needs, the market place, and the life cycle of the company. The wise **Goal Getter** knows that *leadership is always situational*.

Here are some best practices and creative ideas culled from our research to help align knowledge to execution and help you evolve from goal-seeker to goal getter.

"Well done is better than well said."

Determine what you need to learn. Review the self-assessment competency tables at the end of each chapter for the 7 growth stages of the *Leadership Leader* and identify and assess the areas where you'd benefit from additional knowledge.

Determine what you need to unlearn. Have you ever tried to install new upgrades of a particular software program and find that you first need to completely *uninstall* the previous version for the new program to work properly? Learning can be like that too. If you're a veteran MUM whose style has been "command and control" and "inspect-direct-correct," you may find it particularly challenging to break your old habits and apply the more effective *observe, question, collaborate and develop* method of managing your team. If you're supervising your team based on a "parent-to-child" approach, you have to question if that style is still effective, appropriate and relevant to the 21st Century realities of what customers want and how Generation Next learns. It's no longer a case of simply asking "what do I need to learn?" You must first identify what you have to *unlearn*. Learning new things is the easy part. Letting go of what used to work for you in years past and is no longer relevant to today's reality is much harder. Recognize you and your team's knowledge gaps and account for ways to incrementally improve them in each QBP (quarterly business plan) you design. Then work on filling in those gaps daily. *Shoshin*.

Be tenacious. Persistence is what helps make the impossible possible, the possible likely, and the likely definite.

Teach responsibility and accountability. Encourage all managers to believe in their ability to determine and shape their own fate. Do so by collaborative development instead of playing the compliance inspector who merely tells them what to do. Then they in turn must teach this behavior to their junior managers (remember *each one teach one*)*. If your managers (and their team

---

*The performance of Junior Managers impacts over 60% of the weekly shifts, which means that at least 60% of GM and MUM bonuses are being controlled by the actions of your Junior Managers.

The 7 Stages of Building High-Performing Partnerships and Teams

members) aren't accountable and responsible, they will forever be whining about the things they *can't* control like the weather, customers, competition, headquarters, vendors, the economy, and eventually, *you*. Improving GM and Junior Manager performance through coaching and development is the highest-leverage opportunity you have every day to improve your territory and your company's profitability and success.

Every store, every team and every manager is different. When it comes to applying multi unit leadership solutions, one size does not fit all. Be disciplined enough to carefully consider whether a process that worked well at one store will realistically produce similar results in another. Or will the variables of differing marketplaces, customer demographics, personalities and the other endless performance parameters at the second store affect a different outcome? One way to know is by involving the management team at the second store in the proposed solution first. Discuss how it worked at the first unit (have their managers testify to the other store's managers) and collectively brainstorm any challenges to execution that they may foresee. When you tell someone to implement new processes they haven't had involvement in it's always more challenging for self-motivation to kick in. Get over the mistaken belief that collaborative thinking is "wimpy" or a sign of indecision. It is not. Autocratic control is weaker. None of us is as smart as all of us.

Identify your vulnerabilities. Know where you and each of your managers and each of your stores are most vulnerable and dependent. Shore up areas of weakness first, and simultaneously enhance the strengths. Losers let things happen, winners make things happen.

Decide how before you decide what. "The most fundamental obstacle to successful strategic decision making occurs when leaders fixate on the question, 'What decision should I make?' rather than asking 'How should I

"Well done is better than well said."

decide?,'" says author Michael Roberto, author of *Why Great Leaders Don't Take Yes for an Answer* (2005, Wharton School Publishing). When faced with tough big decisions, he suggests engaging in what he calls "pre-mortems" which means envisioning complete failure, imagining the paths that lead there, listing the bigger risks and determine if they're avoidable. "If not, choose another course." If your colleagues or company are in the midst of a big decision, split them up into two teams; Team A comes up with reasons to do it, Team B comes up with reasons not to do it.

Focus higher. Over the Chicago Bulls locker room in the Michael Jordan era of five NBA world championships, a sign was posted that read: "The game is scheduled, we have to play, we might as well win it." It takes just as much time to achieve something great as it does to achieve something "good". You have to aim at something. Why not aim for something big?

Not doing it is as bad as doing it wrong. There are two kinds of leadership sins: sins of commission and sins of omission. This means doing the wrong thing or forgetting to do something. When faced with decision-making beware of paralysis by analysis.

> Reasonable men adapt themselves to their environment; unreasonable men try to adapt their environment to themselves. Thus all progress is the result of unreasonable men.
>
> – G.B. Shaw

Don't correlate cooperation with performance. Just because the team at one of your restaurants gets along with each other does not mean they will naturally perform better. Generally that is the case. However, while you should value cooperation, always be careful to measure it against performance and results.

Keep your eyes on the prize daily. Pay attention to the daily measurements that gauge your success relative to period or quarterly goal achievement, such as KRAs. Use your QBP as the road map every day. Developing your

The 7 Stages of Building High-Performing Partnerships and Teams

managers daily, especially in small doses, are the building blocks of the Dream Team. Measure your progress by how much your team knows and how that knowledge is reflected in the confidence, performance and revenue in each store.

Keep goals focused. For instance, "better service" as a goal is so vague as to be meaningless. Stating the goal instead as: "Improving customer loyalty by behaving in a manner that results in every customer leaving happy and coming back again ," is more effective because the outcome-based objective is crystal clear.

Visualize achieving your goals. Let's "begin with the end in mind" and write down answers to these questions one more time:

- If my stores were ideal, what would they look like?
- How would I know when I got there?
- What kind of development with my team is necessary, today, tomorrow, and the day after that to make certain that the <u>best things happen</u> and the worst things don't?

Shoot for 1%. Constantly search out small improvements, not just big ones. Every day get a little bit better. Don't shoot for 100% improvement; teach your team to be 1% better in a 100 different ways.

Always Over Teach. Why? Your team tends to under-learn and over-forget.

Be "Bi-lingual." In this case I'm not suggesting learning to speak two different languages but rather learning to speak the language of foodservice and the language of business. If you're a foodservice MUM, don't just read the many excellent industry publications like *Nation's Restaurant News*; also subscribe to or read *Forbes, Fast Company, Inc.* and *The Wall Street Journal*. Understand what's happening in retail as well as other industries relative to leadership, team-building,

"Well done is better than well said."

hiring, service, marketing and career-pathing. If you're in the retail world, learn what's going on in the foodservice industry. "Steal" the best ideas; adapt, innovate and improve upon them in your own stores. School is never out for the pro.

Inspire a shared vision. The best way is by consistently developing your team via the *Leadership Ladder* stages we've identified. Continuously improve by feeding the lessons learned back into your planning and development and orientation processes. Learn what your high-performing managers know, then *interpret* it and *integrate it* into the behaviors and routines of your other managers. Again: each one teach one. A major reason for poor service, or inconsistent operations, is because MUMs learn something new then fail to integrate the new idea into and across the entire team. It's been said that the "speed of the leader determines the rate of the pack," but it's also true that the success of your coaching and development efforts in your stores will be determined by the speed of the slowest-many learners, not the fastest-few. Sometimes you have to go slow to get fast.

Be an "Environmentalist." To consistently be a *Goal Getter,* multi unit managers must understand the subtleties of the decision-making process. They must always consider how a policy or procedural change brought about by technology, competition, diversity and in-store leadership (or lack of it) will affect the internal "eco-systems" of each store. An "environmentalist" clearly understands the unique holistic environment of people and processes at each store they supervise and how modifying one facet of its eco-system (equipment, training, talent, procedure or resources) might positively or adversely affect the people or performance of a different internal eco-system. They also know that spreading energy and recognition creates the best environment of all: a culture of kindness. Franchise Business Consultants need to be especially tuned into the environment at the franchise stores they work in and serve to spot innovation and alignment with brand standards.

The 7 Stages of Building High-Performing Partnerships and Teams

Take responsibility and be accountable. Never blame the company. "We" need to get this done, not "They told us to do this". Excuses are for rookies and losers.

Follow-through is not just for golfers. Larry Bossidy, co-author of *Execution* (Crown Business Press, 2002) cites "follow through" as an essential behavior of high-performers. "Follow up meetings with letters," he suggests. "Letters eliminate confusion about what was decided on. If a person gets a letter and discovers it doesn't reflect what he believed was decided, he immediately calls back to have a conversation to resolve it. Secondly, a letter gives you a history. So, when I go to that office or factory the next time, I can take out the letter and ask, 'Now, were these things done? And if they weren't done, why weren't they done?' Another executional behavior is 'Reward the doers.' There's just too much praise in business for the philosophers—people who are good strategists, but don't have the capability to translate that strategy into action. You've got to spend a lot of time making sure you're rewarding the right people." Naturally Mr. Bossidy's "letters" suggestion would apply to e-mail follow-up as well.

Make money. Consistently hitting or exceeding financial goals is the number one shared characteristic of the *Goal Getters* we surveyed. They do it by following the principles and ideas laid out in this book and then teaching and coaching their GMs and junior managers to do the same thing. Invest in a copy of this book for all of your GMs and your junior managers. *Now* teach them how to align their thinking and performance to the next level of MUM leadership. As author Alvin Toffler said: "You've got to think about all the big things while you're doing the small things so that all the small things go in the right direction." After all, the ultimate achievement of every multi unit leader is to *Build Your Replacement.*

"Well done is better than well said."

Assuming that your entire company is able grow to greater heights, you're now facing an even steeper challenge: *sustaining* success. Let's assume you are able to synergize all 7 growth stages on the Leadership Ladder and achieve excellence within your territory. What happens if you lose your way or stumble after achieving your goals? Herein lies a history lesson waiting to be told.

The Lessons of "Cactus Gavvy" Cravath

Ever heard of Clifford Carlton "Cactus Gavvy" Cravath? Most likely you haven't. Nicknamed "Cactus" for his prickly personality, the tobacco-chewing, cussing baseball player was once a household name to hundreds of thousands of Americans. His accomplishments were recounted daily in every newspaper nationwide for over a decade. Cravath was the home run king of major league baseball in the so-called "deadball" era (1913 through 1919), no small feat in a league that also featured hitters like Ty Cobb. Cravath played for both the Red Sox and White Sox, but bloomed with the Philadelphia Phillies in 1913 when he led the Major Leagues with 19 Home Runs and 128 RBI, 35 more runs-batted-in than the runner-up. Over the next six years he won five more Home Run, RBI and batting titles. In 1920—unfortunately for the 38-year-old Cravath—a young Boston Red Sox pitcher was traded to the New York Yankees. This pitcher transformed himself into a slugger who played right field. His name was George Herman Ruth, but most everyone called him Babe. You may have heard of him. They wrote books, staged plays, made movies and built both a legend and a stadium around Ruth. Cravath faded into obscurity.

Is the name Albert Read familiar? Probably not. But surely you recognize Charles Lindbergh, who is famous for making the first transatlantic flight between North America and Europe. Only problem is, you're wrong and he didn't. The first transatlantic flight between the USA and Europe was accomplished by Lieutenant Commander Albert Read of the U.S. Navy and the crew of the flying boat NC-4. They were the first Americans to fly across

The 7 Stages of Building High-Performing Partnerships and Teams

the Atlantic Ocean, and they did it in May 1919, eight years *before* Lindbergh. The transatlantic portion of their flight was from Newfoundland to Portugal with a stop in the Azores, but the entire flight was from North America to Europe. In fact, historical accounts document over 77 other fliers in teams who successfully flew from the US to Europe before Lindbergh. But Lindbergh won worldwide notoriety, fame, accolades and a place in the history books by being the first person to cross the Atlantic Ocean *solo* by air, on May 27, 1927, earning himself the well-known moniker Lone Eagle.*

> **Our achievements speak for themselves. What we have to keep track of are our failures, discouragements, and doubts. We tend to forget the past difficulties, the many false starts, the painful groping. We see our past achievements as the end result of a clean forward thrust, and our present difficulties as signs of decline and decay.**
>
> – Eric Hoffer

So what can Gavvy Cravath and Albert Read teach us about being a successful multi unit leader and operating successful businesses in the 21st Century? Two things: 1) *the early bird may get the worm; but it's the second mouse that gets the cheese,* and 2) *you can learn a lot from the success–and failures—that you, or someone else, makes.*

The foodservice graveyard is littered with names and chains that--like Albert Read and Gavvy Cravath—once dominated their segments and then disappeared quicker than Courtney Love at an O'Doul's kegger. Their stories are cautionary tales of misguided ownership, misplaced priorities, misunderstood customers, mismanaged assets, unwillingness to change, ignorance, hubris, delusionary boards-of-directors, or underestimating new competitors with more energy and focus.

The stories of pioneers, settlers, also-rans, woulda-beens, coulda-beens, mighta-beens and shoulda-beens in the foodservice industry are always more than tales of too little, too early, too late. They're full of deeper lessons for people willing to learn. What critical factors shorten the lifespan of once-thriving concepts?

*Go to **www.sullivision.com** to watch a short video about the importance of being built to last.

"Well done is better than well said."

Timing? Capital? Aggressive expansion? Product innovation? Being first? Fear? Vice? Leadership? Values? Franchising? Family? Markets? Bench strength? Solar flares? Well, the answer is both "all of the above" and "none of the above." For the last ten years our company has advised dozens of emerging concepts and large independent operators how to successfully grow to the next level as chains. And the first thing I advise is that they develop the leadership competencies of their multi unit manager team and then their store managers. Once that process is in place, here are a few suggestions for companies that want to grow strong and grow right with passion and purpose:

- **First be <u>best</u>, then be first.** In the late 1990's, before so many dot-coms dot-bombed, the prevailing business mantra was "be first: first wins" or "grow fast or die." Well, many investors bought into that belief system by shoveling speculative dollars to NASDAQ fund brokers who left them just that—broker. Seeing this fast money, and wanting to get on the same train, many small multi-unit operators jumped at the starry-eyed notion of rapid growth, instant wealth…and possibly early retirement. Suddenly everyone wanted their little concept to be a chain—fast--and we witnessed many a pie-eyed once-thriving operator squander resources, vitality and profits (not to mention falling sway to the narcotic notions of multi-million dollar IPOs) in the name of being "first." History teaches a different lesson: *grow profitably or don't grow at all.* Hurry is the mother of mistake. Study the train wrecks for there are great lessons there; learn from the mistakes of others, you'll never live long enough to make them all yourself. Time gives good advice.

- **Acknowledge reality.** *(The following paragraph is a personal aside to concept founders reading this book, and does not necessarily apply to MUMs.)* This is the most difficult question that executives must ask about a growing entrepreneurial company: *"Are the concept founders and original managers who got us to this level the same people we need to grow us to the next one?"* If you want to grow smartly, you have to be smart and brave enough to know if

The 7 Stages of Building High-Performing Partnerships and Teams

and when to ask the question. And then where to go for help if you need it. Entrepreneurial spirit, hard work and self-assurance will only get you so far in the dog-eat-dog-world of competitive chains, and the naive end up wearing Milk-Bone underwear. The smart, hard-working company founders and concept creators that grew the business to critical first stage levels may not always have the skillsets necessary to create scalability across multi units, regions and marketplaces. It's important to know what you know you don't know and then hire or rent the right expertise to supplement what you don't currently have. After all, 51% of being smart is knowing what you're dumb at. How deep are your smarts? One man's "Simple!" is another man's "*Huh*?"

- **Calculate the "tipping point" of exponential growth.** Opening a second restaurant is a world apart from opening the first. It's more complex because of indirect control and inconsistency issues. Opening the third unit is a little easier. But from there on out it can vary wildly between control and chaos, as any successful chain operator will tell you. At certain unit growth levels, there's a "tipping point" where systems, scalability, personnel, leadership, throughput, bench strength and strategy get bent, stretched or broken. Suddenly the whole company begins to teeter and sway like the town drunk at an all-you-can-drink single malt chug-off. Anticipate that these tipping points will happen, and know that it occurs somewhere between opening units 9 and 10 and again at units 21-22, 50-51 and 99-101. Strong multi unit leadership is the critical glue at each juncture of growth. Be prepared with a strong bench, deep smarts, and the strength to know when you need help, and the kind of help you need. Keep the infrastructure solid and the company's growth focused by putting a premium on systems that are both scalable and promote *habitual consistency* in hiring, training, purchasing, operations, and people development. And get brilliant at the basics.

- **Avoid a condition of ease.** Always celebrate success, and don't ever be satisfied that you or your team has hit the finish line. There is always more to

"Well done is better than well said."

learn and more to be better-than-good at. We have yet to meet a high-performing multi unit manager who was ever satisfied. They all had higher-level goals in mind as they neared accomplishing their most recent goal. Stay on the offense with your team and objectives, and stay self-competitive (remember to ask the question from the earlier chapter: *"If I was the competition, how would I beat us?"*). If you study the history of once-dominant pro sports teams, or businesses that faded from the top, you'll find many reasons but a common shortcoming: instead of playing to win they began playing *"not to lose."* They lost confidence, lacked leadership, and focused more on their fears and shortcomings than their potential. If you're shooting for second place, your strategy will always be determined by the leader. The biggest risk is to take no risk at all.

• **No chipped paint, all the horses jump.** There's a story told about a young and cash-strapped Walt Disney taking his children to an amusement park at a California pier in the 1930's. They spotted a colorful and brightly lit carousel. From a distance and when in motion the horses and lights and ride looked spectacular. His kids clamored for tickets from their Dad. So Walt bought two tickets that he couldn't really afford. But when the ride stopped, the whole family quickly noticed that only the outer ring of horses was actually going up and down. The two

> Whenever a business or individual decides that success has been attained, progress stops.
>
> – Thomas Watson

inner rings of horses were frozen in place, the poles broken. As the passengers got off the ride, the Disney family saw dozens of burned out carousel lights and chipped paint on the horse's bodies and faces; a few even sported missing eyes and broken ears. He felt cheated and resolved to never forget the incident. As he developed his movies and theme parks over the years it is said he had a hand-painted sign over his desk that read: "No Chipped Paint. All the Horses Jump." The little things mean a lot, don't compromise your standards, know your non-negotiables, and never underestimate the importance of the mundane. Your ads, promotions or store itself may attract customers once by chance or by choice. But when they experience you up close, what will they

The 7 Stages of Building High-Performing Partnerships and Teams

see? Brilliance in the basics, or chipped paint and frozen horses? Ask your managers and crew to identify the potential (or actual) chipped paint and frozen horses in your operation. Look for them during your store visits. Identify what your company stands for and also *what it will not stand for.* Ask yourself: "Which values and procedures are so central to our core that if we lose them, we lose ourselves?" Don't water down the brand for the sake of growth.

- **Have an appetite for change.** *Goal Getters* don't fear change, they anticipate it, embrace it, even search it out. Challenge the process and never be satisfied with the status quo. Continuous improvement is a defining characteristic of the *Goal Getter*, all the way to and through the manager team at the store level. Encourage your GMs to ask their hourly team these questions after every shift: *"What Made Our Day Difficult?" "What made our customers mad today?" "What took too long?" "What caused complaints today?" "What was wasted?" "What did we do that was just plain stupid?"* Now get your managers to fix those problems so that you can resolve more challenges and take the stress and complications out of your customer-facing team member's lives every day. Happy teams make happy customers and happy customers buy more (and come back more often with friends.)

- **The most powerful weapon on earth is the human soul on fire.** If your employees and customers are anything like ours, they smell complacency and inertia. Only low performers like it. If high-performers sense decay in an organization (or a leader) they bolt. They want to work for the inspired company or leader who lights the way with a blowtorch, not a handful of uninspired, dispassionate managers holding candles. Overcoming inertia (definition: the property of a body by which it remains at rest or continues moving in a straight line unless acted upon by a directional force) is a primary focus of multi unit *leaders*. If you're no longer personally driven, find a new way to steer your business. If you're no longer passionate, rediscover the romance of your profession. If you've lost the spark, let the sheer *joie de vivre* of this business relight your fire. Passion persuades.

"Well done is better than well said."

- **Preach what you practice.** Create both employee and customer apostles by selecting people, instead of "hiring" them. Choose people who already have the values your company has. Study the U.S. Marine Corps for instance. We have. They recruit from the same age group you do, the potential downside of joining their team is literally fatal, yet they fill their ranks with great success. They develop performance by combining regimen, pride and legacy, wrapped in a layer of deep smarts and covered with a heapin' helpin' of spaced repetition and discipline. I'm not suggesting boot camp orientation, only that excellence exists where excellence is expected. Work toward something bigger: no greatness without goodness. *What do you want to be famous for with customers and associates?* Customers and crew long remember the attributes surrounding passion and excellence. And if you doubt the value of memory as a legacy maker, remember the lessons of Albert Read and Cactus Gavvy Cravath.

- **Throw your cap over the wall.** On November 21, 1963, the day before he was assassinated in Dallas, Texas, U.S. President John F. Kennedy gave a speech in San Antonio. In this speech he referenced a story by an Irish writer concerning a young boy who would scamper across the fields and farms of Ireland's green countryside, where he'd continuously run into stone fences and walls of varying heights that marked property lines. He could climb over most of them, but occasionally would be confronted by a formidable wall that made him feel trapped and intimidated, making him doubt his ability to get over it. On such occasions he would summon courage by throwing his cap over the higher walls. Then he *had* to climb over for he could not return home without the hat. Kennedy knew that bold moves involve risk and courage, and his San Antonio speech likened the USA's publicly-stated goal and resolve to land a man on the moon by decade's end as analogous to "throwing our cap over the wall." When faced with leadership challenges in your territory, opt for the bolder choices, the ones that make you slightly uncomfortable because you've not done them before. These "stretch goals" involve harder work and bigger

The 7 Stages of Building High-Performing Partnerships and Teams

risk but the payoff is always better. Fortune favors the bold. As Kennedy knew, when you make your goals clear and resolve to win, you have taken the first step to achieving them. Once you've read this book and assessed your personal strengths and challenges against each competency of the seven growth stages, "throw your cap over the wall" relative to changing the behavior necessary to bridge your personal learning-doing gap. What you are afraid to do is a clear indicator of the next thing you need to do.

Summary: Goal-Getter™

To be in a leadership role without being goal-oriented is a waste of knowledge, time, treasure and talent. All work is teamwork: if we're not in it together, we're not in it to win it. There is no "A" for effort. Results matter. When your goal is "survival" your objective is to "stay alive", not to win, which means you'd be happy in second place. But "Second Place" is just another way of saying "First Loser". Study companies who have failed and learn their mistakes before you repeat them. Face your fears; throw your cap over the wall. Know what your team needs to learn and unlearn. Be disciplined and align quarterly and period goals to shift execution. Make change your friend. Synergize all 7 Growth Stages into success routines that allow you to apply the right solution to the right challenge; this is the essence of situational leadership. What does your leadership goal look like? Be what you wish others to become.

"Well done is better than well said."

Self-asessment: Goal-Getter™

Review the list of core Goal Getter competencies below. Assess your personal strengths and challenges relative to each competency in one of the boxes to the right. Review the boxes again in six months.

Competency	Good At	Average	Needs Work
My team consistently achieves our goals			
I'm In it to Win it			
I find lessons in mistakes			
I play to win instead of playing not to lose			
I'm a Connector: has know how and know who			
I learn from other industries			
I embrace change			
I meet or exceed my financial goals			

THE END
of the Beginning

"How are you doing as a leader?

The real answer is how are the people you lead doing? Do they learn? Do they visit customers? Do they manage conflict? Do they initiate change? Are they growing and getting promoted?

You won't remember when you retire what you did in the first quarter or the third. What you'll remember is how many people you developed—how many people you helped have a better career because of your interest and your dedication in that development.

When confused as to how you're doing as a leader, find out how the people you lead are doing. You'll know the answer."

—Larry Bossidy

"Faced with the choice between changing one's mind and proving that there is no need to do so, almost everybody gets busy on the proof."

—John Kenneth Galbraith

Goal-Getter™

Synergist™

Marketing Guru™

Head Coach™

Servant Leader

Talent Scout™

Brand Ambassador™

Mastering the 7 Growth Stages of the Multi Unit Leadership Ladder can offer the reader much more than financial success; it can literally transform your work and personal life in dozens of meaningful and rewarding ways. You'll have more time, more fun, more energy, and create a more purpose-driven and fulfilling workplace for you and your team members. The effects of your new-found approach to "Partner Leadership" can have a positive ripple effect on the entire culture, company and customer. Primary benefits are better performance, higher revenues, and happier customers. Secondary benefits include measurably lower turnover, less stress, energized service delivery, and a team aligned with both passion and purpose. In this final chapter let's discuss how to transform knowledge to action. It starts by confronting change and ends with transforming ourselves from multi unit management to multi unit leadership. So let's kick our future off with a look at change, transcendence and finally, Sullivan's Laws.

Change with the times or the times will change you

Compared to our parents and grandparents generations, we now live and work in a lightning-fast and impatient world of constant change. Sixty years ago if your grandfather missed the last train, no problem, he'd catch another one the next day. Today, if people miss one-quarter of a revolving door they're pissed-off. We want results fast, but we want change slow.

The only person who likes change is a baby. The "dirty little secret" of business is that most people hate change, including the leaders. But you only have two options in today's marketplace: you can either lead change or have it thrust upon you. That's the lesson of 21st Century business history. Every single day, markets change, the customer changes, employees change, dining and shopping and buying habits change. So the individuals and companies who choose to compete in those arenas must also change. "Change" is not new; the speed and frequency of change is new. It's hard to see in the present and most difficult to predict the future; change is always most dramatic in retrospect. After all, America's best-known chef was on the label of a can of spaghetti just thirty years ago.

The first step in predicting or embracing change is to face the fears surrounding it. Resistance to change in most companies manifests itself when departments (or stores) segregate themselves into silos and value "turf" over teamwork. Don't be a corporate weenie. Blow up the silos, tear down the walls, and foster collaboration in your company. He who builds a fence always fences more out than he fences in. Think of the people in your company or team who are the most adverse to change. I'm willing to bet they all have reasons and rationale why change is bad. See if this list looks or sounds familiar...

Ten Reasons Why We Can't Change

1. We've never done it before.
2. We've never done it that way before.
3. Nobody else has ever done it.
4. My wife's cousin's brother's company tried it.
5. It has never been tried before.
6. We tried it before.
7. We've been doing it this way for years.
8. It won't work in a small company.
9. It won't work in a big company.
10. It won't work in our company.

You may smile while reviewing the list, but you've no doubt heard these phrases before or possibly even said them yourself. Identify and help transform the naysayer players who are most resistant to change in your team. Remind them that one good definition of insanity is to keep doing the same things over and over again and expect different results. We all have a choice with change; you can fight it or embrace it, but you can't ignore it. Our industry is like an escalator; you can move forward or you can move backward…but you cannot remain still.

What's next is now

One hundred years ago, if you asked a farmer what he needs to improve profitability he might say "a horse twice as strong that ate half as many oats." He would not say he needed "a tractor." The point is, things change so rapidly that people are not sure what the best solutions may be because they're focused only

> **Success should never be confused with wealth or power. Rather, success should be linked to excellence and fulfillment. Success is about who you are not what you have. Successful people work to discover their talents, to develop those talents and then to use those talents to benefit others as well as themselves.**
>
> – Anna Muoio

The 7 Stages of Building High-Performing Partnerships and Teams

on what's in front of them. Anticipating the resources necessary for progress is not about what got the job done yesterday, it's about what can best get it done tomorrow. And the day after that.

Are we endangering long-term performance in our company by applying yesterday's thinking to today's problems? If I asked you right now what you'd need to improve profitability in the next 12 months, you might respond: "sell more, spend less." A good response, but it's a tactical, not a strategic, one. I doubt you'd say: "I must hire better people and develop them daily so I can stop managing them." But that indeed would be the correct answer. An "A Team" of high-performing managers in your stores is priceless and the bedrock of any profitable enterprise. But if we don't change the way we think and the way we act, we won't be able to affect change quicker and better than our competitors. In fact, carve this in stone: we can't "think" ourselves into a new way of acting, we *must act ourselves into a new way of thinking.*

We only *really* know what worked today and yesterday and maybe two years ago. But what will work next? That's our daily challenge. Your job, to paraphrase author Ken Blanchard, is to re-invent your organization on a moment-by-moment basis to accomplish what you have to accomplish on a moment-by-moment basis. Change, therefore, involves a lot of play-calling at "the line of scrimmage." The signs of change are there if we know what to look for, and our teams will be ready for change if we model the way.

Ultimately multi unit leaders have to ask themselves this critical question: *"Which is stronger in my company? The urge to grow or our resistance to change?"* Change is inevitable, *growth is a choice.*

Once you can truly embrace change (at least as best you can), you're ready for the next step: transformation.

Transcending From Manager to Leader: Hit or Myth?

"Leadership is the art of getting someone else to do something you want done because he wants to do it." —Dwight D. Eisenhower, U.S. President

Here are the main things we've learned about 21st Century leadership from our MUM research:

All leadership is collaborative. Instead of trying to overcome resistance to what people are not ready to do, find out what they are ready to do, and direct that motivation and momentum toward the targeted goals. It's sometimes called "leading from the middle."

Leadership is a choice, not a position. You have to be passionate. You have to know the way, show the way and go the way. The biggest risk is to take no risk at all.

Everything rises or falls with leadership. It's rare to read business success stories credited to great "manager-ship." Author Warren Bennis puts it this way: "Managers are people who do things right, and leaders are people who do the right things." Everyday, work <u>on</u> your business not just in it.

Leaders are defined by followers. To help evaluate and improve the leadership skills of your unit managers, assess leadership from the hourly team members perspective. Ask them questions like: "Do you trust your leaders?" "If you had the opportunity, would you work for this person again?" And by the way, these same questions should be posed to your unit or store managers to evaluate their MUMs.

> **Multi Unit Leaders make change and stand for values that don't change.**

Leadership is like Snowboarding or Skiing. You don't plan out every turn ahead of time, you have to be flexible, confident, prepared, and having fun.

The 7 Stages of Building High-Performing Partnerships and Teams

Keep your eyes focused on what's ahead, make adjustments based on prevailing conditions, have fun, and don't fight gravity.

Knowledge is not power, <u>shared</u> knowledge is power. Author Stephen Covey used a farming analogy to illustrate the importance of shared knowledge: "Be certain that the water gets to the end of the rows," he said, "and that once it does, have the people at the end of the row come forward and teach you so you're certain that the translation—and learning—occurred." *Learning has not taken place unless behavior has changed.*

Leadership extends beyond the people you supervise. We work with great companies all over the globe. Through our interaction with partners in China, Japan, India, and Singapore we learned the importance of a popular Asian business philosophy called the "Three Joys". It means that leaders focus on creating value with all three business partners in their triangle of trust: Happy Customer-Happy Employee-Happy Supplier.

> Perhaps the biggest pitfall you face is assuming that what has made you succesful to this point in you career will contine to do so. The dangers of sticking with what you know, working extremely hard at doing it, and them failing miserably are very real.
>
> – Michael Watkins

The team with the most and best leaders wins. A MUM's job is not just to be a leader—it's to make more leaders.

Light the fire within. The best managers today are less focused on being in charge and more focused on helping employees be charged up. "You'll never get the best from employees by trying to build a fire under them," says author Bob Nelson, "you've got to build a fire within them. There's a big difference between getting employees to come to work and getting them to do their best work. Get the best work from employees by expecting it from them, telling them you expect it and helping them attain it in any way they can."

Leadership means learning. Collaborate with talented people outside your area of expertise. When we study or associate with people who know more than we do, our horizons always expand. Research has confirmed that whom you associate with is crucial to who you become. If you spend time with successful people, you're more likely to become successful yourself.

Successful MUMs don't just seek a mentor. They seek multiple mentors, one or more for each of their major personal or professional pursuits. This group of mentors can form a sort of personal "board of advisors" for the brand called "you."

Don't be indifferent. Note to everyone who supervises or helps develop MUMs (including Trainers, Regional Managers, VPs, franchise owners and CEOs): what you do about helping your MUMs get to the next level is up to you. You can do something or you can do nothing. You could invest in their education, share their best practices, relieve their paperwork, help them work smarter, incite their passion, coach them to greatness, and make their work a cause, not a "job." Or, you could do nothing. Or put it off. But not to decide is to decide. You may love your managers. You may hate your managers. But you cannot be indifferent toward your managers.

Be the LEADER of choice. Our industry has long emphasized the goal of being the "employer of choice," but the main reason people leave companies—even good companies—is to get away from a supervisor or boss. Be ethical, create growth potential, pay people fairly and make your company a fun and challenging place to be. Grow future leaders who clearly understand the work, live the culture and teach it to others. Be the leader of choice.

Be supportive and protective of your team. If you provide loyalty down, you get loyalty up.

The 7 Stages of Building High-Performing Partnerships and Teams

Be smart with heart. Leadership is an affair of the heart, not just the head. Getting things done is not the same as getting the right things done. Brains, like hearts, will go where they are appreciated, so don't forget to recognize the performer as well as the performance. "The highest achievable level of service comes from the heart," says Hal Rosenbluth, CEO, Rosenbluth International. "So the company that reaches its people's heart will provide the very best service." Here's an exercise we saw in an e-mail that can help you assess the true value of notoriety versus importance. Unfortunately, the author was not attributed in the e-mail, so we can't identify the source, but it speaks volumes about what really matters:

"Can you name the highest paid CEOs in our industry over the past three years? Can you name the last three Heisman trophy winners? The last three recipients of the Nobel Peace Prize? The last three Academy Award winners for Best Screenplay? Difficult to recall, aren't they? Now try these questions:

- *Name three teachers who helped you get through school.*
- *Name three friends who helped you through tough times.*
- *Name three people who've made you feel loved and appreciated.*
- *Name three people whose company you enjoy.*
- *Name three personal heroes whose stories have inspired you.*

That was a little easier, wasn't it? The moral of the story is both simple and direct; the people who truly make a difference in our lives are rarely the ones with the most hype, the most money, the biggest brains, or the largest accolades. The people who make differences in our lives are the ones who truly care. If you don't recognize your people; someone else will."

"Multi unit leadership," says my friend Jim Buelt, "is like wearing a Speedo bathing suit at the beach. Anyone can, but not everyone should." If you choose to accept the role of multi unit supervisor, and your team members deem you worthy of it by following you, approach the role as a leader, not a manager. And complete the transformation by considering...

Sullivan's Laws

Transforming from multi unit manager to leader is like a casserole—only those responsible for it really know what goes into it. It's a multi-tiered path that has no specific timeline, a complex discipline with a hundred different variables, and a role that is granted not proclaimed. Some seek leadership and never find it. For others, leadership is thrust upon them quickly and they excel at it. People will not follow one-dimensional managers; however, they will follow leaders who have mastered the complexities of *Brand Ambassadors, Talent Scouts, Servant Leaders, Head Coaches, Marketing Gurus, Synergists* and *Goal Getters.* They will respect the discipline and commitment it takes to master each rung of the Leadership Ladder. They will deem these leaders most worthy of their "follower-ship" because true leaders teach them something new each and every day.

So how do we summarize a concept—leadership—so complex that attainment is not guaranteed no matter how much you study it or apply it? One way is by concluding with a list of pointed Performance Proverbs we call *Sullivan's Laws.* They summarize the 7 Stages of Leadership we've detailed throughout the book; read 'em and reap!

The 7 Stages of Building High-Performing Partnerships and Teams

1. Sullivan's Law of Hierarchy: If you're at the top of the ladder, cover your ass; if you're at the bottom, cover your face.

2. Sullivan's Law of "Probability Dispersal": Whatever it is that hits the fan will not be evenly distributed.

3. You're only as good as your last happy customer.

4. The customer doesn't come first, leadership comes first.

5. Nothing is sacred in business other than that the customer comes back.

6. If you don't have time to do it right, when will you have time to do it over?

7. Over-teach. Your team will both under-learn and over-forget

8. Leadership is not what happens when you are there, but what happens when you are not there.

9. Business is like a Dylan song; you don't have to understand it to like it.

10. What isn't tried won't work.

11. Leadership cannot be stored in inventory, it must be 100% available upon demand.

12. Develop don't "direct." Your objective is to be cheering and steering, not domineering.

13. The best leaders have all the <u>questions</u>.

14. It is much harder to ask the right question than it is to find the right answer to the wrong question.

15. Prescription before diagnosis is malpractice.

16. Some turnover is good. It's not the people you fire who make your life miserable it's the people you don't fire. (Of all the people who will never leave you, you're the only one.)

17. There is no "A" for effort. Results matter.

18. Hire people who share your values. Teach them the skills. Give them what they need. Now, and this is most important: get the hell out of their way.

19. Don't lose focus on your core values. The main thing is to keep the main thing the main thing.

20. Planning your day as a MUM is really not that difficult. Just start every morning by asking yourself "now what could possibly go wrong today?"

21. There are no jobs with a future, only people with a future.

22. If you can't win, make the person in front of you break the record.

23. Anthropology will always trump technology in business.

24. Win without boasting, lose without excuses.

25. If you don't like something, change it; if you can't change it, change the way you think about it.

26. The restaurant business is like oxygen. If you're alive, you'll use it.

27. Sullivan's Law of Meetings: the meeting you must attend this week is scheduled on the day you are to attend a seminar that you paid for six months ago. You did not have any meetings the week before. You do not have any scheduled for the next week.

The 7 Stages of Building High-Performing Partnerships and Teams

28. Sullivan's Law of Timing: If you want something to happen it will take twice as long as you expect, if don't want something to happen, it will happen in half the time.

29. Tomorrow when you come to work, if it doesn't make the customer happy, move the business forward and make us money, then don't do it.

30. Different is not always better but better is always different.

31. <u>Acting</u> on a mediocre idea is better than "having" a good idea.

32. "Don't get too far ahead of your customers or you'll confuse them. Don't get too far behind or you'll lose them." – Norman Brinker

33. Compromise is always wrong when it means sacrificing principle.

34. Customers are like spouses, if you don't show appreciation they will go someplace else.

35. "It is not enough to do your best; you must first know what to do, and then do your best."–W. Edwards Deming

36. Blessed are the flexible for they won't be bent out of shape.

37. You don't get better in "general." You get better in specific.

38. There is nothing new except what's been forgotten.

39. One good definition of insanity is to keep doing the same things over and over again and expect different results.

40. A customer will forgive you for higher price but they'll never forgive you for lower quality.

41. Artificial Intelligence is no match for natural stupidity.

42. Service is the invisible product.

43. Because the customer has a need, we have a job to do. Because the customer has a choice, we must be the better choice. Because the customer has sensibilities, we must be considerate. Because the customer is smart, we have to outsmart the competitors they may want to do business with instead of us

44. The devil is in the details. Never overlook the importance of the mundane.

45. Practice does not make perfect. It is the quality and intensity of the practice that makes perfect. — Glenn "Pop" Warner

46. People may doubt what you say, but they will always believe what you do.

47. Management problems always turn out to be people problems.

48. Vision without action is a daydream. Action without vision is a nightmare.

49. What is learned with fun is rarely forgotten.

50. The main thing is to keep the main thing the main thing.

51. Customer complaints provide a clear window into your performance.

52. If you plant crab apples, don't count on harvesting golden delicious.

53. Don't trust a brilliant idea unless it survives the hangover.

54. "If you cannot be an honest lawyer, resolve to be honest without being a lawyer." — Abraham Lincoln

55. Failure is an event, never a person.

The 7 Stages of Building High-Performing Partnerships and Teams

56.   You cannot lead anyone farther than you have gone yourself.

57.   Summary: Since our task is difficult, we dare not relax; since our opportunities are brief, we dare not delay.

58.   If a person needs praise—give it to them. They cannot read their tombstone.

59.   Leaving everything to the last minute is the surest way to make enemies of the other fifty-nine.

60.   Speed is not everything—direction counts.

61.   "There are two things people want more than sex and money... recognition and praise. " – Mary Kay Ash, Founder, Mary Kay Cosmetics

62.   "No matter what business you're in, everyone in the organization needs to know why." – Frances Hesselbein

63.   The man who gets the most satisfactory results is not always the man with the most brilliant single mind, but rather the man who can best coordinate the brains and talents of the people who surround him.
      – General Jack Pershing

64.   The little wheels in the back of the watch are just as important as the hands of the watch.

65.   Correction does much, but encouragement does more.

66.   Forget your mistakes, but remember what they taught you.

67.   Investigate mistakes only when you are calm.

68. When there is nothing for sure, everything is possible.

69. If you consistently do your best, the worst cannot happen.

70. Advice is like snow—the softer it falls, the deeper it goes.

71. People may not remember how fast you did your work, but they will remember how well you did it.

72. Never ruin an apology with an excuse.

73. If you don't give your people the information they need , they'll make up something to fill the void.

74. Once you have the wrong people there is no right way to develop them.

75. "In a large company, managers rely on reports, but you cannot feel reports. You've got to be there—in the field, in the plant, out in the street. You don't learn the business from salespeople or budget planners. You learn the business from the customers—who, by the way, love to teach."
    —Henry Quadracci, CEO, Quad/Graphics

76. "Give a lot, expect a lot, and if you don't get it, prune."
    —Tom Peters, Management Consultant

77. "Having a good time is the best motivator there is. When people feel good about a company, they perform better and produce more."
    —Dave Longaberger, CEO, The Longaberger Co.

78. You can't expect to win unless you know why you lose.

79. "To love what you do and feel that it matters, how could anything else be more fun?" —Katherine Graham

The 7 Stages of Building High-Performing Partnerships and Teams

Finally: the leadership "secret."

The very essence of leadership is that you have to have a vision. It's got to be a vision you articulate clearly and forcefully on every occasion. You can't blow an uncertain trumpet. —Theodore Hesburgh

What's the secret of multi unit manager success? Come closer, I'll tell you the secret...here **IT** is: Success comes to those who make the greatest profit from the fewest mistakes.

Study the sage advice in this book to which over 400 MUMs have contributed, and try to learn first from your mistakes, second from your manager's mistakes, third from your company's mistakes and last from your competitor's mistakes. The main thing to learn is how not to repeat them and profit from the lesson embedded in each mistake. Leaders don't blame—they learn. Learn as you go and you'll quickly turn pro.

So what do we do now? What you know doesn't matter. It's what you do with what you know that matters. Review the self-assessments at the end of each chapter and ask yourself "What do I need to START doing? What do I need to STOP doing? What do I need to CONTINUE to do?" Don't put off the incremental behavior changes that will transform and improve your performance and well-being. Procrastination is the devil's chloroform.

Here's a poem that my grandfather shared with me that sums it up well:

> *Our ends are joined by a common link,*
> *With one we sit, with one we think.*
> *Success depends on which we choose,*
> *Heads we win, tails we lose.*

Please do something: either lead, follow, or get the heck out of the way.

Multi Unit Leadership is not an easy role. Consistently exceeding your goals as you build a high-performing team can be tougher than a woodpecker's lips. It involves pluck, luck and a whoop-ass cup of 21st Century Real Change. Are you ready, willing and able?

Don't Wait Until...

- **Sales go down or**
- **Sales go up or**
- **You hire another person or**
- **You fire another person or**
- **You take a class or**
- **The weather gets better or**
- **The economy gets better or**
- **The time is right or**
- **Your ship comes in or**
- **The "stuff" hits the fan.**

NOW is the Time.

THIS is the Place.

YOU are the person.

This is your Rocket. Let's ride!

"Wow" starts now.

GET GREAT. STAY GREAT. MAKE A DIFFERENCE.

The 7 Stages of Building High-Performing Partnerships and Teams

Road Map for getting the most out of this book

The Next 30 Days *Assessment*

- Fill out the self-assessments for the Leadership Ladder at the end of each chapter. Note where your opportunities for improvement in each competency lie.

- Now write down—in your calendar, not on a "list"—when and how you're going to work on and improve in those competencies.

- Get copies of this book for your fellow multi unit managers and high-performing unit managers. It's the gift that can be opened again and again.

- Work on the *Brand Ambassador* and *Talent Scout* competencies. Re-read each chapter and highlight the behaviors you could improve in.

- Discuss how your company selects and develops new multi unit managers. Specify opportunities for improvement. Detail what needs to be done and how your company will do it.

- Assess the strengths and challenges of each store and unit manager.

- Consider how you conduct store visits. Are there opportunities for improvement? What, specifically?

- Review how you prepare and execute your Annual or Quarterly Business Plans. Is your process aligned with your Key Result Areas and the best practices we detailed in Chapter 6?

- Get our audio book version of *Multi Unit Leadership: The 7 Stages of High-Performing Partnerships and Teams* and use your car as a mobile university.

- Go to **Sullivision.com** and take the free "deeper dive" online Multi Unit Leadership assessment and see where your competencies align and what knowledge gaps may exist.

The Next 60 Days *Begin Application and Transfer*

- Work on the *Servant Leader* and *Head Coach* and *Marketing Guru* competencies. Re-read each chapter and highlight the behaviors you could improve in.

- Now write down—in your calendar, not on a "list"—when and how you're going to work on and improve in those competencies.

- Discuss the strategies and tactics of effective store visits with your fellow MUMs. Decide what you can do collectively and individually to improve the process.

- Conduct your next store visits with partner leadership and collaborative coaching instead of being "Inspector MUM."

- Make certain that GMs are tying period goals to shift execution and pre-shift meetings. Together, watch **The Shift: How to Plan It, Lead It, Make It Pay**, and **Jumpstart: How to Plan and Execute Effective Pre-Shift Meetings** DVDs with your managers. Detail what you need to be doing after viewing.

- Review and download all the great additional free content on Multi Unit Leadership at our website.

- Join the discussion. Share your best ideas or biggest challenges on multi unit management at our free MUM blogspot at **Sullivision.com**

- Listen to and download the free podcasts on multi unit leadership at **Sullivision.com**

The 7 Stages of Building High-Performing Partnerships and Teams

The Next 90 Days *Transformation*

- Work on the *Synergist* and *Goal Getter* competencies. Re-read each chapter and highlight the behaviors you could improve on.

- Design and execute your new Quarterly Business Plan to reflect the template and categories defined in this book.

- Measure the results of your new approach to store visits and manager supervision and area profitability.

- Watch our interactive DVD on Multi Unit Leadership and invest in our MUM e-learning program to enhance your leadership skills.

- Work on your public-speaking skills by seeking out opportunities to speak in front of other professional groups like the local Chamber of Commerce or Convention Bureau breakfast.

- Consider having **Sullivision.com** design and deliver a customized seminar on Multi Unit Leadership or consulting for your company and team.

- Have fun and get the job done.

- Teach it to someone else.

- Get Great. Stay Great. Start Now.

Don't Drop the Ball

Imagine life as a game in which you are juggling some five balls in the air.

You name them—work, family, health, friends, and spirit—and you're keeping all of these in the air.

You will soon understand that work is a rubber ball.
If you drop it, it will bounce back.

But the other four balls—family, health, friends, and spirit—are made of glass.

If you drop one of these, they will be irrevocably scuffed, marked, nicked, damaged, or even shattered. They will never be the same.

Work is a slice of pizza, it ain't the whole pie.

Targeted Training Tools that Drive Revenue

Power Tools for Managers

Every MUM Needs these 2 DVDs for their Managers and their Restaurants

Jumpstart: How to Plan and Execute Effective Pre-Shift Meetings is an award-winning 60 minute DVD that will show your managers the wrong and right ways to deliver effective and goal-oriented "pep rallies" before each shift for every department. Watch and learn realistic examples of how to jumpstart service, sales and cost-control before every shift. Loaded with bonus training features too.

The Shift: How to
Plan It, Lead It, Make It Pay

will help every foodservice manager understand the architecture of the revenue-generating shift. They'll learn how to break down period goals to shift targets, the best practices related to leadership before, during and after the shift, how to coach each member through each shift, and how to make every customer interaction postive in the dining room, drive-through or counter. This 60 minute DVD is used in over 10,000 restaurants worldwide.

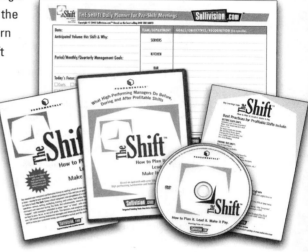

Buy Both & Save!
Jumpstart DVD
AND The Shift DVD

This Dynamic Duo of training DVDs are guaranteed to drive more revenue in any restaurant, every shift. Get them both for a great price at **Sullivision.com**

Go Further Faster!

Free Online Leadership Assessment at Sullivision.com

How well do you measure up in each of the 7 Stage Competencies of High-Performing Multi Unit Leaders? Visit us at our website at **Sullivision.com** and take our **FREE** online Multi Unit Leadership Assessment. You'll clearly assess where your strengths lie and where your opportunities for improvement are. This free assessment is backed by online content and resources that will help you identify and improve in each of your challenge areas. The assessment is effective not only for current Multi Unit Managers but also high-performing GMs who are preparing for the next level in their career.

Serve U

Online learning gets unit managers on the right career path.

Our online learning courses for unit managers—called Serve U—will help your GM's and assistant managers get brilliant at the basics of hiring, service, selling, teamwork, marketing, safety and training. Go to Sullivision.com and click on the E-learning Serve U icon for a full overview and sample of the industry's most popular online learning university!

Multi Unit Leadership E-Learning that Rocks

Available anytime you are.
After taking the free online assessment, check out our e-Learning MUM courses at **Sullivision.com**. Each dynamic and interactive course takes you on a "deeper dive" of the 7 core leadership competencies: Brand Ambassador, *Talent Scout, Servant Leader, Head Coach, Marketing Guru, Synergist and Goal Getter.* These fun and insightful courses are chockablock-full of creative content and realistic simulation, focused on guided practice and execution, not "theory". You can progress at your own pace, start and stop at the times most convenient to your schedule, and access richer content, insight and expertise than a book alone can provide. Learn while you earn.

Targeted Training Tools that Drive Revenue

▶ *Customize this Book: If you'd like to talk about cost-effective ways to customize this book for your concept, logo, menu, products and multi unit management team, just send an e-mail to jim@sullivision.com.*

About Jim Sullivan

Maybe you've seen him on CNN, NBC, ABC, the BBC, CBC, the Food Network, or heard him on Larry King, or National Public Radio. Over a half million foodservice and retail managers, executives and franchisees worldwide have read his newsletters, books, or columns and seen his DVDs, webcasts, e-learning programs and live seminars. His products and programs have been featured in the *Wall Street Journal, the New York Times, Newsweek, Fast Company, The London Times, Der Spiegel, Inc.* and *USA Today.*

Jim Sullivan, is the founder and CEO of Sullivision.com, and a veteran of over 20 years the hospitality and retail industries as an award-winning operator and best-selling author. Sullivision.com has built their reputation designing successful sales, marketing, training and customer service programs for the "Top 200" restaurant, hotel, and retail chains worldwide. Jim is the author of two books that have sold over 400,000 copies worldwide, and two of his DVDs, *Jumpstart! The Art of Effective Pre-Shift Meetings* and *The Shift: How to Plan It, Lead It, Make It Pay* are used in over 10,000 foodservice operations worldwide.

Jim is a visiting professor at *Penn State University, Purdue,* the *University of Delaware, Cal Poly* and the *Culinary Institute of America.* You can reach Jim at **www.sullivision.com.**

NOTES

The 7 Stages of Building High-Performing Partnerships and Teams

The 7 Stages of Building High-Performing Partnerships and Teams

The 7 Stages of Building High-Performing Partnerships and Teams

The 7 Stages of Building High-Performing Partnerships and Teams

_____
_____
_____
_____
_____
_____
_____
_____
_____
_____
_____
_____
_____
_____
_____
_____
_____
_____
_____
_____
_____
_____
_____
_____
_____
_____
_____
_____
_____
_____
_____
_____
_____
_____
_____

The 7 Stages of Building High-Performing Partnerships and Teams

The 7 Stages of Building High-Performing Partnerships and Teams

The 7 Stages of Building High-Performing Partnerships and Teams

The 7 Stages of Building High-Performing Partnerships and Teams